# Make it Easy

**Age 5-6**

**English**

## Contents

### Learning Activities

### Quick Tests

### Answers

**Lynn Huggins-Cooper and Louis Fidge**

# Rhyming words

Look at this sentence. All the words in bold rhyme. That means they contain the **same sound**. They all end in the letters *at*.

The **fat cat sat** on the **mat**, watching a **bat**!

 Draw a line to join each word with its rhyme partner.

a  can          red
b  pink         sack
c  bug          dot
d  bed          stink
e  pot          plug
f  back         fan

 Look in the box to find words that rhyme with each word below. Write the words in the blank spaces.

a  yell    Smell
b  dark    park
c  dog     frog
d  box     fox
e  win     bin
f  sock    rock
g  big     pig

fox
frog
pig
smell
rock
bin
park

2

# The alphabet

abcdefghijklmnopqrstuvwxyz

When people say words are in **alphabetical order** it means they appear in the same order as the alphabet. **A** words come first, then **b** words right up until the end of the alphabet.

> **bat zebra ant** put into alphabetical order is **ant bat zebra**.

**I** Write these letters in alphabetical order.

a  f b a d c e g        a b c d e f g

b  z x y w v u        _____

c  p r q t s u v        _____

d  g f i h k j m l        _____

e  m l n k j o p        _____

f  s t v u w r x        _____

g  d f e h i g j k        _____

**II** Write each set of words in alphabetical order.

a  cat     egg     box        _____

b  bag     dig     apple        _____

c  cup     art     pig        _____

d  car     baby     dog        _____

e  wall     bed     door        _____

f  book     sun     leg        _____

g  tree     bird     peg        _____

# Spelling simple words

Learning to spell is easy when you use:
**look, cover, write, check**.

First **look** at the word. Look to see if there are any letters with tails that hang below the line, or sticks that 'stick up' above the line. Try to see the word in your head.

tail _y_     | — stick

Then **cover** the word up and try to **write** it. Uncover the word and **check** it. See if you were right. Keep practising!

**I** Learn these words. Use look, cover, write, check.

a saw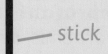

b say

c now

d yes

e did

f not

g was

h but

i run

**II** Add the missing letter to each word. Use the letters in the box to help you.

a m_a_n

b f_i_n

c p_i_g

d p_i_n

| |
|---|
| a |
| i |
| o |
| u |

e d_o_t  ●

f w_i_g

g s_u_n

h b_a_ll

# Writing practice

It is important to **write neatly**, so that people can read your writing. Before you start, make sure you are sitting comfortably and you are holding your pencil in the right way between your finger and thumb.

**I** Trace over these words.

a  way        us        to
b  too        how       her
c  him        old       one
d  or         out       saw
e  so         not       now

**II** Copy each word three times.

a  see    _see_     _see_     _see_
b  ran    _ran_     _ran_     _ran_
c  our    _our_     _our_     _our_
d  pot    _pot_     _pot_     _pot_
e  that   _that_    _that_    _that_

# Full stops and capital letters

A sentence always **starts** with a capital letter and most sentences **end** with a full stop.

It is hot today.
/ capital letter      full stop \

**I**   **Write these sentences again, adding capital letters and full stops.**

a  i like you  _____

b  this is my sister  _____

c  sausages are my favourite  _____

d  i am going out  _____

e  i want to read  _____

**II**   **These sentences are mixed up. Write them out in the right order. Use a capital letter and a full stop in each sentence.**

a  like brother i my

_____

b  dog my walking likes

_____

c  smell the cat food can its

_____

d  eat we sweets

_____

e  wet makes rain you

_____

# Names

The name of a **person** or **place** should **start** with a capital letter.

> My cat is called **W**iggy.
>
> I come from **B**righton.

**I** Circle the letters that should be capitals.

a **b**rian

b **m**rs jones

c **a**ndrew

d **e**ngland

e **m**r brown

f **m**iss lacey

g **l**ondon

h **m**r smith

i **f**rance

j **j**anet

k **d**octor doolittle

l **c**ambridge

m **a**frica

n **s**cotland

**II** Now underline all of the letters that should be capitals in these sentences. Do not forget to add the full stops!

a my friend jamila comes from yorkshire ·

b my dog is called bertie ·

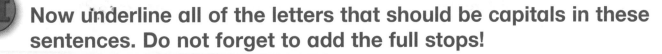

c auntie jane lives in edinburgh ·

d bruce, stella and jodi are my friends ·

e we sailed down the river thames ·

f dad's name is john ·

g i am going on holiday to portugal with my sister sarah ·

h i went to durham to see the pantomime cinderella ·

# ff words

Words are made when letters and groups of letters are put together. Learning the way that groups of letters are put together helps you to **build new words**.

> **o + f = of    o + ff = off**

The two *ff*s sound different to one *f* on its own.

**I** Look at these letters and groups of letters. Write the words they make in the puffs of smoke.

a flu + ff = *fluff*

b pu + ff = *puff*

c bu + ff = *buff*

d cu + ff = *cuff*

e sni + ff = *sniff*

f sti + ff = *stiff*

g mu + ff = *muff*

h stu + ff = *stuff*

i sta + ff = *staff*

j whi + ff = *whiff*

**II** Write the correct *ff* word next to each picture. Use the words in the box to help you.

| muff | cliff | giraffe | puff | whiff | sniff |

a _____

b _____

c _____

d _____

e _____

f _____

8

# ll words

Some words end in *ll*. These letters always have a vowel in front of them.

a e i o u

tall

**I** **Make words using the endings in the ball.**

a  b *all bull bill bell*

b  y *ell*

c  s *ell*

d  c *ill*

e  h *ill*

all
ill  ell
ull  oll

f  d *oll*

g  f *ull*

h  p *ill*

i  t *all*

j  w *ill*

**II** **Write the *ll* word for each picture.**

a

_ _ _ _

c

_ _ _ _

e

_ _ _ _

b
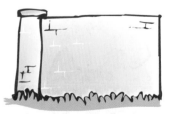
_ _ _ _

d

_ _ _ _

f

_ _ _ _

9

# *ss* words

Some words end in *ss*.

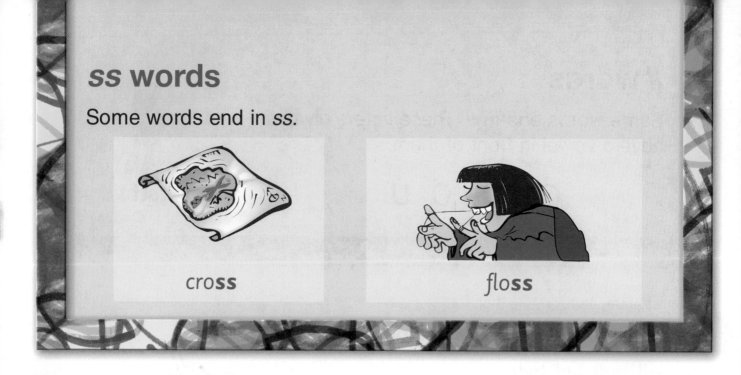

cro**ss**

flo**ss**

## I Join the *ss* word to the right picture.

a address

b chess

c pass

d dress

e cress

f floss

## II Choose an *ss* word from the box to complete each sentence.

| hiss | floss | mess | grass | kiss | cress |

a I sat on the _____.

b The mud made a _____.

c I like egg and _____ sandwiches.

d Candy _____ is sweet!

e I _____ my granny.

f The snake went _____.

10

# *ck* words

In English a word **never starts** with *ck*. But sometimes *ck* is found in the middle or at the end of a word.

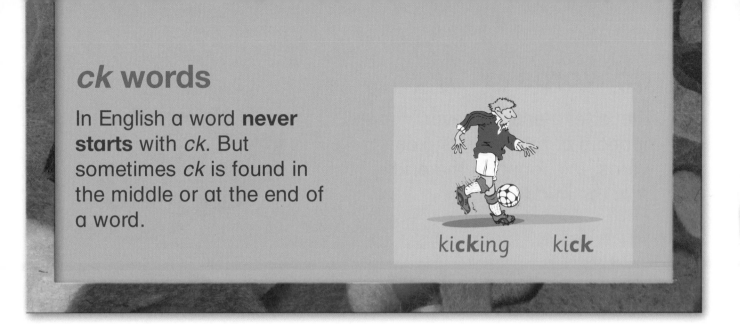

ki**ck**ing    ki**ck**

 **Draw a picture for each *ck* word.**

a clock

c sock

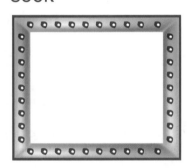

e lock

b block

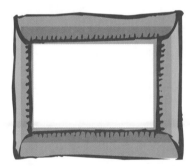

d rocket

f duck

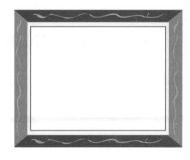

 ***ick* or *ock*? Add the letters to complete the words. Some words can use both – but can you say which ones?**

a s _ick  sock_____

b kn_____

c w_____

d fl_____

e p_____

f r_____

g l_____

h st_____

i sm_____

j tr_____

# *ng* words

The letter blend *ng* never appears at the beginning of words. It is found at the **end** or in the **middle**.

I'm laughing.

**I** **Circle the words that use *ng*.**

a square rectangle circle

b apple lemon orange

c monkey orangutan ape

d sing laugh shout

e queen prince king

f triangle cymbal drum

g penguin walrus seal

h swing slide roundabout

i necklace ring bracelet

j finger thumb hand

k sting hurt burn

l herring cod eel

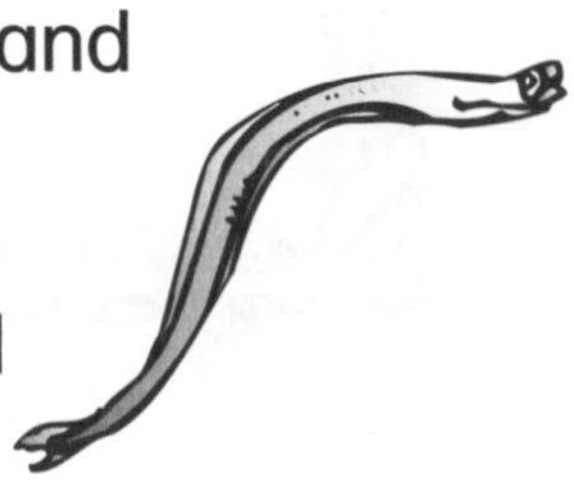

**II** **Write a sentence using each *ing* word.**

a cooking _____

_____

b running _____

_____

c calling _____

_____

d shouting _____

_____

e looking _____

_____

# *bl* words

*b* and *l* make the letter blend *bl*. Lots of words **start** with *bl*.

blew                    bloom

**I**  Tick the words that start with the blend *bl*.

a  back   dark   bland        f  bleat   bran   bill

b  black   bright   big        g  burn   bleep   ball

c  baby   bin   blue           h  bloat   bunny   barn

d  blend   bark   brave        i  brand   bit   bleak

e  bus   blank   broom         j  blade   brass   bust

**II**  Draw a picture for each *bl* word. This will show that you know what it means.

a  blade              c  blow               e  blast

b  blink              d  blue

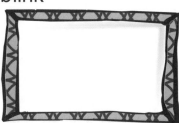   

# *cr* words

The letters *c* and *r* blend together at the beginning of words to make the sound *cr*.

---

**I** Draw a line to match each picture to the correct *cr* word.

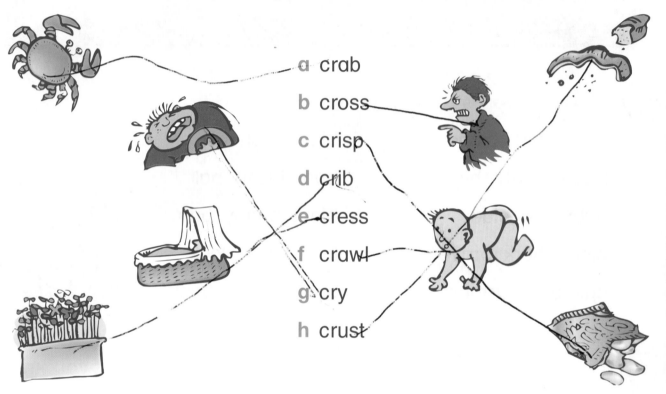

a crab

b cross

c crisp

d crib

e cress

f crawl

g cry

h crust

---

**II** Draw a picture that contains each of the things described by these *cr* words.

a crack          b crane          c crazy          d crawl

# *tr* words

Lots of words **start** with the letter blend *tr*.

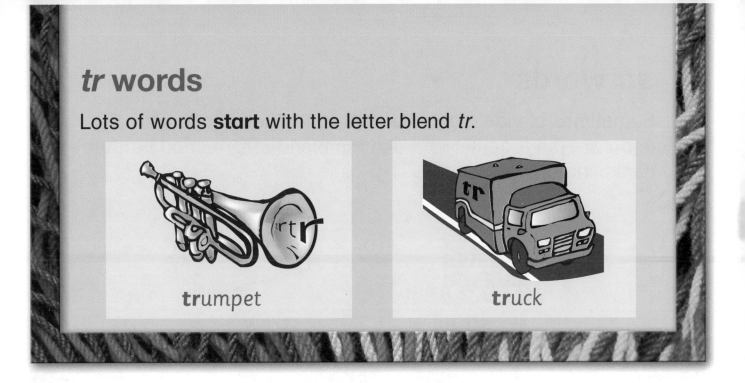

**trumpet**          **truck**

**I** Find the *tr* words in the box below. Then write them down.

> take  trade  tick  tramp  trash  table  travel  tray
> telly  trip  tank  true  trumpet

a _____          e _____

b _____          f _____

c _____          g _____

d _____          h _____

**II** Write the correct *tr* words in the spaces.

a I walked down the _____.

b The farmer drives a _____.

c I went to my grandad's house on a _____.

d The fly was caught in the spider's _____.

e When you cross the road, watch for _____.

f The bird made a nest in a _____.

g I always _____ my best.

tree

track

train

tractor

try

trap

traffic

15

# *str* words

Sometimes blends are made from more than two letters. *S*, *t* and *r* are put together to make the blend *str*. You find it at the beginning of many words.

**str**ing

**str**aw

**I** Circle the word that begins with *str*.

a strap soft sell

b stall string stink

c strong sand sit

d save street sell

e straw sold saw

f seen so stream

g sick sit stretch

h strange silly smell

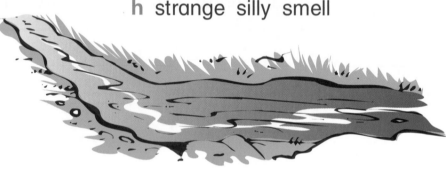

**II** Now write a sentence using each word you circled.

a _____

b _____

c _____

d _____

e _____

f _____

g _____

h _____

# *nd* and *lp* words

*lp* and *nd* are letter blends found at the **end of words**. Like *ck* and *ng*, they never appear at the beginning of words.

gu**lp**

wa**nd**

**I** Write *lp* or *nd* to finish each word.

a wi_____

b ki_____

c ba_____

d gu_____

e ha_____

f la_____

g pu_____

h he_____

i fi_____

j sa_____

**II** Draw a line to match the *lp* and *nd* words to the pictures.

a band     b hand     c yelp     d help     e gulp

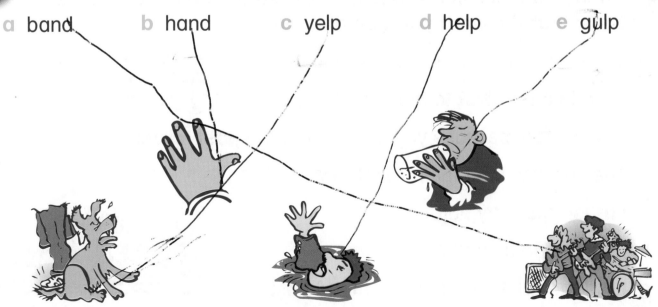

# Words using *st*

The letters *s* and *t* appear in many words to make the blend *st*.

**st**amp        po**st**age        po**st**

**I**   **Tick the word in each pair that ends in *st*.**

a post [✓]   pole [ ]
b pick [ ]   last [✓]
c blast [✓]   plate [ ]
d fake [ ]   fast [✓]
e just [✓]   jump [ ]

f bin [ ]   bust [✓]
g trust [✓]   take [ ]
h make [ ]   must [✓]
i beast [✓]   drink [ ]
j least [✓]   lady [ ]

**II**   **Choose the correct *st* word, so the sentences make sense. Cross out the word you do not need.**

a There was **dust mast** everywhere.

b I used **yeast dust** to make my bread.
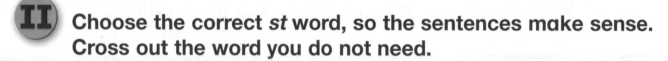

c I like history because you learn about the **past crust**.

d The sail flew from the **mast feast**.

e I **must mast** try harder!

f Mum made us a tasty **past feast**.

g I like the **dust crust** on the bread best.

# *ee* words

The letters *ee* together sound like someone is squealing!

**I**  Draw a line to match each *ee* word to the right picture.

a  sleep

b  sheep

c  feet

d  sleet

e  sheet

f  beer

g  deer

h  beep

**II**  Draw a circle round the *ee* word in each sentence.

a  The water is deep.

b  Have you seen my dad?

c  Where have you been?

d  My sister is a teenager.

e  I shall creep up the stairs, because my brother is sleeping.

f  Have a peep at these chicks!

g  The car horn went beep.

h  In the winter we get sleet as well as snow.

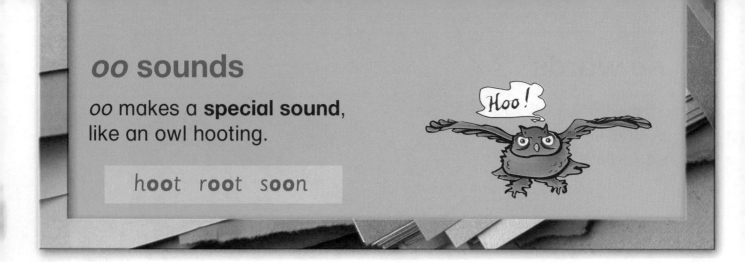

# *oo* sounds

*oo* makes a **special sound**, like an owl hooting.

h**oo**t  r**oo**t  s**oo**n

**I** Draw a picture of the missing *oo* words in the boxes below. Use the words in the box to help you.

| stool | pool | food | school |
|---|---|---|---|

a The cat sat on the _stool_.

b Who would like to swim in the _pool_?

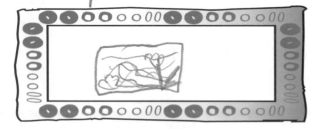

c The _school_ was very noisy!

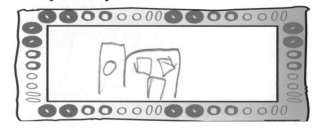

d What is your favourite _food_?

**II** Write the correct *oo* word in each sentence.

a The _sun_ was bright in the sky.

b The lemonade was lovely and _light_.

c I eat yoghurt with a _spoon_.

d Can I come _home_?

e _wool_ is made into jumpers.

too

moon

wool

cool

spoon

20

# *oa* words

There are lots of words that use the letters *oa* together. They make a sound like the name of the letter *o*.

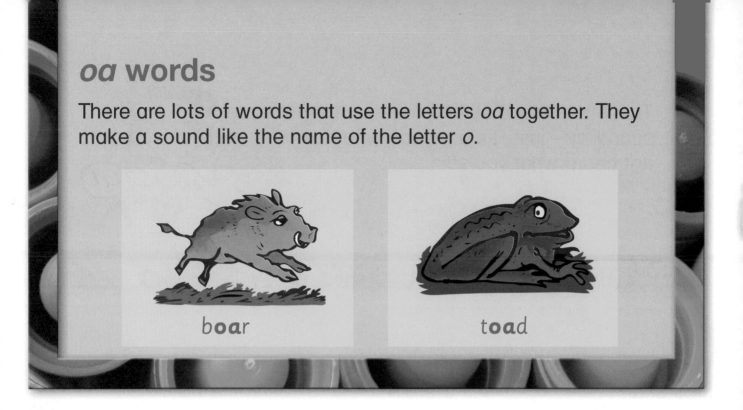

boar                    toad

**I** Which pictures are *oa* words? Circle the ones you choose.

a

b

c

d

e

f

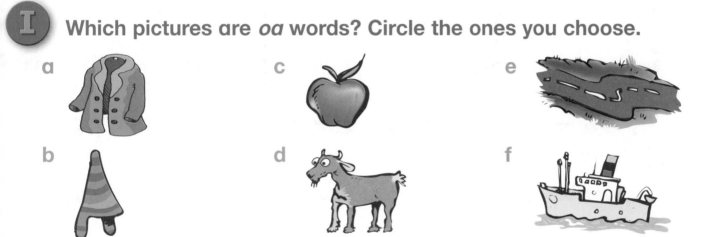

**II** Draw a line to match each *oa* word to its clue.

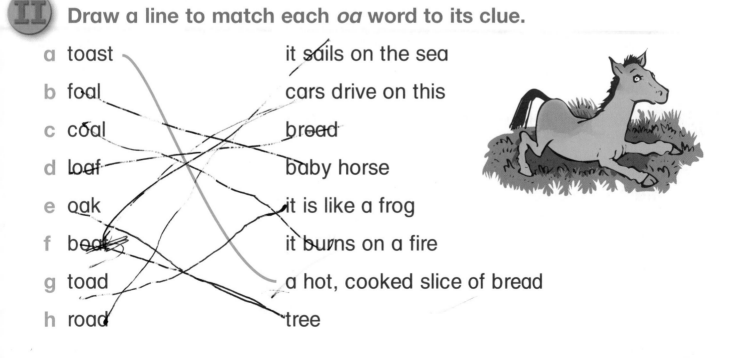

a toast            it sails on the sea

b foal             cars drive on this

c coal             bread

d loaf             baby horse

e oak              it is like a frog

f beak             it burns on a fire

g toad             a hot, cooked slice of bread

h road             tree

## *ai* words

The letters *a* and *i* blend together to make the sound *ay* – just like a person who has not heard what you said!

**I** Draw a picture for each *ai* word.

a snail

c brain

e train

b rain

d tail

f nail

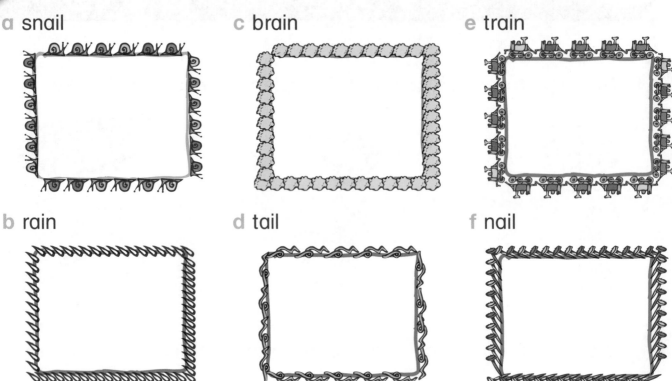

**II** Write a sentence using each *ai* word.

a snail    _____

b main    _____

c pail    _____

d fail    _____

e rain    _____

f pain    _____

# *ie* and *y* words

The letter blend *ie* sometimes makes the same sound as the letter *y* when it is at the end of a word – so it can be confusing!

pie

why

 **Which letters are correct? Underline the right answer.**

a pie    py

b tie    ty

c die    dy

d ly    lie

e thyf    thief

f trys    tries

g why    whie

h flie    fly

i cry    crie

j by    bie

 **Complete the words. They all end in *y* or *ie*.**

a d _____

c cr _____

e t _____

b fl _____

d sp _____

23

# Making words

You can **build words** by adding different groups of letters together.

$$cr + isp = crisp$$

**I** Add these groups of letters together and write the words you make.

a th + at = _that_

b th + is = _____

c th + en = _____

d wh + at = _____

e wh + en = _____

f wh + ip = _____

g tr + ap = _____

h dr + op = _____

i cr + op = _____

j br + an = _____

**II** Join together the groups of letters with a line to make words. Use a different colour felt pen for each word.

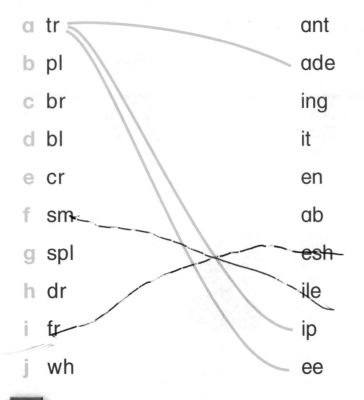

a tr          ant

b pl          ade

c br          ing

d bl          it

e cr          en

f sm          ab

g spl         esh

h dr          ile

i fr          ip

j wh          ee

# Question marks

**Question marks** look like this **?**. They are used at the end of a sentence to show it is a question.

Some words give us a clue that a sentence is being asked:

What...? When...? How...?
Why...? Who...?

Where is my hat?

 **I**  Add a question mark or a full stop at the end of these sentences.

a  Do you like football

b  I am glad we are going there

c  Can we go now

d  May I have one please

e  You can play

f  This is my dog

g  What was that noise

h  What time is it

**II**  Write questions of your own using the words what, when, how, why, who. **Do not forget the question mark!**

a  _____

_____

b  _____

_____

c  _____

_____

d  _____

_____

e  _____

_____

# Plurals

Where there is more than one thing, we say it is a **plural**.

To make the word **frog** plural, add an *s*. This shows there is more than one.

one frog

two frog**s**

**I** **Circle all the plural words.**

a The horses eat hay.

b The birds flew away.

c Some girls like swimming.

d The flowers are pretty.

e Have you seen my comics?

f These are my favourite sweets.

g The dogs are barking.

h Would you like some crisps?

**II** **Some plurals do not add an *s*. Join the word to the plural with a line.**

a woman          mice

b goose           men

c mouse           women

d man             geese

e louse           lice

# In the past

When the **action word** in a sentence ends in *ed* it means the action happened in the past.

I walk**ed** to school yesterday.

Some words change completely

I **run** fast changes to I **ran** fast

**I** **Change the action word to the past tense. The first one has been done for you.**

a I lik*ed* the games best.

b I talk____ to my friend.

c I look____ at the picture.

d She play____ with her brother.

e He paint____ a picture.

f I call____ my sister.

g They wash____ their hands.

**II** **Write the correct present tense word next to the past tense word. The first one has been done for you.**

a jumped _____*jump*_____

b hopped _____

c tried _____

d called _____

e ran _____

f lifted _____

g skipped _____

h cried _____

i helped _____

| run | jump | skip | help |
| try | hop | call | cry | lift |

## Vowels

The letters

# a e i o u

are called **vowels**.

Sometimes *y* acts as a vowel in words like 'cry' and 'why'.

**D**o h**a**v**e** s**o**m**e** t**ea**.

---

**I** Circle the vowels in these words.

a cottage

b seaside

c woods

d babies

e school

f computer

g picture

h doctor

i berries

j leaf

---

**II** Fill in the missing vowels to make these words.

a h____ ____se

c gl____ss____s

e c____k____

b b____ ____ks

d m____lk

f st____rs

# Consonants

**Consonants** are all the letters of the alphabet except the vowels *a e i o u*.

The consonants are:

## b c d f g h j k l m n p q r s
## t v w x y z

---

**I**   Underline the consonants in these words.

a  b o a t

b  b a b y

c  m o u s e

d  s a n d

e  s u n s h i n e

f  d e s k

g  p e n c i l

h  s c i s s o r s

i  e n v e l o p e

j  t a b l e

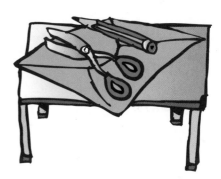

---

**II**   Write the names of the things under the pictures. Use pairs of consonants in the box to help you.

a
___ a ___

c
___ e ___

e
___ a ___

b
___ a ___

d
___ a ___

ct  lg  mn

jm  cn

# Same meanings

Sometimes, different words can be used to say the **same thing**.

shout  yell  roar

These words can all be used to mean someone is talking very loudly.

**I** What words mean the same thing? Draw a line to link the matching words.

a big

b small

c shiny

d noisy

e dash

f gently

g flower

h chair

run

blossom

loud

tiny

softly

seat

sparkly

huge

**II** Think of a word that means the same as these words. Write your word in the space.

a smelly ___stinky___

b sleepy _____

c jump _____

d walk _____

e cry _____

f sad _____

g happy _____

h angry _____

i wet _____

j squashy _____

# Opposites

**Dark** and **light** have opposite meanings.

During the day, it is light.

At night, it is dark.

**I** **Draw a line to match the opposites.**

a open     shiny

b big      shut

c tidy     horrible

d dull     dry

e hard     soft

f wet      quiet

g loud     messy

h lovely   small

**II** **Think of a word that means the opposite of each of the words below. Write your words in the spaces.**

a happy    _sad_          f full    _____

b awake    _____     g slow    _____

c out      _____     h man     _____

d up       _____     i run     _____

e after    _____     j low     _____

# Test 1 The alphabet

All **words** are made up of **letters**. There are **26** letters in the **alphabet**.

**Fill in the missing letters.**

a b 1.c d e f

j 3.i h 2.g

k l 4.m n o

r q 5.p

6.s

7.t

u

8.v w 9.x y 10.z

Colour in your score

10 9 8 7 6 5 4 3 2 1

# Test 2 Making some words (1)

The sound of the **first letter** of each of these words is the **same**.

sun          saw          sink

**Choose one of these letters to start each word.**

**m     p     h**

1. _peg

2. _pan

3. _hop

4. _pin

5. _mat

6. _hut

7. _hen

8. _mop

9. _mug

10. _pen

Colour in your score

33

# Test 3 Making some words (2)

We use **letters** to make **words**.

b + a + t = bat

**Do these sums. Write the words you make.**

**1.** s + a + d = _sad_

**2.** d + i + g = _dig_

**3.** b + a + g = _bag_

**4.** t + o + p = _top_

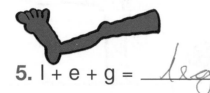

**5.** l + e + g = _leg_

**6.** f + o + x = _fox_

**7.** n + e + t = _net_

**8.** t + u + b = _tub_

**9.** d + o + g = _dog_

**10.** j + u + g = _jug_

10
9
8
7
6
5
4
3
2
1

Colour in your score

# Test 4 Labels

Many pictures have **labels** to help you.

**Write the correct name under each animal.**

| | | | | |
|---|---|---|---|---|
| monkey | goat | horse | tiger | kangaroo |
| donkey | bear | zebra | camel | panda |

1. camel
2. horse
3. kangaroo
4. zebra
5. bear
6. tiger
7. monkey
8. goat
9. donkey
10. panda

Colour in your score

# Test 5 Sentences

A **sentence** must make **sense**.

I to hop like. ☒    I like to hop. ☑

**Write the words in order to make some sentences.**

1. sun yellow.  The is _____

2. green.  is grass The _____

3. read.  like to I _____

4. lay eggs.  Hens _____

5. lion A roar.  can _____

6. raining.  is It _____

7. in You water.  swim _____

8. ball.  You a kick _____

9. door The shut.  is _____

10. stripes.  A has tiger _____

10

9

8

7

6

5

4

3

2

1

Colour in your score

36

# Test 6 Missing words

A **sentence** must make **sense**.

A roars. ☒        A lion roars. ☑

**Choose the best word to finish each sentence.**

| elephant | sun | money | cup | kangaroo |
|---|---|---|---|---|
| banana | star | spade | bike | umbrella |

1. You ride a _____ .

2. The _____ shines.

3. A _____ twinkles.

4. You spend _____ .

5. You eat a _____ .

6. A _____ hops.

7. You need an _____ in the rain.

8. You drink from a _____ .

9. An _____ has a trunk.

10. You dig with a _____ .

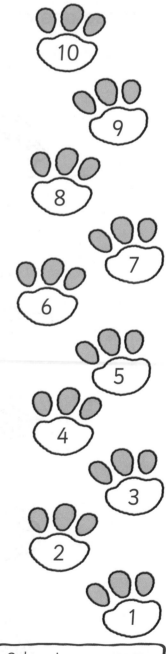

Colour in your score

# Test 7 Last letters

The sound of the **last letter** of each of these words is the **same**.

pen     pin     pan

**Choose one of these letters to finish each word.**

t     g     p

1. ba_g_

2. ma_p_

3. zi_p_

4. cu_p_

5. ha_t_

6. wi_g_

7. ne_t_

8. do_g_

9. ru_g_

10. po_t_

Colour in your score

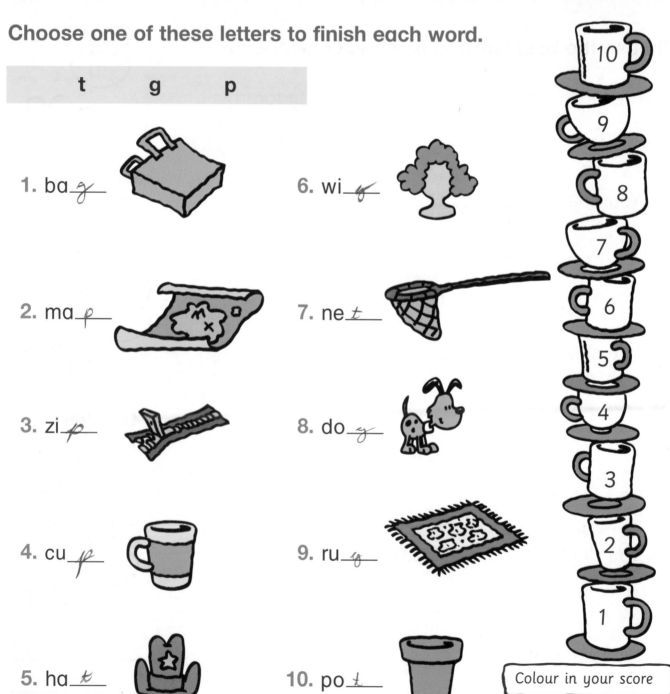

38

# Test 8 Groups of words

We sometimes **group** words together. These are all **birds**.

hen      parrot      sparrow

bike     rocket     helicopter     bus     aeroplane

boat     yacht     car     ship     lorry

**Sort these things into groups.**

Things that go on land.

1. _____     3. _____

2. _____     4. _____

Things that fly in the sky.   Things that go on the water.

5. _____     8. _____

6. _____     9. _____

7. _____     10. _____

10
9
8
7
6
5
4
3
2
1

Colour in your score

# Test 9 **Word building**

We can **build** words from **letters** and **groups of letters**.

b + ag      r + ag      w + ag

bag      rag      wag

**Do these sums. Write the words you make.**

1. f + an = _fan_

6. r + od = _rod_

**6**

2. s + ix = _six_

7. p + eg = _peg_

3. v + an = _van_

8. c + ut = _cut_

4. n + od = _nod_

9. m + ix = _mix_

5. l + eg = _leg_

10. n + ut = _nut_

10
9
8
7
6
5
4
3
2
1

Colour in your score

40

# Test 10 Middle letters

The sound of the **middle letter** of each of these words is the **same**.

pan          bat          bag

**Choose the correct middle letter to make each word.**

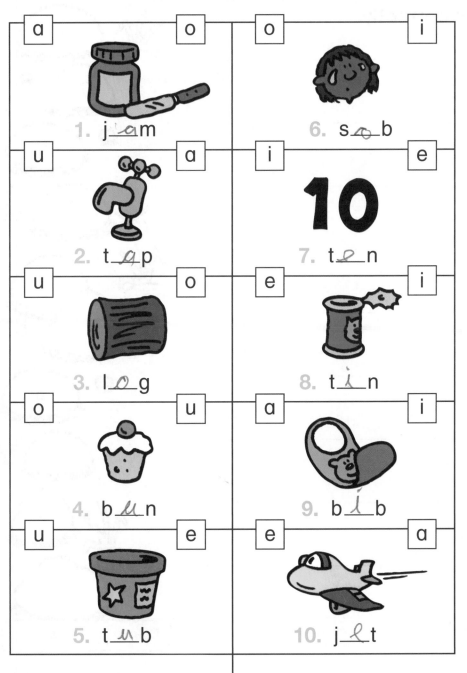

| a | | o | | o | | i |
|---|---|---|---|---|---|---|
| 1. j_a_m | | | | 6. s_o_b | | |

| u | | a | | i | | e |

2. t_a_p                    7. t_e_n

| u | | o | | e | | i |

3. l_o_g                    8. t_i_n

| o | | u | | a | | i |

4. b_u_n                    9. b_i_b

| u | | e | | e | | a |

5. t_u_b                    10. j_e_t

10
9
8
7
6
5
4
3
2
1

Colour in your score

41

# Test 11 Capital letters and full stops

A **sentence** always begins with a **capital letter** and often ends with a **full stop**.

The girl fell off her bike!

**Write these sentences correctly.**

1. the rain falls _____

2. a tree grows tall _____

3. the sky is blue _____

4. my cup is full _____

5. a cow moos _____

6. we like books _____

7. you bang a drum _____

8. it is sunny _____

9. a ball is round _____

10. i like to sing _____

10
9
8
7
6
5
4
3
2
1

Colour in your score

42

# Test 12 The letters *ff*, *ll* and *ss*

Some words end with **double letters**.

Pa**ss** the ba**ll**.

| | doll | off | bell | |
|---|---|---|---|---|
| hill | toss | puff | fall | |
| | hiss | cuff | fuss | |

**Write the words that end with ff.**

1. _____          3. _____

2. _____

**Write the words that end with ll.**

4. _____          6. _____

5. _____          7. _____

**Write the words that end with ss.**

8. _____          10. _____

9. _____

Colour in your score

# Test 13 The letters *ck*

Many words end in **ck**.

A du**ck** says qua**ck**.

**Do these sums. Write the words you make.**

1. b + a + ck = _back_

2. p + a + ck = _pack_

3. n + e + ck = _neck_

4. p + e + ck = _peck_

5. k + i + ck = _kick_

6. s + i + ck = _sick_

7. l + o + ck = _____

8. d + o + ck = _____

9. l + u + ck = _____

10. s + u + ck = _____

Colour in your score

# Test 14 The letters *ng* and *nk*

Many words end in **ng** and **nk**.

I can si**ng**.

I can thi**nk**.

**Find and write the ng or nk words that are hiding.**

1. a b a n g w    *bang*

2. b a n k t y    _____

3. h g k i n g    _____

4. b s o n g m    _____

5. f v s a n k    _____

6. h a n g j b    _____

7. s a r i n g    _____

8. z l i n k n    _____

9. b u n k x c    _____

10. j h p i n k    _____

10

9

8

7

6

5

4

3

2

1

Colour in your score

# Test 15 Letter blends at the beginning of words

These words all have **l** as a second letter.

slide    fly    clock    black    glue

**Write the new words you make.**

1. Change the **fl** in **fl**ip to **sl**.    _slip_

2. Change the **pl** in **pl**ot to **sl**.    _____

3. Change the **sl** in **sl**at to **fl**.    _____

4. Change the **cl** in **cl**ick to **fl**.    _____

5. Change the **fl** in **fl**ap to **cl**.    _____

6. Change the **bl** in **bl**ink to **cl**.    _____

7. Change the **cl** in **cl**ot to **bl**.    _____

8. Change the **sl** in **sl**ack to **bl**.    _____

9. Change the **cl** in **cl**ass to **gl**.    _____

10. Change the **cl** in **cl**ad to **gl**.    _____

10

9

8

7

6

5

4

3

2

1

Colour in your score

# Test 16 Letter blends at the end of words

Say these words slowly. Listen to the way they **end**.

bolt　　shelf　milk　help　　gold

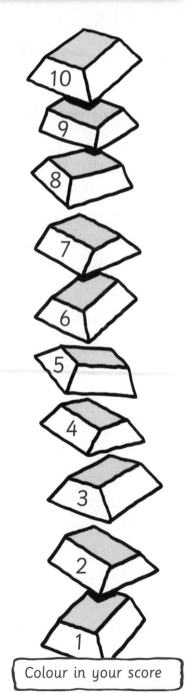

| | hold | elf | milk | |
|---|---|---|---|---|
| yelp | belt | silk | gold |
| | help | shelf | melt | |

**Write the pairs of rhyming words.**

**Write the words that end with ld.**

1. _____ 2. _____

**Write the words that end with lf.**

3. _____ 4. _____

**Write the words that end with lk.**

5. _____ 6. _____

**Write the words that end with lp.**

7. _____ 8. _____

**Write the words that end with lt.**

9. _____ 10. _____

Colour in your score

47

# Test 17 **Plurals**

**Plural** means when there is **more than one**.

We add **s** to many words to make them plural.

one rabbit                     three rabbit**s**

**Fill in the missing word.**

1. one hat but two _____.

2. one leg but two _____.

3. one tin but two _____.

4. one pot but two _____.

5. one mug but two _____.

6. one _____ but two pans.

7. one _____ but two pets.

8. one _____ but two lips.

9. one _____ but two dogs.

10. one _____ but two sums.

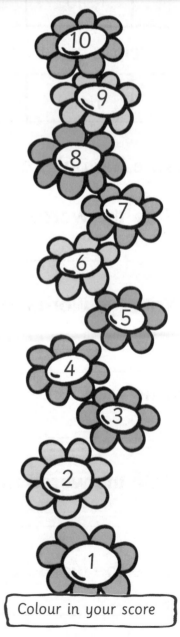

Colour in your score

48

# Test 18 Sets of words

This is a **set** of fruit.

orange   banana   apple

This is a **set** of animals.

lion   monkey   elephant

potato   butterfly   cabbage   onion   ant

carrot   beetle   cauliflower   earwig   turnip

**Write the names of the vegetables.**

1. _____     4. _____

2. _____     5. _____

3. _____     6. _____

**Write the names of the insects.**

7. _____     9. _____

8. _____     10. _____

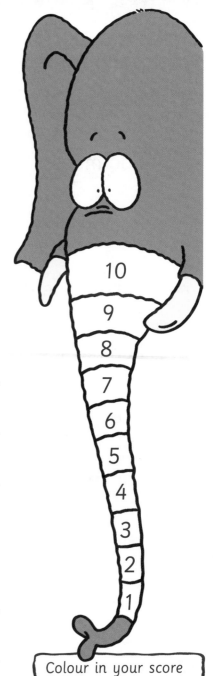

10
9
8
7
6
5
4
3
2
1

Colour in your score

# Test 19 Silly sentences

A **sentence** must make **sense**.

The dog ate the bone. ☑    The bone ate the dog. ☒

**Write each sentence correctly.**

1. A cow barks. _____

2. A dog moos. _____

3. A duck hisses. _____

4. A horse cheeps. _____

5. A hen neighs. _____

6. A sheep chirps. _____

7. A snake quacks. _____

8. A bird bleats. _____

9. A bee brays. _____

10. A donkey buzzes. _____

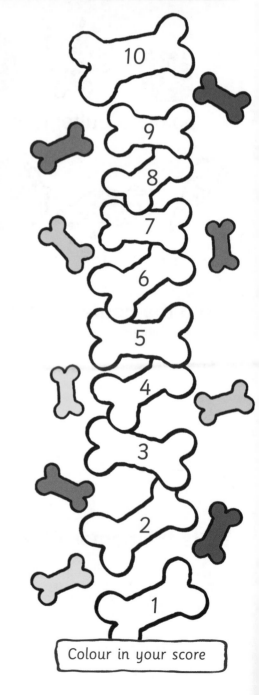

Colour in your score

# Test 20 The letters *sh* and *ch*

You will find **sh** and **ch** in many words.

fi**sh** and **ch**ips

**Choose sh or ch to complete each word.**

1. _____est

2. _____ell

3. _____ip

4. di_____

5. _____eep

6. ben_____

7. _____icken

8. tor_____

9. _____eese

10. bru_____

10
9
8
7
6
5
4
3
2
1

Colour in your score

51

# Test 21 The letters *ee* and *oo*

The letters **ee** and **oo** are two common letter patterns.

I have some b**oo**ts on my f**ee**t.

**Choose ee or oo to complete each word.**

1. _____l

2. st_____l

3. p_____l

4. br_____m

5. m_____n

6. tr_____

7. w_____p

8. f_____d

9. sw_____t

10. b_____

Colour in your score

52

## Test 22 **The letters** *ay* **and** *ai*

The letters **ay** often come at the **end** of a word.

The letters **ai** often come in the **middle** of a word.

tr**ay**

tr**ai**n

**Choose ai or ay to complete the word in each sentence.**

1. It is a lovely d_____.

2. The r_____n is falling.

3. I hit the n_____l with a hammer.

4. You can swim in the b_____.

5. You can make things with cl_____.

6. The sn_____l went slowly.

7. I had to w_____t for my dinner.

8. You can pl_____ in the park.

9. The plates are on a tr_____.

10. You will have to w_____t and see.

10
9
8
7
6
5
4
3
2
1

Colour in your score

53

# Test 23 Vowels and consonants

There are **26** letters in the **alphabet**.

| a | b | c | d | e | f | g | h | i | j | k | l | m |
|---|---|---|---|---|---|---|---|---|---|---|---|---|
| n | o | p | q | r | s | t | u | v | w | x | y | z |

The five **vowels** are **a, e, i, o, u.**

All the other letters are called **consonants**.

**Fill in the missing vowel in each word.**

1. m_a_t

2. s_u_n

3. b_e_d

4. n_e_t

5. b_i_b

6. b_a_g

7. f_o_x

8. s_i_x

9. m_u_d

10. b_u_n

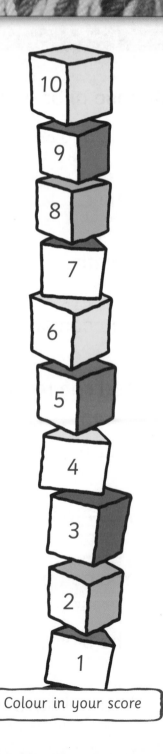

10
9
8
7
6
5
4
3
2
1

Colour in your score

# Test 24 Names

Whenever we write **someone's name** we should always **start** with a **capital letter**.

Humpty Dumpty sat on a wall.

**Write the names of these nursery rhyme characters correctly.**

1. humpty dumpty *Humpty Dumpty*

2. little bo peep *Little Bo Peep*

3. margery daw *Margery Daw*

4. tommy tucker *Tommy Tucker*

5. jack horner *Jack Horner*

6. polly *Polly*

7. mary *Mary*

8. lucy locket *Lucy Locket*

9. georgie porgie *Georgie Porgie*

10. bobby shafto *Bobby Shafto*

Colour in your score

10
9
8
7
6
5
4
3
2
1

# Test 25 **The endings** *ing* **and** *ed*

We can add **ing** and **ed** to the ends of some words.

*I am wash**ing** my face.*
wash + ing = washing

*Yesterday I wash**ed** my feet.*
wash + ed = washed

**Add ing to each word. Write the word you make.**

1. talk    *talking*

2. lick    *licking*

3. draw    *drawing*

**Add ed to each word. Write the word you make.**

4. shout    *shouted*

5. kick    *kicked*

6. crawl    *crawled*

**Take the ing off. Write the word you are left with.**

7. sniffing    *sniff*

8. sleeping    *sleep*

**Take the ed off. Write the word you are left with.**

9. turned    *turn*

10. passed    *pass*

Colour in your score

56

# Test 26 Questions

A question must begin with a **capital letter** and end with a **question mark**.

**capital letter**

**question mark**

How many legs has a spider?

**Write these questions correctly.**

1. what is for tea

   _____

2. when are you coming

   _____

3. what shape is a ball

   _____

4. who is making that noise

   _____

5. where do you live

   _____

6. how many sweets have you got

   _____

7. what is your address

   _____

8. who is your teacher

   _____

9. when is it time for dinner

   _____

10. where is London

    _____

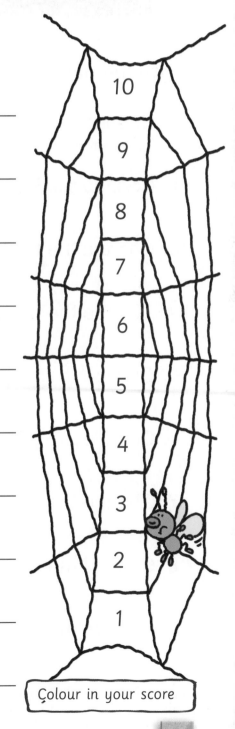

10
9
8
7
6
5
4
3
2
1

Colour in your score

57

# Test 27 The letters *ea* and *oa*

The two letter patterns **ea** and **oa** are common.

a b**oa**t on the s**ea**

**Write the new words you make.**

1. Change the **s** in se**a** to **t**. _____

2. Change the **b** in **b**eat to **s**. _____

3. Change the **l** in **l**eap to **h**. _____

4. Change the **b** in **b**eak to **l**. _____

5. Change the **t** in **t**each to **b**. _____

6. Change the **g** in **g**oat to **b**. _____

7. Change the **f** in **f**oal to **g**. _____

8. Change the **t** in **t**oad to **r**. _____

9. Change the **c** in **c**oast to **t**. _____

10. Change the **p** in **p**oach to **c**. _____

10

9

8

7

6

5

4

3

2

1

Colour in your score

# Test 28 Magic *e*

Look what happens when we add **e** to the **end** of some words.

hop + e = hope

**Do these sums. Write the words you make.**

1. mad + e = _____

2. slid + e = _____

3. mak + e = _____

4. can + e = _____

5. cub + e = _____

6. rob + e = _____

7. shin + e = _____

8. cut + e = _____

9. tap + e = _____

10. bit + e = _____

Colour in your score

# Test 29 The months of the year

It is important to know how to spell the **months of the year** correctly.

**Here are the months of the year in the wrong order.**

| | | | |
|---|---|---|---|
| August | May | December | January |
| February | June | October | March |
| September | April | November | July |

**Fill in the missing months in order. Spell them correctly.**

|  |  |
|---|---|
| <u>January</u> | 5. _____ |
| <u>February</u> | 6. _____ |
| 1. _____ | 7. _____ |
| 2. _____ | 8. _____ |
| 3. _____ | 9. _____ |
| 4. _____ | 10. _____ |

10
9
8
7
6
5
4
3
2
1

Colour in your score

60

# Test 30 Rhyming

**Rhyming** is important in spelling.

A plane can **fly** in the **sky**.

| | ring | bake | train | |
|---|---|---|---|---|
| goat | cool | king | coat |
| | chain | pool | cake | |

## Write the pairs of rhyming words.

**Write the** ing **words.**

1. _____

2. _____

**Write the** ain **words.**

7. _____

8. _____

**Write the** ool **words.**

3. _____

4. _____

**Write the** ake **words.**

9. _____

10. _____

**Write the** oat **words.**

5. _____

6. _____

Colour in your score

# ANSWERS

**Page 2**

I  a  fan     d  red
   b  stink    e  dot
   c  plug     f  sack

II a  smell    e  bin
   b  park     f  rock
   c  frog     g  pig
   d  fox

**Page 3**

I  a  a b c d e f g
   b  u v w x y z
   c  p q r s t u v
   d  f g h i j k l m
   e  j k l m n o p
   f  r s t u v w x
   g  d e f g h i j k

II a  box, cat, egg
   b  apple, bag, dig
   c  art, cup, pig
   d  baby, car, dog
   e  bed, door, wall
   f  book, leg, sun
   g  bird, peg, tree

**Page 4**

I  Spellings remembered.

II a  man     e  dot
   b  fin      f  wig
   c  pig     g  sun
   d  pin     h  ball

**Page 5**

I  Words overwritten neatly.

II Words copied correctly;
   rounded letters, correctly
   formed, sitting on lines.

**Page 6**

I  a  I like you.
   b  This is my sister.
   c  Sausages are my
     favourite.
   d  I am going out.
   e  I want to read.

II a  I like my brother.
   b  My dog likes walking.
   c  The cat can smell its food.
   d  We eat sweets.
   e  Rain makes you wet.

**Page 7**

I  a  (B)rian
   b  (M)rs (J)ones
   c  (A)ndrew
   d  (E)ngland
   e  (M)r (B)rown
   f  (M)iss (L)acey

g  (L)ondon
h  (M)r (S)mith
i  (F)rance
j  (J)anet
k  (D)octor (D)oolittle
l  (C)ambridge
m  (A)frica
n  (S)cotland

II a  (M)y friend (J)amila comes
     from (Y)orkshire.
   b  (M)y dog is called (B)ertie.
   c  (A)untie (J)ane lives in
     (E)dinburgh.
   d  (B)ruce, (S)tella and (J)odi are
     my friends.
   e  (W)e sailed down the (R)iver
     (T)hames.
   f  (D)ad's name is (J)ohn.
   g  (I) am going on holiday to
     (P)ortugal with my sister
     (S)arah.
   h  (I) went to (D)urham to see
     the pantomime (C)inderella.

**Page 8**

I  a  fluff     f  stiff
   b  puff     g  muff
   c  buff     h  stuff
   d  cuff     i  staff
   e  sniff     j  whiff

II a  giraffe    d  whiff
   b  puff      e  cliff
   c  sniff     f  muff

**Page 9**

I  Children will not know all of
   the words below, but they are
   given for correctness.
   a  ball, bull, bill, bell
   b  yell
   c  sill, sell
   d  call, cell, cull
   e  hill, hall, hull, hell
   f  doll, dell, dull, dill
   g  fall, fill, full, fell
   h  pull, pill, pall, poll
   i  till, tall, tell, toll
   j  will, wall, well

II a  ball     d  bull
   b  wall     e  well
   c  bell     f  doll

**Page 10**

I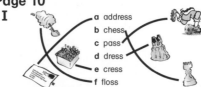
a  address
b  chess
c  pass
d  dress
e  cress
f  floss

II a  grass    d  floss
   b  mess    e  kiss
   c  cress    f  hiss

**Page 11**

I  Check child's pictures of each
   'ck' item.

II a  sick, sock
   b  knock
   c  wick
   d  flick, flock
   e  pick, pock
   f  Rick, rock
   g  lick, lock
   h  stick, stock
   i  smock
   j  trick

**Page 12**

I  a  rectangle    g  penguin
   b  orange     h  swing
   c  orangutan   i  ring
   d  sing       j  finger
   e  king       k  sting
   f  triangle     l  herring

II Any reasonable sentences
   containing the words.

**Page 13**

I  a  bland    f  bleat
   b  black    g  bleep
   c  blue     h  bloat
   d  blend    i  bleak
   e  blank    j  blade

II Check child's pictures of the
   words listed.

**Page 14**

I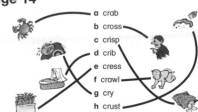
a  crab
b  cross
c  crisp
d  crib
e  cress
f  crawl
g  cry
h  crust

II Check child's pictures of the
   words listed.

**Page 15**

I  (in any order)
   a  trade    e  true
   b  trip      f  trumpet
   c  tramp    g  travel
   d  trash    h  tray

II a  track    e  traffic
   b  tractor   f  tree
   c  train     g  try
   d  trap

**Page 16**

I  
a strap    e straw  
b string    f stream  
c strong    g stretch  
d street    h strange  

II Sentences using the circled words.

**Page 17**

I  
a wind    f land  
b kind    g pulp  
c band    h help  
d gulp    i find  
e hand    j sand  

II a band  b hand  c yelp  d help  e gulp

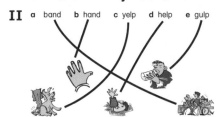

**Page 18**

I  
a post    f bust  
b last    g trust  
c blast    h must  
d fast    i beast  
e just    j least  

II The correct words are:  
a dust    e must  
b yeast    f feast  
c past    g crust  
d mast  

**Page 19**

I

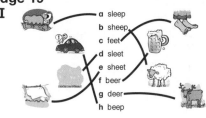

a sleep  
b sheep  
c feet  
d sleet  
e sheet  
f beer  
g deer  
h beep  

II  
a deep  
b seen  
c been  
d teenager  
e creep, sleeping  
f peep  
g beep  
h sleet  

**Page 20**

I Pictures of the items mentioned:  
a stool    c school  
b pool    d food  

II a moon    d too  
b cool    e wool  
c spoon  

**Page 21**

I Circled: a, d, e, f

II  
a a hot, cooked slice of bread  
b baby horse  
c it burns on a fire  
d bread  
e tree  
f it sails on the sea  
g it is like a frog  
h cars drive on this  

**Page 22**

I Check child's pictures of the items listed.

II Sentences using the words listed.

**Page 23**

I  
a pie    f tries  
b tie    g why  
c die    h fly  
d lie    i cry  
e thief    j by  

II a die    d spy  
b fly    e tie  
c cry  

**Page 24**

I  
a that    f whip  
b this    g trap  
c then    h drop  
d what    i crop  
e when    j bran  

II  
a trade, trip, tree  
b plant  
c bring  
d blade, blab, blip (bling, if the child knows this word)  
e crab  
f smile  
g split  
h drab, drip  
i fresh, free  
j when, while, whip, whee  

**Page 25**

I  
a ?    e .  
b .    f .  
c ?    g ?  
d ?    h ?  

II Questions written using the question words provided.

**Page 26**

I  
a horses    e comics  
b birds    f sweets  
c girls    g dogs  
d flowers    h crisps  

II  
a women    d men  
b geese    e lice  
c mice  

**Page 27**

I  
a liked    e painted  
b talked    f called  
c looked    g washed  
d played  

II  
a jump    f lift  
b hop    g skip  
c try    h cry  
d call    i help  
e run  

**Page 28**

I  
a c(o)tt(a)g(e)  
b s(ea)s(i)d(e)  
c w(oo)ds  
d b(a)b(ie)s  
e sch(oo)l  
f c(o)mp(u)t(e)r  
g p(i)ct(u)r(e)  
h d(o)ct(o)r  
i b(e)rr(ie)s  
j l(ea)f  

II  
a house    d milk  
b books    e cake  
c glasses    f stars  

**Page 29**

I  
a boat    f desk  
b baby    g pencil  
c mouse    h scissors  
d sand    i envelope  
e sunshine    j table  

II  
a cat    d can  
b jam    e man  
c leg  

**Page 30**

I  
a huge    e run  
b tiny    f softly  
c sparkly    g blossom  
d loud    h seat  

II Any suitable words such as:  
a stinky    f unhappy  
b tired    g glad  
c leap    h cross  
d stroll    i soaked  
e weep    j spongy  

**Page 31**

I  
a shut    e soft  
b small    f dry  
c messy    g quiet  
d shiny    h horrible  

II Any suitable words such as:  
a sad    f empty  
b asleep    g fast  
c in    h woman  
d down    i walk  
e before    j high

**Page 32**
1. c
2. g
3. i
4. m
5. p
6. s
7. t
8. v
9. x
10. z

**Page 33**
1. peg
2. pan
3. hop
4. pin
5. mat
6. hut
7. hen
8. mop
9. mug
10. pen

**Page 34**
1. sad
2. dig
3. bag
4. top
5. leg
6. fox
7. net
8. tub
9. dog
10. jug

**Page 35**
1. camel
2. horse
3. kangaroo
4. zebra
5. bear
6. tiger
7. monkey
8. goat
9. donkey
10. panda

**Page 36**
1. The sun is yellow.
2. The grass is green.
3. I like to read.
4. Hens lay eggs.
5. A lion can roar.
6. It is raining.
7. You swim in water.
8. You kick a ball.
9. The door is shut.
10. A tiger has stripes.

**Page 37**
1. bike
2. sun
3. star
4. money
5. banana
6. kangaroo
7. umbrella
8. cup
9. elephant
10. spade

**Page 38**
1. bag
2. map
3. zip
4. cup
5. hat
6. wig
7. net
8. dog
9. rug
10. pot

**Page 39**
1. bike
2. bus
3. car
4. lorry
5. rocket
6. helicopter
7. aeroplane
8. boat
9. yacht
10. ship

**Page 40**
1. fan
2. six
3. van
4. nod
5. leg
6. rod
7. peg
8. cut
9. mix
10. nut

**Page 41**
1. jam
2. tap
3. log
4. bun
5. tub
6. sob
7. ten
8. tin
9. bib
10. jet

**Page 42**
1. The rain falls.
2. A tree grows tall.
3. The sky is blue.
4. My cup is full.
5. A cow moos.
6. We like books.
7. You bang a drum.
8. It is sunny.
9. A ball is round.
10. I like to sing.

**Page 43**
1. off
2. puff
3. cuff
4. doll
5. bell
6. hill
7. fall
8. toss
9. hiss
10. fuss

**Page 44**
1. back
2. pack
3. neck
4. peck
5. kick
6. sick
7. lock
8. dock
9. luck
10. suck

**Page 45**
1. bang
2. bank
3. king
4. song
5. sank
6. hang
7. ring
8. link
9. bunk
10. pink

**Page 46**
1. slip
2. slot
3. flat
4. flick
5. clap
6. clink
7. blot
8. black
9. glass
10. glad

# HOW TO
# PROPAGATE

# HOW TO
# PROPAGATE

## techniques and tips
## for over 1000 plants

## John Cushnie

Kyle Cathie Limited

# To my lovely daughter Laura

First published in Great Britain in 2006 by
Kyle Cathie Limited
122 Arlington Road
London NW1 7HP
general.enquiries@kyle-cathie.com
www.kylecathie.com

10 9 8 7

ISBN 978 1 85626 612 3

Project editor Caroline Taggart
Design Isobel Gillan
Copy editor Catherine Ward
Picture research and editorial assistance Vicki Murrell
Index by Helen Snaith
Production by Sha Huxtable & Alice Holloway

A Cataloguing in Publication record for this title is available
from the British Library.

Printed in Singapore through Tien Wah Press

Title page: *Pelargonium* 'Merlot'
This page: *Lewisia cotyledon* 'Regenbogen'

# Contents

# introduction

Not so many years ago, everyone who had a garden propagated most of their own plants. Today we tend just to nip down to the garden centre or, if we are planning something on a grander scale, we rely on a landscape contractor to tell us what to do and to supply the plants. Which is a shame, because most of the plants that we grow, whether they are bedding plants, perennials, shrubs or even trees, can be propagated with ease. There are hundreds of shrubs and perennials that root like weeds. With a certain amount of know-how, a degree of patience and little else you can have fun and fill your garden to overflowing. The only danger is that, like me and a lot of other gardeners, you may become obsessed with propagation.

Nature, of course, has been propagating since time began. Long before humans learned to garden, she employed the services of birds, furry animals, wind and water to transport seeds far and wide. Today, in every garden as well as in the wild, seed is spread naturally by those same means. Birds love to eat berries and most seeds pass through their digestive system unharmed. The seeds are often dropped miles from where they were eaten, which is one of the reasons that unsolicited new plants may appear in your garden. Some seeds, including those of weeds such as thistles and cleavers, cling to the coats of wild creatures and are spread through the countryside and the suburbs as these animals go about their daily lives. Tree seeds are at the right height to be carried on the wind and those of the sycamore and maple are designed by nature to make sure they travel first class. Their 'wings' allow them to spin on the slightest breeze

Some plants have a habit of growth that promotes natural propagation. Left to themselves, suckering trees such as poplars and aspens produce well-rooted young plants that will eventually flower profusely. Strawberries spread by runners, rooting where they come in contact with the soil, and this is the recognised method of propagating commercial fruiting varieties.

Where plants such as rhododendrons, dogwood and hydrangea grow in the wild, low-growing branches root where they touch the ground. These become plants and leap-frog at an alarming rate. Eventually, a single plant may become a small copse or cover vast expanses of land, as in the case of wild rhododendrons growing on the sides of Scottish hills.

Gardeners call this layering and have adapted this method to propagate these plants in a more controlled fashion.

Over millennia, gardeners have copied Mother Nature, improving on her techniques and using heat, cold and chemicals to encourage pieces of plant to root or seeds to germinate. And it is the improvement on those techniques that this book is about.

## Why propagate?

The obvious answer is to have more plants. Commercially, it is big business with billions of pounds' worth of plants being sold worldwide annually. On the domestic level, it is fun to do. I love to see seeds germinating and then watch as they turn into plants with flowers or edible crops. Whether the original seed was finer than dust or, like a broad bean, as large as my thumbnail, the marvel of the resulting plant never ceases to amaze me. There is an enormous sense of satisfaction when something that is difficult to root starts to grow. Compared with buying all your plant requirements, there is also a lot

of money to be saved. When growing from seed, you may even be lucky enough to produce a brand new variety and end up having a new plant named after you!

Anomalies, mutations and plant 'sports' occur naturally. If the portion of the plant that is different in some way is propagated, then the world and its gardeners have a new plant. Most variegated forms of shrubs such as hollies and elaeagnus first appeared as sports growing on plants that had previously had all green foliage. Cuttings of the variegated shoot were taken and now they are available to us all.

When you take a cutting and propagate it, the resulting plant is identical to the parent. The same cannot be said of seeds. Quite often the resulting seedlings will be a mixture, with some resembling one or other of the parents and others a cross between the two. Just like humans!

Starting on page 19, I give detailed instructions for all the methods of propagation that the home gardener is likely to want to use. I've been propagating plants for over forty years and I have never ceased to find it exciting. I hope you will too.

# materials and equipment

Some forms of propagation – such as rooting hardwood cuttings in the open ground – require only a pair of secateurs or a sharp knife. For others, a container, some compost and a clear polythene bag are sufficient. Difficult-to-root plants may require specialist compost mixtures, rooting hormone powders or gels and heated propagators where the bottom heat under the pots and the air temperature may be controlled.

*Clay pots may be old-fashioned, but they are a joy to work with and there is less risk of compost becoming waterlogged.*

## Before you begin

As with all aspects of gardening, prevention is better than cure and it is common sense to pay careful attention to hygiene. Keep all tools scrupulously clean. Disinfect them after taking every batch of cuttings, as some disorders, such as virus disease, can be spread throughout a batch of cuttings by the infected sap on the blades of knives or secateurs. And be vigilant: look out for pests and signs of disease; don't let one infected plant ruin all your efforts (see page 106 for more details of symptoms). Damping off disease can wipe out a tray of seedlings overnight unless preventative measures are taken. A few greenfly introduced to the propagating frame via a single cutting could result in every plant being plastered with them before the rooted cuttings are ready to pot up. When propagating by cuttings, avoid taking them from a plant that is distorted or where the leaves are mottled or streaked with yellow. These symptoms suggest that the plant is infected with virus disease. If using hormone powder or gel to assist rooting, use only small quantities at a time. That way, if a cutting is diseased, any contamination via the powder is restricted to a small batch of plants.

If you are reusing pots and seed trays, make sure you sterilize them in disinfectant and scrub them thoroughly before filling with compost. Buy sterilized seed and cuttings compost and sterilized loam soil. Ordinary garden soil will be contaminated with pests, disease spores and weed seeds.

Greenhouses, propagating units and garden frames should be cleaned on a regular basis. Wash the inside of the glass with a fungicide and, if the greenhouse is empty, use a power hose to eliminate pests from cracks and corners. Remove all debris and don't use the greenhouse as a store for pots, trays and compost where pests may overwinter.

In addition to basic hygiene, there are a few points of common sense that will make sure your efforts are not wasted.

■ Strong direct sunlight can cause cuttings to transpire and wither before roots can form. Sun scorch can be a serious problem, burning the leaves of tender seedlings. To avoid this, screen the propagating area, and seedlings in particular, from direct sunlight. Cover cuttings with horticultural fleece (readily available in garden centres) or polythene to cut the glare and retain a humid atmosphere around the cuttings.

■ Waterlogging will cause cuttings to rot prior to rooting and provide ideal conditions for diseases such as black leg and damping off. Pots and trays should have an adequate number of drainage holes. If you are reusing containers, check that the holes in the base are not blocked.

■ Use rooting compost with added grit to keep it open and free draining (see **Composts**, page 10). After the seed is sown don't pack down the surface of the compost too hard. Stand the container in water, allowing it to rise up through the drainage holes and wet the compost. Use mains water in preference to rainwater that has been stored in a butt, which may contain impurities such as fungus, spores or bacteria that harm young seedlings.

■ Nutritional problems may occur where seedlings are retained for too long in the seed compost. The definition of 'too long' varies from plant to plant but, as a general rule, a seedling should be potted on before it has produced four or six leaves. By this

*Clean glass inside and out provides maximum light, especially in early spring and autumn, when the sun is less powerful and light levels are lower.*

*Below left* Ensure that there are no lumps in the compost by sieving it over the seed. Lumps prevent tiny seedlings from reaching the surface of the compost.

*Below right* A single seedling per container avoids the need to prick out.

time the growth of leaves will be demanding nutrients not to be found in seed compost, which contains little or no fertilizer. If these developing plants run out of nutrients they will suffer, the foliage will turn yellow and growth will be stunted. Transplanting them into a suitable potting compost will usually solve the problem.

■ Hardwood cuttings take a season to root properly and the layering of shrubs may require two seasons or more. By that time, the available nutrients may leach out of a free-draining, sandy soil. If the foliage is yellowing, an application of a balanced liquid fertilizer will usually help the plant recover.

## Composts

In the good old days (I wonder when that was?) gardeners made up their own compost mixtures and the recipes were closely guarded secrets. Today, with the benefit of research, there are no secrets and excellent seed, cuttings and potting composts are available off the garden centre shelf.

The most common materials used to form composts for propagation are peat, sand, vermiculite and perlite.

**Peat** is a sterile compost with no nutrients added, which helps to retain moisture when mixed with free-draining materials.

A fine grade of peat is ideal for seed sowing and cuttings. If it is allowed to dry out, it is the devil to get wet again.

**Sand** can be used to cover seed in place of compost. There are many grades of sand from fine silver sand to horticultural grit. Coarse grades are excellent for mixing with other materials to improve drainage and to aerate the compost. Always wash sand before use, as it may contain fine particles of clay that could clog up the sand, drying to mud. Never, ever use sand from the beach as it will be contaminated with salt.

**Vermiculite** is a form of expanded mica (a silicate mineral) that retains moisture. It may be used in the same way as sand.

**Perlite** consists of expanded volcanic granules. It is sterile and, when mixed with other materials, will retain moisture and encourage aeration. It is available in several grades – as a rule of thumb, the larger the seed the coarser the grade.

**Leaf mould** or decayed leaves is an excellent substitute for peat in potting compost. However, because it is not sterile, I would never use it in seed compost, though I have used sieved leaf mould when rooting semi-ripe cuttings.

**Composted bark** is, I feel, similar to leaf mould. While it has uses in potting mixtures for acid-loving plants, it is not suitable for propagation.

**Coir** is a by-product of coconut waste. It can be used in potting composts, but I have never had great success using it for propagation.

You can make your own soil-based seed compost by mixing two parts (by bulk) sterilized loam soil, one part moss peat and one part sharp sand. Add 90g super-phosphate (to aid the formation of roots) to a barrow load of mixture. For plants that prefer an alkaline soil, add 60g ground limestone. For cutting compost, use equal parts of peat and coarse sand or grit.

### Ready-made composts

For the busy gardener there is every conceivable type of compost available pre-packed on the garden centre shelf. The main types to interest the propagator are seed, cuttings and potting composts. There are also specialist mixtures for ericaceous plants (lime haters), cacti and succulents where the compost needs to be very free draining, bulb compost and compost suitable for growing orchids.

Seed and cuttings composts may double up, although I prefer a very fine mixture for seed sowing and one with a coarser mixture and added grit for good drainage when rooting cuttings. Both contain minimal quantities of nutrients as they are for short-term use only: seedlings and rooted cuttings will soon be moved on.

For propagation, avoid anything labelled multi-purpose compost. It will contain too many nutrients, encouraging seedlings and cuttings to become leggy and thin. The soil in potting composts such as the John Innes range has been sterilized and is free from pests, diseases and weed seeds. John Innes composts are graded No 1, 2 and 3, depending on their nutrient content. No 1 is used for potting on seedlings or rooted plants, No 2 for repotting young plants. The strongest mixture is No 3 for repotting mature plants. Multi-purpose compost is also available peat free and can be used for potting, but is more likely to dry out than peat- or soil-based mixtures. I can't recommend garden soil for propagation purposes. It will be contaminated with weed seeds, pests and diseases. If you must use it, then small amounts can be drenched in boiling water but it is messy, turning to mud and taking days to dry out.

*A fine spray of water at room temperature will settle the soil around transplanted seedlings.*

Cuttings of larger shrubs, such as philadelphus, choisya and escallonia, will root well in an open, coarse compost. Use a seed compost with added grit, or mix your own using equal parts by bulk of peat and grit. Heather roots are thread-like and prefer fine compost with fewer air spaces and here I prefer an ericaceous seed compost.

## Basic equipment

**Containers** Whenever possible, use new pots and seed trays for sowing seed and rooting cuttings. As I've already said, if you are reusing containers they must be thoroughly cleaned by scrubbing in hot water with added disinfectant and

fungicide. Pests can lurk in crevices, especially in older clay pots.

Plastic containers are light, cheap and therefore disposable, so are a good choice for seedlings and cuttings. To save wasting compost, they need not be deep since the seedlings or rooted plants will be potted up or transplanted before the roots grow longer than 5–7.5cm.

Pots made of peat or other fibres can be used. Strips of expanded polystyrene trays are light and used extensively for growing annual bedding plants from seed.

Compressed peat modules are space saving. They expand when saturated with water, leaving a small depression for seed or cutting. Do not allow them to dry out as they need to be plunged in water to allow them to become moist.

**Labels** Make sure that plant labels are large enough to hold important information, such as the date when the cutting was taken or when the seed was sown. Always record the full plant name, including the species and variety. I also like to note the source of the cutting: who gave it to me or where it came from. Make sure that the marker ink won't wear off or fade. Names written with an HB pencil on white plastic remain clear for a considerable period.

**Polythene bags** A supply of clear polythene bags is essential to cover small containers of germinating seeds or cuttings. Freezer bags can be purchased in a variety of sizes, making them ideal for fitting over different-sized pot rims.

Add to the list clear polythene sheeting for covering trays. Horticultural fleece is better than polythene for rooting cuttings of some plants, such as lavender and hypericum, which require a less humid atmosphere.

## Extra equipment for propagating seeds

A wooden board is useful for firming the seed compost to produce a level surface ready for sowing. If the base of the board is cut slightly smaller than the seed tray all the compost will be firmed uniformly. You will also need a plastic or wooden dibber slightly thicker than your index finger and without a point to make suitable holes in the compost for transplanting seedlings. I like to use a table fork for lifting the seedlings out of the seed tray ready for transplanting. It's

*At this stage labels are essential, as lots of seedlings look very similar.*

an ideal size and easy to clean, but if you are male ask the head gardener before stealing it from the kitchen!

## Extra equipment for propagating cuttings

When it comes to propagation, sharp and clean are the two golden words. Secateurs, pocket knife and budding knife (for grafting and bud grafting) are essential. I prefer by-pass secateurs where the two blades make the cut. The anvil type, where a single blade cuts through to a flat strip of metal, can occasionally cause bruising to the base of a softwood cutting. Hygiene is critical to prevent the spread of infection. Clean blades with disinfectant after every operation and always before you store them at the end of the day to

prevent spreading diseases from plant to plant. Change disposable blades regularly. Sharpen blades regularly to ensure a clean cut and replace razor blades and carpet knife blades before they lose their edge. Store all equipment with sharp edges or points in a safe place away from children and non-gardeners who might be tempted to use them to cut bamboo or wire!

Many gardeners use a rooting hormone in powder or gel form to encourage their cuttings to root more quickly. These also contain a fungicide which offers the cutting some resistance to soil- and waterborne diseases. You will also need a hand-held sprayer with a misting nozzle to damp over cuttings to prevent loss of leaf moisture through transpiration.

## Propagators and cloches

Propagators come in all shapes, sizes and prices. They allow the amateur gardener to control the temperature of the air and the humidity surrounding the seeds or cuttings. Bottom heat can be provided to keep the compost at a suitable temperature to encourage rooting (see page 16). Within the controlled environment, plants can be sown earlier to flower or produce crops out of season.

On a very basic level, a clear polythene bag placed over the top of the pot and secured with a rubber band will provide a warm, humid atmosphere to encourage rooting or germination. One step up from this is an empty plastic bottle with the base cut off. This may be used to protect pots of young seedlings or individual seedlings planted in the open ground – being more solid, a bottle is less likely than a bag to suffer wind damage. If the bottle contained a sugary drink, wash it out beforehand to remove any remaining sugary liquid that may attract mould. Leave the screw cap on to begin with, but once cuttings have rooted, take it off so that the plants can harden off (see below).

The main drawback of polythene bags and plastic bottles is that condensation tends to build up on the inside. This layer of moisture reduces the available light and, by keeping the leaves wet, can cause fungal diseases such as botrytis and grey mould so make sure you remove them once a week and wipe the insides.

Unheated propagators are useful for germinating seeds and propagating cuttings. They have a solid base to hold the containers of compost and a hard, transparent lid with a sliding vent to control humidity, you can buy them cheaply from garden centres or DIY stores. The best place to keep them is in a spare room where there is plenty of natural daylight, although the smallest ones would fit on a kitchen windowsill.

Glass cloches are constructed of sheets of glass supported on a wire frame and used to protect young or tender plants growing in the garden. Polythene cloches are tunnel-shaped with clear polythene draped over wire hoops and made secure. Both provide shelter from the elements, help to warm up the soil in spring and encourage strawberries to crop earlier than those growing without protection.

*Small-scale propagation does not require you to spend a lot of money on equipment. This basic electric propagator will serve most domestic purposes well.*

## Adding heat and artificial light

If you are an adventurous gardener, constantly trying to root difficult plants requiring bottom heat and seeds that will only germinate in a high temperature, you should ask Santa Claus to be kind and bring you a heated propagator. Electrically heated propagators controlled by a thermostat removes the element of luck involved in propagating plants, providing you with 'green fingers' and making the rooting of cuttings more of a certainty. They come in various sizes, being rated between 20–65 watts to suit your budget, with a cover made of glass or plastic. Larger systems incorporate a misting unit with an artificial 'leaf', which dries out at the same rate as the leaves of the cuttings, causing the mist unit to switch on automatically. This misting keeps the foliage covered with a film of water, preventing transpiration and ensuring excellent results.

Make sure you position a heated propagator in good natural daylight to prevent seedlings becoming leggy, which is what will happen if they have to strain to find enough light. The best position is on a greenhouse bench near to an electricity and water supply.

Another way of adding heat is with an electrically heated soil-warming cable, preferably one that is connected to a thermostat with an on-off switch to maintain an even temperature. The main advantage of a soil-warming cable is that the plants are heated from below, which speeds up rooting of semi-ripe cuttings in particular, giving them a kick-start. Soil-warming cables need to be powered off the mains supply, but they are cheap to run and are ideal in a propagating frame. The best way to install them is to line the base of the propagating frame with a layer of sand, 2.5cm deep, and then wind the cable up and down across the base like a snake, leaving 15cm between lines of cable and avoiding any sharp bends or kinks. Cover with another layer of sand, this time 10cm deep, and place your containers or seed trays on top. A word of caution: water and electricity don't mix. Make sure that any cables outdoors or in the greenhouse are installed by a qualified electrician using armoured cable and

*Protective frames can be imaginative and stylish.*

waterproof connections and switches. Where there are electric plugs, take the power through contact breakers for safety.

**Hot beds** If Santa is hard of hearing and your heated propagator never arrives, try an old method that I use all the time – a hot bed. Place a 15–25cm layer of fresh, farmyard manure with straw in a garden frame (see below). Water it well, add a handful of nitrogenous fertilizer, pack it down and cover with a layer of coarse sand, 5cm deep. Set your containers of compost and cuttings on the sand, cover with clear polythene and replace the frame lid. As the manure decomposes it should give off enough warmth to provide your cuttings with bottom heat for six to eight weeks.

**Artificial light** will allow you to sow seeds earlier in winter without them becoming straggly. On average, a 150 watt fluorescent lamp suspended 75cm above the propagator will provide artificial light to an area 60cm in diameter.

**A garden frame or cold frame** (also sometimes called a propagating frame) makes an ideal halfway house for hardening off rooted cuttings and transplanted seedlings prior to moving them outside, and is also useful for overwintering hardwood cuttings in pots. It resembles a large box made of wood, bricks or concrete blocks with a hinged lid of glass or clear plastic sloping down from back to front. The base can be clean sand, gravel or a layer of concrete on a sheet of landscape fabric to deter weeds.

The best place to position a garden frame is close to the greenhouse or wherever the plants are being propagated to allow for easy access. If possible, position it so that it is facing the midday sun. If you are making a garden frame from scratch, aim to make it no more than 90cm by 120cm to allow you to reach to the back of the frame, and 45cm high at the rear to provide sufficient height for pots of hardwood cuttings. The front wall should be no higher than 25cm, otherwise the front half of the frame area will be shaded in summer. Where there is a solid base, slope it slightly towards the front with drainage weep holes to allow water to drain away.

The one major disadvantage of a garden frame is the lack of temperature control, especially in winter when they can get very cold. A good tip to keep in the warmth is to cover the lid with a layer of carpet or bags stuffed with straw, especially at night when the temperature drops. On hot, sunny spring days, the lid can be raised and shading material draped in front to cut the glare of the sun.

*The design of the garden frame should allow for maximum ventilation on warm, sunny days.*

# propagation techniques

Trust me, it is not difficult for the home gardener to turn single leaves, 5cm long stems of shrubs or 2m high branches of willow into plants with roots. Propagation is a rewarding job and after your first few successes you, like me, will be hooked, spending the rest of your gardening life propagating plants by every conceivable means.

The beauty of most forms of plant propagation is that all the newly rooted plants will be replicas of the parent plant, a good example being the millions of identical plants of × *Cupressocyparis leylandii* 'Castlewellan Gold' that are being grown around the world. They are all from one chance seedling found in Castlewellan Forest Park in County Down, Northern Ireland – just down the road from where I live.

Occasionally a plant will produce a branch that is different in leaf, habit or flower from the parent, and nurserymen and growers are constantly on the lookout for anything strange or different. Cuttings are taken and quickly propagated until there are sufficient plants to launch the new variety on the market. Plant breeders deliberately produce new plants by cross-pollinating flowers and sowing the resulting seed. A great new rose is the result of such breeding with the best few plants being selected from the thousands of seedlings that germinate. Saving and sowing the seed of a pink-flowering sweet pea will result in a selection of colours.

But for most of us, the joy of propagation is to reproduce more of a plant that we already know and love. The following pages will show you how to do it in a variety of ways.

*Propagate magnolias by layering, roses by bud graft and sweet pea from seed.*

# sowing seed

I love to see seeds germinating with their green leaves emerging from the compost, and then watch as they turn into plants with flowers or edible crops. Propagation from seed can be undertaken directly in the garden soil or in seed trays. When the weather is cold and wet, you can sow seed under cover in the shed, greenhouse or kitchen.

*Majestic oak trees from small acorns grow. As always in gardening, nature shows the way.*

## The principles of sowing seed

The principles of sowing seed remain the same for a row of lettuce, annual flowers, a garden lawn, a chestnut that will grow to become a 30m tree, or a field of cabbages. The secrets of success are common sense and taking the time to do it properly.

The key to reproducing from seed is germination, which simply means beginning to grow, producing a shoot and root. In the wild, seed ripens on the plant, falls to the ground and, if conditions are favourable, germinates straightaway or in the spring when the weather improves and the soil warms up. Lightweight seeds, such as those of the foxglove tree (*Paulownia tomentosa*), are easily transported by wind to germinate and grow well away from the parent tree.

However, in the wild, not every seed will survive. Those that do germinate may be eaten or damaged, most of them never growing to become mature plants. Many will 'fall by the wayside'. In the garden, we can improve the odds imposed on nature and increase the percentage of seeds that become seedlings.

The essential requirements for germination are heat, air and water. Warmth is necessary to break dormancy (with most plants this is the 'wake-up call' in spring after the cold of winter has passed), but the temperature required varies from plant to plant. As a general rule, plants indigenous to a hot climate require higher soil and air temperatures than those from colder climates. Without air, seed will suffocate and die. Some seeds in desert locations remain viable for years until sufficient rain falls to trigger germination. Moist compost will permit water to enter the seed and mobilize the enzymes necessary for germination to take place. This action will only occur when the air and compost are warm.

### Germination times

There are seeds, such as cress, that will germinate within three to five days of sowing. Others, including many species of trees, may not appear for six months, while still others are erratic, appearing in ones and twos over a period of as long as 12–18 months. As so often with gardening, your best friend is patience. Sometimes seed

# Golden rules for collecting seed

As flowers die, the plant's energy is diverted to producing seeds that form in the ovary. In some cases a single seed is produced, as in plums, chestnut and coconut. Other plants, such as the edible pea, give us pods containing many seeds. After the flower dies the seed starts to ripen and this process may take weeks or months, depending on the plant.

*Collect seed on a dry, sunny day and label immediately.*

- Check your plants daily to establish when the seed is ripe and ready for collection. Some plants, such as the hardy *Cyclamen hederifolium*, disperse their seed as soon as it is ripe (the seed pod is held on a coiled, spring-like stem which releases the ripe seed, scattering it away from the parent plant). Timing is critical. The seed should be fully ripe before you remove it from the plant. As a general guide, the skin of unripe seed will be soft. The time to collect seed is when its containers dry out and change colour and berries have ripened.
- If possible, choose a sunny, dry day and wait until the afternoon when the overnight dew has lifted. Never collect or store damp seed, which will either try to germinate or rot in storage.
- Separate and discard detritus and bits of seed pod as soon as possible, as these might carry fungal spores. Cleaning the seed can be a laborious operation. First spread the seed on a sheet of clean white paper, making sure that each species is dealt with separately to avoid mixing seed. Use your fingers to remove the larger pieces of debris; gentle blowing should help to dislodge smaller pieces of seed pod. A very fine sieve is a useful piece of equipment, but for tiny seeds such as those of begonia and lobelia you will have to remove unwanted material using tweezers.

- Check to see if the seed should be sown fresh or stored until a later date. With the exception of some tender plants and those where the seed has to be stratified to break its dormancy (see page 22), I tend to sow seed in spring as the weather is improving and there will be a long period of growth before the onset of winter. Some seed, such as that of the hellebore, stores its food as fats and oils and should be sown as soon as the seed is ripe; delayed sowing will result in poor germination. Candelabra primulas will also germinate better if they are sown straightaway. If seed needs to be sown as soon as it is ripe that information is recorded in the directory.
- Always store seed in porous paper bags or envelopes and never in plastic bags (which would not allow moisture to dissipate). Keep it in an airy room at an even temperature, avoiding direct sunlight. Dry seed can be stored in a plastic container, such as an old photographic film box.
- Always label packets of seed on the outside with a permanent marker and, for safety, place another label inside the packet with the seeds.
- Avoid collecting seed from plants that are classified as F1 hybrids, which are the result of hybridizing two interbred lines of one variety – the result being a cultivar of uniform colour and quality. The (F2) offspring will be variable and mostly below an acceptable standard for quality.

simply doesn't germinate and there may be a number of reasons for this: it might have been sown too deeply in the compost, resulting in the seed dying before it reaches the surface; it may not have been viable (fertilized) in the first place, it may have been badly stored, or it may simply have been past its best.

Seed packets often state the approximate germination period. If nothing shows after the stated time, poke about in the compost with the point of a pencil to find the seed and see if there are any signs of life. If tiny white shoots or roots are visible then all will be well and the cotyledon leaves will soon appear. Where there are no shoots or roots but the seed hasn't rotted, be patient and continue to encourage it to germinate. If germination has failed, throw the whole lot away and don't be tempted to resow in the same compost.

## Collecting seed

Saving the seed from our own garden plants is not only practical, but it can save us a lot of money. For me there is something magical about collecting seed from the garden, storing it and then sowing it. However, seed collection can be a frustrating business. Collect it too early and the premature, unripe seed will not germinate. Leave it too long and it will be past its best or, worse still, the birds will have got there before you.

### Extracting seed
Nature has its own way of dealing with fleshy fruit and berries. When they fall to the ground in autumn, the outer, edible flesh rots or is eaten by birds and small animals, while the inner seed is left exposed to the prevailing temperature and moisture. We can speed up this process in the garden by sieving fleshy fruit such as tomatoes to separate the seed from the flesh. Larger seeds, such as those of apples and pears or the stones of peaches, plums and cherries, are easy to remove when the fruit is cut up or eaten.

### Stratification
Many trees, shrubs and other berrying plants are unable to germinate until they have experienced a period of low, winter-like temperatures in damp conditions. This allows the hard outer skin to soften. If you don't want to wait for nature to do the work for you, you can help the seeds along through a process called stratification.

Break or cut open the outer coat of the berry to expose the seed. Mix the seed with sharp, clean sand and place in a tray. Leave the tray of sand and seed outside where it will be exposed to the winter elements, but do not allow it to become waterlogged. Cover the tray with fine mesh wire to prevent vermin getting at and eating the seed. In spring, the sand and seed mix or the seed on its own can be sown in compost and allowed to germinate normally. Alternatively, place the seed in a clear, labelled polythene bag in the refrigerator for six to eight weeks, depending on the variety of seed. After this time, the seed will be convinced that it has just emerged from a cold winter.

## Storing self-saved seed

When you purchase a packet of seed it comes in an airtight, waterproof packet with a use-by date. Unlike fresh food, it is not dangerous to use seed after that date but the chances of germination are reduced. With home-saved seed it is not possible to recommend use-by dates, as ripeness and storage conditions play a part. Sow a few 'old' seeds to check their viability. If germination levels appear to be low, sow more seed. If the seed fails to germinate, put it out on the bird tray.

Some seeds have longer life spans than others; on the whole, seeds that are naturally dry are viable for longer than those with a high moisture content, such as oak, which should be sown as soon as it is ripe Recommended storage times for seeds varies from plant to plant with viability rates for many species dropping dramatically after the second or third year. Celery, marrow and cabbage seed remains viable for four to five years, whereas sweet corn isn't worth sowing after a year's storage.

## Chipping seed

Sweet peas have a very hard seed coat that prevents moisture being absorbed. To encourage the seeds to swell, soak them in water heated to room temperature for up to two hours prior to sowing. Once the seeds start to swell, sow immediately in compost. Alternatively, scrape off a portion of the hard, outer coating using sandpaper or a nail file, taking care not to damage the 'eye' of the seed (the small scar visible on the outside). If you have lots of seed to chip, try the James Bond

*Layers of rosehips being stratified in sand to speed up germination.*

method. Slip a rolled sheet of sandpaper into a clean, dry jar with a lid, sanded side facing into the jar. Drop in the seeds and replace the lid. The jar should be shaken not stirred, allowing the seed to be abraded against the sandpaper.

## Temperature

Both air and compost temperatures can be critical for successful seed germination. Seed that is too cold or too warm will refuse to germinate. Few seeds will germinate in soil temperatures below 5°C, although ash seed will germinate at 2°C.

Seeds of plants from countries with defined seasons will germinate in warm air temperatures but not high ones. The seed likes to 'think' that it is spring rather than mid-summer. Plants from temperate climates require 8–18°C; those from tropical climates 15–24°C, though night-time temperature can be lowered to 12.5°C. At lower temperatures it will take longer for seed to germinate.

# sowing outdoors in the open ground

Outdoors we have little control over the elements and while it is essential to wait for the right sowing conditions, it can be a bore and very frustrating. Where I live in Northern Ireland and across similar northern latitudes, gardeners may have to delay sowing for several weeks compared with those living in warmer parts of the country.

*Sprouting beans on a grand scale.*

The one piece of comfort on offer is that waiting those extra few days until the weather and soil conditions do improve will not seriously effect the time of flowering or harvest. The result will be better germination and sturdier seedlings. On the other hand, sowing into cold, wet, lumpy and sticky soil drastically reduces the number of seeds that germinate. Those that do grow will sulk, making little growth until the soil conditions improve.

Imagine the germinating seed sending out its small, fine roots in one direction and its vulnerable shoot stretching to reach the surface and daylight. Any small obstacle can stop it in its tracks. So ideally the soil should be well cultivated with any large stones and weed roots removed.

If you are starting from scratch in a new garden, then a considerable amount of ground cultivation will be necessary. Grass or weeds should be removed or killed with a chemical weedkiller such as one containing glyphosate. Break up the ground by digging or rotovating to a depth of at least 20cm.

*Opposite Poppy seed can survive in the soil for thousands of years, waiting until the conditions required for germination are just right.*

Building-site gardens are often a nightmare to cultivate with churned-up clay mixed with all sorts of building materials and a thin layer of topsoil to make it look presentable. In such cases there are no short cuts. The debris has to be removed and additional topsoil imported. If the builder is still on site he may take pity on you and supply you with more.

Whether in a new or an established patch, when sowing seed outside the surface should be firm but crumbly without large lumps; any lumps should shatter easily when the soil is raked. Compacted soil takes longer to dry out, so avoid walking on uncultivated soil, especially if it is heavy or wet. If you use a glass or clear plastic cloche or frame to cover and protect the soil, it will dry out and warm up more quickly, allowing the sowing dates to be brought forward.

At the final raking, apply a general purpose, balanced granular fertilizer such as Growmore at 30g per square metre and tickle it into the top 2cm of the soil. If time allows, leave the prepared soil for a week to allow seedling weeds to germinate, then spray with a contact weedkiller such as paraquat or use a flame gun. Disturbing the soil by hand weeding at this stage will only bring more weed seed to the surface. If you now sow immediately with the minimum of soil movement, your new seedlings will be well advanced and better able to tolerate the competition by the time the next batch of weed seeds germinate. If using chemicals, make sure you are properly protected with waterproof clothes, gloves and face mask.

## Planting depths

As a general rule, small seeds should be scattered close to the surface and covered with a thin layer of sand or fine soil without lumps or stones. When small seeds are sown too deeply in soil or compost, one of two things will happen. Either the seeds will germinate and die before they reach the light; or they will remain dormant, eventually rotting in the ground. Exceptionally, they can remain dormant and viable for thousands of years, germinating when the soil is cultivated and they are brought closer to daylight. Sheets of red poppies can suddenly appear when old pasture ground is ploughed.

Larger seed should be sown more deeply. Sowing depth need not be so precise with larger seeds such as peas and beans, which have sufficient food reserves within the seed to keep it growing until the shoot reaches the surface and light and starts to manufacture food for itself. Brassicas can be sown 1–2cm deep, while broad beans should be planted 5cm deep.

### five tips for successful seed sowing

1 Think hygiene. Containers and compost should be new and clean. Saved seed must be from healthy plants. If you smoke, wear gloves when handling seeds.
2 Whenever possible use fresh seed. Germination rates may be low with older, stored seed.
3 Use a proprietary seed compost. Potting and multi-purpose composts contain too much nutrient.
4 Sow the seed at the correct depth. Small seeds need to be closer to the surface. Very fine seed is sown on the surface of the compost.
5 Sow thinly or space the seeds to give the seedlings room to grow.

**1** Mark out the line of each row, using a string and pegs.

**2** Use the back of a rake to excavate a shallow furrow (known as a drill) in the prepared soil. The depth of the drill will vary according to the size of your seed.

**3** When sowing seeds in rows, a clever tip is to pour boiling water along the open drill a few minutes before sowing. Not only will this kill any weed seeds, but it should help to warm up the soil and encourage your seeds to swell.

**4** Sow the seeds thinly and evenly along the seed row to avoid having to space the young plants later.

**5** Rake the soil back into the drill to cover the seeds. Water the row with a fine rose on the watering can, so as not to wash the seeds away.

## successional sowing

With some plants, especially salad crops, it is best to sow little and often. A few lettuce seeds will provide you with more than enough green leaves to eat before they become tough and start to flower. The same applies to radishes, spring onions and cress. Each time you sow sufficient for your requirements, reseal the seed packet ready for another sowing in a week or fortnight's time.

# sowing under cover

There are clear-cut advantages to sowing seeds in a greenhouse: you (and the seeds) are not at the mercy of the elements, temperatures can be controlled, the compost can be kept uniformly moist by watering and weeding is kept to a minimum. That's because bagged seed compost purchased from the garden centre is weed free.

*Heat, light and moisture levels are easy to control in a greenhouse.*

To reinforce what I said in the previous chapter, compost for seed sowing may be peat based or peat free. Both sorts need to be retentive of moisture but free draining. The important thing is to choose compost that is specifically for seeds. On no account use any type of potting compost. The level of nutrients will be too high, forcing the seeds into soft growth with little root. (Seeds have little need for nutrients until the seedlings are potted up or planted out.)

Despite the advantages, growing seed under glass is not without its problems. Pests such as slugs and snails can cause havoc in the greenhouse, munching their way through the soft stems, and these should be baited and trapped on a daily basis. Seedling diseases, such as damping off, can destroy a pot or tray of seedlings within days of germination. Watering with a solution of Cheshunt compound will reduce the risk of an attack (see pages 106–111 for more details).

*Peppers are readily grown from seed. For best results I recommend buying seed rather than saving your own, as mixed parentage may result in poorer plants and fruit.*

## tips for sowing very fine seed

When you open a packet of begonia seed it is difficult to see the seed, never mind get it out of the corner of the packet! Once you have managed that, these tips will help you to sow it.

- Use a small pot and fill it to the top with seed compost. Lightly firm the compost with a wooden block, leaving the surface level. Carefully open the packet of seed and add half a teaspoon of dry, silver sand. Shake to mix the seed and sand. Sprinkle the sand with the seeds evenly over the surface of the compost. Press the sand/seed into the compost using the wooden block, dusting off any of the mixture that may stick to the wood. Don't cover the seed with compost.
- Water the compost by standing the container in a tray of tepid water, which will soak up through the drainage holes to the surface.
- Cover the container with a sheet of glass or clear polythene to retain moisture. Keep the container away from direct sunlight.
- The tiny seedlings should not be pricked out until there are three to four true leaves, which are not to be confused with cotyledons or seed leaves. Most plants produce a pair of cotyledon leaves (dicot or dicotyledon) before the true leaves appear, though some, such as grass, crocus and lily, have a single cotyledon leaf (monocot or monocotyledon). The seedling cotyledon leaves soon fall off.
- Hold the seedlings by the leaf and never the stem. At this stage protect the young seedlings against slugs and snails. They can devour a lot of seedlings overnight, leaving little more than a mucous trail to mark their journey to the restaurant.

*Looking at the abundant leaves and flowers gives no indication that begonia seeds are minute.*

**1** With large seed, such as marrow or cucumber, push one seed at a time into the compost at the recommended depth.

**2** Space 1–2cm apart to give each seed room to grow and make transplanting easier.

**3** With fine seed, trickle thinly over the compost and cover with a thin layer of compost. I prefer to tip the seeds out of the packet onto the palm of my left hand. I lift the seed between the index finger and thumb of my right hand and by gently rubbing my fingers together allow the seed to fall onto the compost.

**5** When the seedlings are large enough to handle, prick them out (that is, transfer the healthiest to a larger growing space). Use a dibber or an old kitchen fork, taking care not to damage the tender root system.

**6** Always handle seedlings by the cotyledons (first leaves) rather than the stem, which bruises easily.

**4** Most varieties of seed need light, and prefer to be kept in subdued light away from the glare of the midday sun. A good method is to cover the tray with glass and newspaper until the seedlings appear.

# spores

Spores are the equivalent of seeds in plants such as ferns, mosses, lichen and fungi. They are microscopic in size, allowing them to be transported far and wide by the slightest breeze. A single fern will produce millions of spores, few of which will survive in the wild. Unlike seeds, spores, once germinated, do not immediately produce a new plant, taking weeks to form a union between male and female before the young fern is apparent.

*Spores – a fern's equivalent of seeds – form on the back of the frond.*

Ferns are the spore-bearing plants that gardeners are most likely to want to propagate, so here are a few ferny terms that you might need to know. Seeds are spores, leaves are fronds. The spores are held in sporangia (seed pods) and a group of them is known as a sorus (plural sori). But don't worry, that is the vocabulary lesson finished.

The good news is that propagation by spores is not difficult. The sporangia form on the underside of the frond and by late summer or early autumn they will have turned brown and will be ripe and ready for collection. Fern spores are best sown as soon as they are ripe, especially those of the beautiful osmunda fern, which remain viable for only a few days.

1 Cut the fronds before the sporangia split open and store them in a paper bag until ready for use. As they dry out, you will be able to shake the tiny spores free.

2 Seal the bag to prevent the tiny spores escaping. For goodness sake don't sneeze before the bag is closed! When you are ready to sow, make sure that the container, the compost and the water are all sterilized, since algae thrives in the same conditions as fern spores.

**3** Fill the container to within 2cm of the surface. I prefer to use a John Innes seed compost with added moss peat to improve drainage. Water the compost with cooled boiled water; even rainwater should be boiled before use. Allow the compost to drain, then scatter the spores thinly over the surface. If you like – and if you have an old brick handy – you can cover the compost with a layer of brick dust, which stops the spores slipping or being washed down into the compost. Press down into the surface using a sterilized block of wood, but do not cover the spores with compost.

**4** Cover the container with a sheet of clear, sterilized glass. Stand the tray in good light but away from strong, direct sunlight. Avoid a situation where there is a cold draught. Where possible, use a propagator with the air temperature set at 20°C. Wipe over the glass daily to remove any condensation.

**5** Be patient and after about five to seven weeks a thin green slime-like layer will form on the surface. This is a mass of baby spores called sporelings and each individual piece covers male and female cells. These form unions... and after another four weeks they become new tiny fern plants. At this stage only, water the compost by sitting the container in a tray of cooled, boiled water. Where ferns are congested in the container, small clumps can be spaced out to allow extra room for them to develop. At this stage there are no roots and they are positioned so as to stand on the compost.

When the plantlets are 2cm high, you can prick them out into individual pots or trays as for seedlings. Keep the young plants in humid conditions for a few days until they settle in and start to grow. Tender ferns grown as house plants can be potted up before their roots fill the pot. Hardy ferns can be planted out in the garden, but take care not to damage the roots.

# cuttings

I have always enjoyed propagating plants from cuttings. While I was still at school, I rooted hundreds of chrysanthemums and grew them on for their flowers. Today I still love turning cuttings into plants but I have a wider interest that encompasses shrubs, trees, perennials, house plants and alpines. For me and millions of other gardeners, there is still the thrill and pleasure when something unusual starts to grow.

*I have rooted chrysanthemums since childhood and they remain a favourite.*

A stem cutting is a piece of a plant, with or without leaves, that is encouraged to produce roots and form a replica (clone) of the parent plant. A root cutting is different. Here a section of root is encouraged to produce leaves and stems. Many plants are easy to root from cuttings, particularly stem cuttings, but there is more than one method of stem cutting to choose from. The directory which starts on page 114 explains which method is likely to work best for which plant, but do experiment for yourself.

What works for me and is the perceived method of propagation may fail miserably for you and yet a completely different system might bring you good results.

## Some general advice

The ideal compost for rooting cuttings is a free-draining one without added nutrients. A home-made mixture of equal parts of peat, coarse horticultural grit and perlite will be every bit as successful as a proprietary mixture of peat-based or peat-free compost. If you are buying compost off the shelf, make sure you choose one for seeds or cuttings rather than a John Innes mixture designed for more mature plants. The latter will contain too many nutrients and force your new plants into soft growth without a strong root system. For best results, the compost should be damp, not wet, and should form a ball when squeezed in your hand. If it is very crumbly, it is too dry; if water drops out, then it's too wet and should be left in an airy room protected from the rain until it dries out.

*A moisture-retentive compost will help roots to become established.*

How long should a cutting be? Well, size matters. With fuchsias and some chrysanthemums, it is the very tip of the new shoot that is propagated (sometimes known as a tip cutting). With these plants, the smaller the cutting the better, so you might take a sprig that has only three or four leaves on it, each no larger than your fingernail.

At the other end of the scale, willow and poplar trees taken as hardwood cuttings up to 2m in length may be rooted after leaf fall in winter. For most purposes, shrub cuttings tend to be around 5–10cm long.

There are tricks to learn and tips to help you put roots on whatever plant you fancy. Whenever possible, take cuttings from low down on the plant. Those taken close to the base of the plant will root more quickly than those from higher up. You will have better success rates from rooting thin shoots rather than thick stems and you will find that cuttings of shrubs grown in shade (where growths are thin and drawn up towards the daylight) will root more quickly than the same plant grown in full sun.

And a final word of advice: avoid at all costs taking cuttings from plants that are diseased or infested with pests. Your mission is to increase your stock of a particular plant, not to spread pests and diseases that may destroy other plants.

*Get to know your plants. A plant grown from a cutting of a grafted weeping willow will not behave in the same way as one grown on its own roots.*

# softwood cuttings

I tend to use the term 'softwood' to describe two different types of cuttings that are technically known as greenwood and basal. Greenwood refers to the soft, young growth of plants such as pelargoniums, whose stem never firms up or becomes woody. Basal refers to the fleshy shoots of herbaceous plants such as delphiniums, which appear at soil level directly from the base of the plant. Greenwood and basal cuttings are both rooted in the same way so, for the purposes of this book, I have lumped them together under one heading, softwood cuttings.

*With a plant whose leaves are crowded together to form a rosette, the whole piece is rooted as a softwood cutting.*

## Basic technique

The earlier the plant comes into leaf and commences growth, the sooner the softwood cuttings may be taken. The best time to take softwood cuttings is first thing in the morning before the plant starts to lose moisture in a process known as transpiration. Use a sharp knife or secateurs to remove a shoot from the parent plant, cutting immediately above a leaf or pair of leaves using a sloping cut. (However, when you come to prepare your cutting for planting you should trim it immediately *below* a leaf or pair of leaves.) The area below a leaf has the highest concentration of plant hormones, which will assist rooting. For plants such as cistus or euonymus, pull the cutting off the main stem complete with a strip of the older bark, known as a 'heel', and trim it back close to the joint with a sharp knife (see page 38). Cuttings of plants that produce leaves crowded together on the stem to form tight rosettes are taken in the same way, with the lower leaves removed to leave 1–2.5 cm of stem.

To prevent the cutting from wilting, immerse it in a bucket of clean water, making sure that all the foliage is wet, and place in a polythene bag. Store in a cool, shaded area until you are ready to plant it – which should be as soon as possible and certainly within a couple of hours. Label the cutting as soon as you remove it from the parent plant, using waterproof ink, and place the label inside the bag.

Seed trays are ideal for rooting large numbers of cuttings, however small numbers are best rooted in shallow pots. It is a waste of compost to use pots deeper than 10cm because the newly rooted plants will be transplanted before the roots have time to reach the bottom of the pot.

Always use a dibber or pencil to make a hole in the compost for the cutting, but don't make it deeper than about 1–2cm. In order for the cutting to root, it must be in direct contact with the compost, not an air pocket, and even the lowest leaves of the cutting should be above soil level. Firm the compost by hand and water overhead using a fine rose.

Most softwood cuttings will root quickly in high humidity, which is easy to maintain in a propagator. Simply place the pots or trays of cuttings inside the propagator and set the temperature. Where there isn't a propagator, cover the container with a clear polythene bag and secure it with string or a rubber band. Condensation will collect on the inside of the bag, so wipe it off every few days to ensure the cuttings get enough light – a sharp tap or a shake of the bag should do the trick, and any drips that fall on the leaves will help keep them damp.

The best place to put the cuttings is on a sunny windowsill in a warm room, avoiding strong direct sunlight. If you have a greenhouse, place the pots of cuttings in good light.

Softwood cuttings tend to root quickly – from three to five weeks, depending on the plant and how warm the compost is. When the tips of the cuttings commence growing, you may be fairly sure they have produced roots. Look for white roots emerging from the base of the pot or container. Once this happens, don't be tempted to disturb the cuttings straightaway. Leave them for another week to ten days to allow a good root system to develop before potting the young plants up individually in small containers. Avoid potting into large

containers or the roots will have too much space to move through, resulting in poor growth. Young plants prefer to grow through the compost and round the side of the pot, forming a rootball.

Protect young plants from the extremes of winter. Keep tender plants in a warm room or in a heated greenhouse or conservatory. Hardy shrubs such as hebe and philadelphus can be overwintered in a garden frame and planted out in late spring; they will flower the same summer.

Occasionally, you will wake up to find your cutting has withered and its leaves have fallen off. If this happens, it's as good as dead. If the cutting looks healthy, but no new growth has formed – say after four or five weeks – ease it gently out of the compost to check for roots. If the stem is black or discoloured, dump the cutting and throw away the compost. However, if the stem looks healthy, re-insert it in the compost and give it a second chance.

*With plants such as this euonymus, pull the side shoot down to remove a 'heel' of the older wood. The heel can then be trimmed to the required length and helps the cutting to root more quickly.*

2 Use a sharp knife to trim the cutting to the required length, slicing immediately below a leaf joint. If you pulled the cutting from the parent plant, remove the 'heel'. For most plants, the required length will be 5–10cm. Remove any leaves on the part of the stem that is going to be buried in the compost, taking care not to damage the stem.

1 Choose a young side shoot; if you are propagating a plant whose stems eventually become woody and firm, make sure your shoot is still soft. Separate the cutting from the parent plant early in the morning in late spring or early summer. You can do this either by cutting it with a sharp knife or by pulling the cutting away from the main stem.

3 Wound the base of the cutting by removing a sliver of the outer skin, then dip it into a small container of hormone rooting powder.

**4** Fill a small pot or seed tray with suitable compost to within 2.5cm of the rim. Make a small planting hole using a wooden dibber or pencil, just deep enough for the base of the cutting to rest on the base of the hole, with no air pocket. Insert the cutting, making sure that all the leaves are above the compost.

**5** Plant other cuttings in the same pot or tray, about 5cm apart.

**6** If you don't have a propagator, cover the container with a see-through polythene bag to keep the atmosphere humid. (If you are going to put the cutting on a sunny windowsill, use white polythene to prevent sunlight scorching the leaves.) In either case, secure the bag with string or a rubber band.

# semi-ripe cuttings

Semi-ripe cuttings (sometimes referred to as semi-hardwood) are the preferred method of rooting evergreen plants, especially conifers, and are also my only sure way of propagating evergreen ceanothus. Material for propagation is taken from midsummer until early autumn, and comes from lower down the current season's growth. The stem will have started to firm up and become slightly woody at the base, while the top growth is still soft and pliable. Cuttings will root more quickly in a heated propagator with bottom heat, but the kitchen windowsill will do.

*This glorious red is the winter foliage of Nandina domestica, an evergreen bamboo that can be rooted by semi-ripe cuttings in summer.*

## Basic technique

Take cuttings in the same way as described for softwood cuttings (see page 34), but make them slightly longer at 7.5–12.5cm. I prefer to prepare semi-ripe cuttings with a 'heel' (see page 36), as this provides a greater area of exposed cambium to encourage rooting. I also find the firmer wood is less likely to rot. To reduce transpiration from cuttings of plants with large leaves such as abutilon and hydrangea, the foliage may be cut in half horizontally. I always remove the growing tip of the cutting, which encourages it to form side shoots as soon as it is rooted and starting to grow. The result is a bushy plant with shoots lower down on the stem.

*With skimmia I take semi-ripe cuttings with a heel and root them in a propagator in early autumn.*

When propagating without the use of a propagator, cover the cuttings with clear polythene and place them on a well-lit windowsill but away from strong, direct

sunlight. Check regularly for signs of disease, removing any dead or yellowing leaves. Water as necessary but avoid overwatering the compost. There are some plants with hairy leaves, such as lavender, and those which form rosettes of leaves, such as saxifrage and sedum, that root better when there is less humidity to cause leaf rot. I find that these plants root more quickly under horticultural fleece rather than the more usual clear polythene. In a propagator, allow air to circulate freely and remove condensation from the cover.

Some plants may root within four or five weeks, while others may take up to six months, only showing movement late the following spring. The firmer the wood, the longer it will take for the cuttings to root. If, after four or five months, the cutting looks healthy but there is no sign of growth at the tip, ease it out of the compost and see if it has

produced roots. If there is no sign of white roots and the lower part of the stem is black or brown, then dump the cutting and the compost.

Some plants, particularly skimmia and conifers, have a habit of forming a large amount of callus at the base of the cutting without any roots. Where this occurs, try scraping most of this growth off and reinserting the cutting – it will probably now produce roots in a matter of weeks.

It is desirable to encourage newly rooted deciduous plants to make some top growth before winter. If not, they may not come out of their dormancy in spring and end up rotting in the pot. For best results, these plants are best overwintered in a cool greenhouse or a garden frame, out of strong, direct sunlight.

*Evergreen ceanothus such as this root readily as semi-ripe cuttings. The deciduous species do better with softwood cuttings.*

1 Choose a side shoot that is slightly woody at the base, but which has soft, pliable top growth. Pull the side shoot away from the parent stem, taking a 'heel' of bark with it, rather than making a clean cut with a knife.

2 Trim the heel of the cutting, removing the thin 'tail' of older wood. If the tip of the shoot is very soft, nip it out along with any flower buds that are showing. Dip the base of the cutting in hormone rooting powder to encourage roots to grow.

**3** Fill a container with suitable compost to within 2.5cm of the rim. Insert the cuttings around the circumference of the container, leaving enough room for each one to grow.

**4** Place the container in a propagator or cover with a clear polythene bag, secured with a rubber band. Put the cuttings in a light place such as on a windowsill, but away from direct sunlight.

**5** With large-leafed plants such as hydrangea, cut the leaves in half horizontally to reduce transpiration.

# hardwood cuttings

There is something particularly satisfying about propagation by hardwood cuttings. It requires no specialist equipment and can be done out in the garden without protection or heat. Although it takes a full year for the cuttings to root, the wait is worth it because the results are so spectacular – producing large plants ready for planting out or potting up. This method is most often used to propagate deciduous shrubs and trees.

## Basic technique

Take hardwood cuttings in late autumn and winter. Choose stems of the current year's growth that are firm and have hardened. Make the bottom cut straight across immediately below a node or leaf joint, and the top sloping cut above a bud and angled away from it to run water away from the bud. The length of the cutting depends on the amount of growth made during the year but should be 20–30cm. Given sufficient growth, you can make two or more hardwood cuttings from each branch. If stems are uniformly thick, make sure you know which is the top and which is the bottom. This is why we make a sloping cut at the top and a horizontal cut at the base. Inserting the cutting upside down will result in 100 per cent failure!

I always root hardy plants outside in a sheltered part of the garden but, where space allows, you may wish to place them in a container of soil-based compost in a garden frame over winter and set them outside in spring. Evergreen conifers are less prone to wind or frost damage if you put them in containers in a garden frame. With rows of hardwood cuttings lined out in open ground, lay landscape fabric between the rows and cover with bark or gravel to keep down weeds.

The following summer, the cuttings will produce side shoots and in autumn (a year after taking the cuttings) you will have strong, well-rooted, bushy plants ready to dig up and plant out. Depending on the species, rooted plants will be bushy, 45–60cm high with side shoots. Some cuttings will simply die. The stem will turn dark brown or black and become brittle. Pull these out of the ground and burn them.

*Mophead hydrangeas will root from hardwood cuttings if you follow my tip below.*

*Opposite Hardwood cuttings of Virginia creeper root like weeds. Don't plant too many, as you will have 100 per cent success.*

## a tip for hydrangeas

Hydrangeas may be rooted as hardwood cuttings, but the pithy stem is inclined to rot before the cutting is able to form roots. To guard against this, cut immediately below a leaf where the stem is toughest and seal the end of the cut with wax. Wound the sides of the stem to expose some of the cambium layer before inserting in the ground.

# Hardwood cuttings method A: for most plants

**1** Choose a little used area of the garden, preferably one that is well drained and protected from the wind. Dig a trench 15cm deep, making one side vertical. If your soil is heavy, spread a 2.5-cm layer of coarse grit or sand in the base of the trench to assist drainage.

Choose a fully-ripe stem of the current year's growth that is firm and has hardened. Make a straight cut at the base of the stem, immediately below a node or leaf joint. At the top, make a sloping cut above a bud, angling it away from it. The cutting should be 20–30cm in length. Plants such as roses or gooseberries are easier to handle if the thorns or spines are removed at this stage.

Space the prepared cuttings vertically, 15cm apart in the trench, making sure that the base of each cutting is in direct contact with the grit (with no air pocket underneath). Position the cuttings close to the vertical side of the trench to keep them upright when the trench is backfilled with soil.

**2** Backfill the trench...

**3** ...then use your feet to firm the topsoil around the cuttings. Take care not to damage the portion of the cutting that is above the ground. Finally, use a fork or a rake to loosen the surface of the soil and apply a deep mulch of bark or compost to deter weeds.

# Hardwood cuttings method B: for taller plants

**1** For larger plants such as willow or poplar, saw a length of straight branch about 1.2–2m long, after leaf fall.

**2** Use a crowbar to make a 30cm deep hole in the ground.

**3** Insert the cutting and firm it in with your foot.

**Alternatively**, cut 'pegs' of willow 30cm long and 3cm in diameter. Make a hole in the ground with a crowbar and hammer the pegs 15cm into the ground, making sure you get them the right way up.

# leaf cuttings

When I want to grow more house plants, either for my own use or as presents for friends, I tend to choose those that can be propagated from a single leaf. That way, the original plant isn't abused and the leaf that has been removed isn't missed. The highly ornamental *Begonia rex*, mother-in-law's tongue *(Sansevieria* spp.) and Cape primrose *(Streptocarpus* spp.) can all be propagated by leaf cuttings and a single leaf is capable of producing lots of young plants. Cuttings may be propagated between spring and late autumn, but in late spring they will root more quickly.

## Leaf cuttings method A: for most plants

**1** Select a healthy leaf of a plant such as *Begonia rex* and remove it together with its stalk. The stalk is not needed, but should not be left on the parent plant or it will encourage botrytis fungal disease.

**2** Using a sharp knife, cut completely through the main veins, making the cuts 2cm apart.

**3** Fill a tray with moist cuttings compost and lay the leaf down flat, right side up on the surface. The cut veins must be in contact with the compost to encourage them to root, so either peg the leaf down firmly with U-shaped pieces of light wire resembling hair clips, or weigh it down with small pebbles. I know a lady gardener who uses coloured glass beads to hold the leaf in place, and very nice they look too. Ensure the compost remains damp by placing the container in a tray of water and allowing the water to soak up. Avoid wetting the leaf as this will cause it to rot.

**4** Plantlets will form at the cut veins. When the plantlets have produced three or four leaves, they will be rooted and ready to lift and pot up individually.

## Leaf cuttings method B: for long, narrow leaves

**1** Cut the leaves of Cape primrose (shown here) or mother-in-law's tongue into horizontal sections 5cm deep or...

### a quick tip

Cuttings taken from the base of the leaf will root more quickly than those that are closer to the leaf tip.

**2** ... just for a change, cut the leaves lengthways. With a sharp knife cut along either side of the main, central vein. Discard the vein and keep the two 'side pieces'.

**3** Dust the lower 'cut' edge of each leaf section with hormone rooting powder and insert upright in a tray of moist cuttings compost so that the cut side is in contact with the compost. To prevent leaf scorch, avoid placing the cuttings in strong sunlight. A propagator with bottom heat will give quick results but covering the cuttings with a clear polythene bag will work perfectly well.

**4** Keep the compost moist, but avoid dampening the foliage of Cape primrose as the fine hairs on the leaf surface rot easily. After eight to ten weeks, plantlets will appear at the base of each section of leaf where the vein is in contact with the compost. When each plantlet has three or four leaves, separate them from the original piece of leaf and pot them into moist, free-draining compost. For the first two weeks, grow them on away from bright sunlight.

# Leaf cuttings method C for African violets

Leaf propagation of African violets (*Saintpaulia* spp.) is slightly different, because you keep the leaf stalk attached to the leaf. Healthy, mature leaves may be rooted at any time of the year.

**1** Cut the leaf off the parent plant with as long a stalk as possible. Trim the end of the stalk, making a clean cut straight across and taking care not to bruise the stalk. I don't use hormone rooting powder with African violet leaves, as they seem to root better without it.

**2** Fill a pot with cuttings compost to which you have added a little extra grit to ensure good drainage. Use a pencil to make a hole towards the edge of the pot – the new plant will grow from the inside base of the existing leaf, so it needs space towards the centre of the pot. Insert the leaf stalk, keeping the lower edge of the leaf slightly above the surface of the compost and facing into the pot. You can plant several leaves in the same pot, as long as you give them plenty of space.

**3** Place in a heated propagator. Within six weeks a new plant should have formed on the surface. Separate the new plant from the old leaf and pot on into a soil-less compost with added grit.

# leaf bud cuttings

This type of cutting is made up of the leaf attached to part of the plant stem. Check that there is a growth bud where the stem and leaf stalk join (the axil). This is the method I use to propagate camellias, and the one most likely to succeed without the advantage of bottom heat in a propagator. Take the cuttings in midsummer from the current year's growth that has started to firm up.

**1** Cut the stem immediately above a leaf with a healthy bud...

**2** ... and again about 2.5cm below the leaf.

**3** I like to split the stem in half lengthways at this point...

**4** ... to make a larger wound, but most growers don't do this.

**5** Dip the stem in hormone rooting powder and insert it in moist, gritty, free-draining compost. Position the leaf at, or just above, the compost surface.

Place the pot in a heated propagator and spray regularly with a fine mist of tap water at room temperature. Ericaceous plants such as camellias prefer rainwater, but as this is more likely to contain harmful bacteria and disease spores that would damage the vulnerable cuttings I always use tap water for propagation.

If you don't have a propagator, cover the pot with a clear polythene bag or the top half of a plastic drinks bottle. Place the container in a warm, shaded position and keep the air and the compost moist.

In the case of camellias, the cutting should be well rooted within 10–12 weeks. Take care when potting the rooted plant as, at this stage, its roots are brittle and vulnerable to drying out. Camellias prefer acid soil, so use an ericaceous compost for potting. Keep the newly potted plants in light shade for a few weeks.

# root cuttings

This is propagation with a difference. The previous pages describe how to encourage stem cuttings and leaves to produce roots. Here, we want the root to produce new roots as well as stems and leaves. In nature this is a regular occurrence: a small piece of bindweed (*Convolvulus* spp.) root will regrow as a nasty, twining weed; and a small piece of dandelion in the lawn will regrow as vigorously as ever. Fortunately, there are lots of perennials, shrubs and trees that can be propagated in the same way.

*Chaenomeles – better known as Japanese quince or japonica – is easily multiplied by root cuttings.*

Root propagation takes place any time from late autumn to late winter, when the plant is dormant. It is practical to dig up herbaceous perennials, such as phlox and acanthus, but for large shrubs and ornamental trees, such as *Paulownia tomentosa,* it is best to expose the roots without lifting the tree. The best roots to remove are the young, fibrous, pencil-thick roots, which can be found in line with the perimeter of the tree's canopy of branches. Check that they belong to the plant to be propagated first! In the case of the Japanese quince (*Chaenomeles* spp.), take portions of young root from close to the centre of the rootball. The ideal diameter of root is pencil thickness, although thicker can be used.

*Propagating phlox by root cutting avoids any risk of spreading eelworm problems, which in this plant tend to affect the stems.*

# Root cuttings method A for plants with thin roots

**1** For plants with thin, thread-like roots, such as phlox, cut the roots into 5–7.5cm lengths without bothering to make a sloped end.

**2** Lay them horizontally 5cm apart on a seed tray of cuttings compost. Lightly cover with more compost and water the surface. Keep the cuttings in a cold frame or in a sheltered position outdoors over the winter months. In spring, the cuttings will have produced more roots and the growth buds will have produced shoots and leaves. By summer, the plants will be well rooted and may be transplanted into potting compost.

# Root cuttings method B for plants with thick roots

**1** Dig up the dormant plant with a fork.

**2** Wash excess soil off the roots.

**3** Remove a small number of roots from the parent plant, making clean cuts with a sharp knife. Store the roots in a polythene bag until you are ready to use them. If you have dug up the parent plant, replant it as soon as possible.

**4** The best roots to propagate are the side roots. You will need to know which end of the root is the top and which is the bottom, so always cut the top of the root (the part that was closest to the crown of the plant) straight across...

**5** ...and cut the base of the root cutting at an angle. The sections of root should be 7.5–10cm long. Dust both cut ends with flowers of sulphur or a fungicidal powder to reduce the risk of fungal disease.

**6** With the aid of a dibber, insert the cuttings vertically, 5cm apart in moist, free-draining, rooting compost with extra coarse grit added.

**7** The top (straight cut end) should be level with the surface of the compost.

**8** Cover with a layer of coarse, washed grit and do not water until new roots have formed.

# runners, suckers and stolons

One of nature's most efficient ways of propagating plants is by runners, suckers or stolons. These are all forms of stem, often confused but subtly different. For the most part, plants that reproduce in this way manage perfectly well on their own, but there are ways of helping them along.

*The results shown here are the best reason for propagating plants.*

A runner spreads horizontally above the ground. Plantlets form at the ends of long stems, rooting into the ground before producing a further plant and eventually a line of connecting rooted plants. The best example of this is the fruiting strawberry. Early rooting can be encouraged by plunging a pot of compost into the ground and pinning the runner onto the surface with a U-shaped piece of wire or a small stone. Plants rooted in midsummer will produce some fruit the following summer. Some ferns and succulents produce new

plants at the end of stems produced above the ground, known as stolons. These root quickly and, if not removed and potted up, will form large clumps or colonies surrounding the original plant.

On grafted plants such as apples or roses, suckers are a nuisance. They are produced by the rootstock and will eventually weaken the plant. With other plants, suckers can be a cheap and quick method of propagation: separate them from the parent plant complete with roots and grow them on as identical plants.

*Nature is very capable of producing new strawberry plants without assistance.*

# Irishman's cuttings

This is a quick and easy way of propagating plants that multiply by producing runners or suckers that root while they are still attached to the parent plant. I have no idea why it is called an Irishman's cutting, unless it is the 'luck of the Irish', but it is extremely effective and requires no specialist equipment.

Plants such as ajuga (shown here), dogwood and cotoneaster that tend to layer themselves where a stem touches the ground (see page 68) are ideal for self-rooted cuttings. The rooted sections can be removed from the parent plant with secateurs to provide a ready-made plant complete with roots.

**1** Using a garden fork, ease the rooted pieces out of the ground and separate them from the parent plant (above). Reduce the foliage of the rooted 'cutting' to a quantity that can be maintained by the existing roots. This will encourage the plant to become established.

**2** Pot the plant in a suitable compost until it develops a good root system and starts to grow. Then plant out in a permanent position.

# division

Clump-forming plants such as herbaceous perennials and some alpines that produce more than one stem at ground level may be split apart to create several plants. Each portion will be complete with roots, centre crown and growth buds.

*Hostas may be divided every year or, as large clumps, every third year.*

There are two periods when division is most practical: early spring, just as growth is about to commence; or late autumn, just as the plant's foliage is dying down for the winter. I prefer to divide plants that come into growth early in spring, such as hostas and agapanthus, in late autumn or winter when there is less risk of damaging the new shoots. In gardens where the soil is cold and wet in winter and growth is late to start, spring is usually a more reliable time for dividing.

Clump-forming perennials with fine roots, such as asters, polyanthus and gentians, are easy to tease apart with your fingertips and don't suffer from being lifted out of the ground in early spring. Dig up the clump and gently tease it apart without damaging the roots or top growth.

Some larger clump-forming perennials produce a congested mat of roots that is impossible to divide with your hands and you may have to resort to using two garden forks. I have never been very successful with this method, but try it for yourself. I usually end up with a stubborn clump like a bad hair day and sprained wrists.

Hostas are tolerant of a reasonable level of abuse. During winter or early spring, cut the clump into pieces using a sharp spade or a hatchet. It's best to keep it the right way up so as not to damage the growth buds.

## Dealing with old, congested plants

As clump-forming plants grow and spread, the centre of the clump (which is the oldest part) tends to become woody with few roots. This is also the area most likely to be suffering from disease, such as virus disease. Where this is the case, cut out the woody centre of the clump and dump it, retaining only the youngest and most vigorous roots towards the edge of the clump. Plant out or containerize the young plants using a soil-based potting

## five tips to guarantee success

1 Only propagate from healthy plants. Those with discoloured leaves or distorted stems should be burnt.
2 Split the clump when it is dormant.
3 Make sure there are growth buds or shoots on each piece.
4 Pot up or plant out immediately after dividing.
5 Whenever possible, tease out the roots rather than cutting them.

compost. Soil-less composts are more difficult to keep moist. Plant at the same depth as previously grown and firm the soil as you pot to eliminate air pockets. Water to settle the soil around the roots and keep in light shade for a few days to prevent wilting. Perennials divided in spring will flower that same summer or autumn. This operation should be repeated every three or four years as the new plants grow old.

Some house plants lend themselves to division. We have already discussed propagation by leaf cuttings of mother-in-law's tongue (see page 50), but when these plants become old and start to form a clump in the pot with numerous leaves growing directly out of the compost on fleshy roots, division is a better option. Remove the parent plant from the pot and tease out some of the rooted offsets, cutting them away from the main plant using a sharp knife. Plant up individually in separate pots and re-pot the parent plant.

*Both agapanthus and water lilies are easily propagated by division just as they are coming into growth.*

## Division method A: for plants with fine roots

**1** Dig up the plant (here a montbretia) in early spring.

**2** Tease out rooted pieces from the edge of the clump.

**3** If necessary, prise the pieces apart using two digging forks. Push them into the centre of the clump, back to back, and lever them apart. The prongs should separate the mass of roots without too much stem or shoot damage. Plant out or pot up at once.

1 Dig up a clump of hostas in late autumn or winter, when there is little risk of damaging new shoots.

## Division method B: for clump-forming plants

2 Use a sharp spade to separate small sections of plant from the main clump.

3 Dump the central congested root section and replant your new plants at the same depth as before. Space them far enough apart to accommodate the future spread of the plants.

4 Press the soil in place with your foot to remove air pockets and water well to settle the soil round the roots.

# simple layering

There are many forms of layering, all of which are practical for the home gardener. The most common system is simple layering and nature has been propagating this way since long before man and woman appeared. Where a branch of dogwood (*Cornus* spp.) touches the ground, it will send out roots and become a plant. Brambles root in the same way, and this is how they manage to leapfrog far and wide.

*Where there is a low branch of witch hazel that can be bent to ground level, layering is the ideal method of propagation.*

*Opposite Daphne cneorum will often layer naturally.*

In the garden, there are many plants that we can encourage to root by simple layering. I have one hundred percent success with expensive shrubs such as witch hazel (*Hamamelis* spp.), rhododendron and daphnes that are difficult for the home gardener to root by other means. One of the advantages of this method is that you can encourage quite sizeable branches to produce roots, giving you a large plant ready for planting out in the garden.

## Basic technique

This form of propagation may be undertaken at any time of the year, but the time taken to root will be speeded up if the layer is made when the plant is actively growing during spring and summer.

The age of the shrub or tree isn't important, but make sure the young branch you select is no more than two years old. Older wood may take a long time to form roots or may not root at all.

Simple layering will only work where a branch is at ground level or can be bent to touch the soil. At the point where the branch meets the ground, the soil is loosened and enriched with mixed coarse sand and peat to provide a free-draining medium that will encourage rooting. The stem is then wounded where it will be in contact with the soil and stripped of any leaves either side of the wound to encourage all the plant's energy into producing roots. The stem is then pegged firmly in place and covered with more compost or prepared soil and water, before

## five tips for success with simple layering

1  Select a one- or two-year-old branch that will bend to touch the ground midway along its stem.
2  Prepare the ground where the branch is to be rooted by loosening the soil and removing stones.
3  Secure the branch to prevent it moving in the wind and damaging the young roots.
4  Keep the ground moist by adding peat or compost to the soil and mulching the surface. Water during dry periods.
5  Have patience. Don't check for roots for at least 15 months.

being weighed down with a large stone to prevent movement and disturbance.

Most plants root in 12–18 months, though some take two years. During this time, keep the ground well watered. After about 15 months, ease the branch out of the ground with a garden fork. If it is well rooted, cut the stem on the side closer to the parent plant. (If not, leave it and check again in a month or so.) Lift the newly rooted layer with as much soil as possible to reduce the check to the roots.

Pot the plant up and grow it on for a season to allow it to form a good rootball in the container. I prefer to use a soil-based compost as it is less likely to dry out during summer. With acid-loving plants, choose an ericaceous compost. Alternatively, plant the rooted layer in the garden. Be prepared to stake the plant for the first year to prevent the leafy head loosening the roots during windy weather.

**1** Prepare the ground by digging over the soil, adding a shovelful of mixed coarse sand and peat into the top few inches. Scoop a depression in the soil where the stem will be positioned.

**2** Select a young (one- or two-year-old) branch that can be bent down to ground level.

**3** Where the branch comes into contact with the soil, make a long shallow cut part way through the stem between two leaves to form an open 'wound'. Wedge it open with a matchstick and dust the wound with rooting hormone. Alternatively, twist the stem to crack it at the right position. Strip off any leaves within 15cm either side of the wound.

**4** Place a U-shaped piece of wire on either side of the cut area to hold the branch in place on the ground, with the wound against the soil.

**5** Make a mound of soil or moisture-retentive compost over the cutting, water generously and cover with a large stone or brick to keep the branch in place. If necessary, tie the portion of stem beyond the area for rooting to a cane, or stake it to prevent the wind from blowing it about and damaging the young, newly formed roots. This will also encourage the plant to grow vertically and not at an angle.

# serpentine layering

This form of simple layering is especially suited to climbers, such as clematis, honeysuckle, jasmine (shown here), fallopia and wisteria. The selected stem should be current season's growth and must be capable of being laid along the ground. As with simple layering, propagation may be carried out at any time of the year, but rooting will be quicker during spring and early summer.

**1** Prepare the soil along the line where the stem is to be rooted in the same way as for simple layering (see page 70). If space is limited, the stem may be curved to form a circle around the parent plant, but make sure it is well away from the root zone. Instead of laying the stem flat along the ground, you are going to loop it in and out of the soil until it resembles the Loch Ness monster.

**2** Allowing at least four or five leaves to each section that is going to remain above ground, prepare the sections that are to be buried by removing the leaves and wounding the stem below a node where a leaf was removed, as for simple layering.

**3** Securely peg each loop using U-shaped wires pushed into the ground.

**4** Cover the flat sections of stem with cutting compost and ensure the soil remains moist.

**5** The layers should be well rooted within 12 months, when you can dig up the whole stem exposing the rooted sections. To separate each section, cut immediately behind the roots to give a rooted plant with a looped area of top growth above ground level. Either pot up in a container or plant out in the garden to grow on for a year before moving to its permanent position. Use a bamboo cane to straighten and support the stem.

# mound or stool layering

Mounding is an easy, if slow, way to propagate woody plants such as cornus (shown here), weigela, philadelphus, gooseberry and blackcurrant.

**1** In winter, cut a healthy, vigorous growing shrub to within 45cm of ground level.

**2** Allow the shoots to grow during the following spring and summer, but prune them down again in winter to within 2.5cm of ground level.

**3** The following spring, lots of new, strong shoots will commence growing. When they are 15cm high, heap up loose, stone-free topsoil, to which sand or grit has been mixed, around the stems to form a mound. Leave the tips of the shoots exposed. As the shoots grow, add more soil, in a similar way to earthing up potatoes, to a finished height of 25–30cm.

**4** In late autumn, gently remove the soil. Each shoot will have produced roots. Cut the rooted shoots from the parent plant, leaving a 2.5-cm stump. The rooted layers may be potted up or lined out in the garden to grow on for a season. Repeat the mounding practice the following spring when there will be additional shoots ready to root.

# drop layering

Also known as plunge layering or sink layering, this is the opposite of mounding. It involves digging the stock plant out of the ground and replanting it in a deeper hole to encourage the stems to form roots. There is less risk of damage to the rooting stems if the summer is hot and dry. This method is best suited to heaths *(Erica* spp.), heathers *(Calluna* spp.) and *Gaultheria mucronata*.

**1** Dig up a healthy plant during spring or early autumn.

**2** Enlarge and deepen the planting hole so that when the plant is reinserted, only the growth tips are above ground level.

**3** Add a handful of bone meal as a slow-release fertilizer.

**4** Replant the plant with only the tips of the shoots above ground.

**5** Spread out the shoots and carefully fill in between them with free-draining cuttings compost.

**6** Water several times to settle the compost around the stems. Six to seven months later, dig the whole plant up. The stems will be well rooted and may be cut off and potted up or lined out in the garden. Pinching out the growing tip will encourage the new plant to produce side shoots and become bushy.

# air layering

So far, all the forms of propagation by layering that have been described have involved bringing the plant into contact with soil. However, there are many instances where this isn't possible. With air layering, the gardener brings the rooting compost to the plant – which is ideal if the only branches available for propagation are stiff and upright, and therefore unsuitable for simple layering.

*The rubber plant was the first plant I ever air layered. I got a thrill when it was successful and I have enjoyed the same experience many times since.*

Mature plants of witch hazel (*Hamamelis* spp.) and rhododendron, in particular, are often without young, low branches that can be bent to ground level.

Some fast-growing house plants are also suitable for air-layering – especially the rubber tree (*Ficus* spp.) and croton (*Codiaeum* spp.) which can quickly become too tall for the average room. Air layering allows you to produce small plants that can be grown for a few years before they too become too tall.

**1** In spring or early summer, select a firm, healthy one-year-old branch. Midway between leaf joints (nodes), make a sloping cut part way through the stem.

**2** Wedge the cut open with a piece of matchstick or a small amount of sphagnum moss to prevent it healing over.

**3** Dust the wound with hormone rooting powder.

**4** Pack damp sphagnum moss around the wounded area and wrap a bandage of clear polythene tightly around the moss to prevent it drying out. Seal it around the stem, top and bottom.

**5** Cover the see-through polythene with an outer covering of black polythene.

Remove the black covering occasionally to check on progress. If the moss appears to be drying out, loosen the top tie, pour in some water and reseal. Eventually, white roots will appear in the moss and these can be seen through the clear polythene. In the case of house plants, rooting may take eight to ten weeks; trees and shrubs, on the other hand, may need 12–18 months to become well rooted.

Once roots have formed, carefully unwrap the stem and remove any loose moss. Using sharp, clean secateurs, cut through the stem immediately below the rooted area and pot up the new plant. Trim the stem of the parent plant back to just above a leaf. This will encourage it to produce side shoots, forming a bushy rather than a tall plant.

# grafting

Simply put, grafting involves placing the cut surfaces of two plants together and encouraging them to bond and grow as one plant. The two pieces are known as the rootstock (the plant retaining its roots) and the scion (the plant being grafted onto it that will form the new plant).

*The blooming good results of grafting an ornamental cherry.*

Why graft? One of the main reasons is to combine the best attributes of two plants into one. In commercial nurseries, grafting is widely practised on fruit trees and roses to give us a wide choice of plant sizes and vigour. Dwarf fruit trees, for example, are created by grafting a scion that is a top fruiting performer with a rootstock that promotes less growth. (While it is possible to root apples and roses from cuttings, they usually make weak plants with poor root systems.) So the choice of rootstock determines the type of growth; attributes of the scion, such as flower colour, fragrance or leaf shape, are transferred to the new plant.

Grafting is a great way of reviving old plants to give them a new lease of life. The first graft I attempted was on an old apple tree with small, sour fruit that I grafted with a better quality dessert fruit. The result was a first-time brilliant success, but since then I have had some failures. All the same, I still get enormous satisfaction every time a graft 'takes'.

Another reason for grafting is to propagate lilac and other plants that are difficult to root by other means. Please don't be deterred from grafting plants because of the detailed and skilled knifework involved. Practice makes perfect. If you succeed, you too will have the enormous satisfaction and pleasure of creating plants that would be expensive to buy in the garden centre.

There are many forms of grafting, but the most successful for a range of plants are whip and tongue and saddle grafting. The ideal time for both methods is in late winter or early spring, just before trees and shrubs commence their annual growth. The rootstock will be at its best in spring when the sap is rising. However, if the scion wood starts growing early it may die before the graft union is working. To

## five tips for success with grafting

1 Select healthy material to use as the scion graft. Don't use diseased shoots or those that have yellow, mottled or distorted leaves.
2 Chose a suitable rootstock with the required vigour.
3 Make clean cuts with a sharp knife.
4 Select a rootstock and scion stem with similar diameters that will match when grafted.
5 Treat the grafted plant with care. The union will be weak for the first season.

avoid this problem, collect the scion wood in late winter when it is dormant. Wrap it in a damp cloth and store in a cool shed until you make the graft.

Rootstocks may be purchased as young plants suitable for grafting from specialist nurseries. However, it is possible to grow many rootstocks, especially roses, rowan, cherry and ash, from seed.

The main thing to bear in mind when choosing two plants for grafting is to pick a scion that is related to the rootstock – that is, one from the same family. So you might graft a rowan tree *(Sorbus* spp.) with an apple or hawthorn because they all belong to the family Rosaceae. *Sorbus sargentiana* may be grafted onto the common species *Sorbus aucuparia*. The beautiful yellow-barked ash, *Fraxinus excelsior* 'Jaspidea' uses the common ash *Fraxinus excelsior* as its rootstock. Different species of wild rose are used as rootstocks for a number of rambler, bush, shrub or climbing rose varieties.

*Grafting in winter is a quick way to bulk up your supply of* Sorbus commixta.

# whip and tongue grafting

When I see a dovetail joint at the corner of a wooden drawer, I am reminded that cabinet makers would be good at grafting. The aim is to bring the cut edges of the rootstock and the variety (scion) together so that they lock in place and the graft unites the two pieces of plant.

*I once had 100 per cent success with 18 whip and tongue grafts of an* Acer japonicum aconitifolium. *Only once.*

I prefer to graft when the rootstock is planted, leaving both hands free for making the graft. However, if you have more than a few to graft, the constant bending down to work just above ground level is hard on your back. Alternatively, you might prefer to work at a table and plant the completed graft back in the ground afterwards.

**1** Make the first cut on the rootstock 10–15cm from the ground.

**2** Use a sharp knife and cut upwards with a sloping cut 3.5–5cm long.

**3** Starting with a good clean cut (right), one third of the way down the slope from the top, make a 1-cm vertical cut to form the 'tongue' (far right).

**4** Select your scion material, which should be of similar diameter to the rootstock. Make a sloping cut at the same angle as for the rootstock, finishing just below a growth bud. Now make a vertical cut one third up from the bottom of the sloping cut, again 1cm deep.

**5** Check that the two ends of stem are a good fit without any gaps between the wood. Cut the scion down to two or three buds. These will form the branch system when the plant commences growth next spring.

**6** Bring the two stems together, locking the tongue and the groove in place. Ensure that both cambium layers (the layer below the bark) are touching around most, if not all, of the cuts. Bind the union with clear polythene tape. Paint the wrapping with pruning paint to form an airtight seal. A dab of the same on the cut tip of the scion finishes the job and reduces the risk of disease entering the open wound.

# bud grafting

This technique is normally referred to as budding. It is a popular and reliable method for grafting bush roses. Budding takes place in summer, usually on roses that are growing in the ground or in containers.

*Rosa 'Irish Eyes'. Like the eyes, this rose is irresistible and it produces plenty of bud 'eyes' to aid propagation.*

The difference between budding and grafting is in the material used. Both whip and tongue and saddle grafting use stems of the desired species or variety. With budding, only a single growth bud is used. The top growth of the rootstock is removed after the bud has formed a union.

The bud is taken from a healthy, well-ripened stem of the current year's growth. Cut a 15–25cm length of stem, making sure that there are dormant buds at the leaf axils. Remove the leaves, leaving only the leaf stalks. Stand the stem upright in water and cover with damp hessian sacking until you are ready to use it.

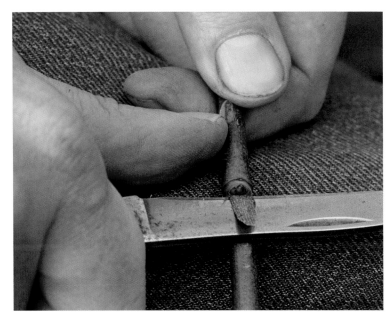

**1** Prepare the bud before opening the rootstock. Any sharp knife may be used, but a special budding knife is best as it has a flattened end to the handle for easing open the bark flaps on the rootstock.

**2** Cut a single healthy bud from the selected stem with the minimum of wood. The leaf stalk is useful for holding the bud and will drop off at a later time. The sliver of wood behind the bud is not required and should be removed from under the bark with the point of the knife, leaving the bud and the cambium layer attached to the bark. The bud must be kept moist until the rootstock is prepared. The simplest method is to hold it between your lips.

**3** Now prepare the rootstock. Clean the stem 2.5–5cm above ground level with a piece of hessian. Make a 'T'-shaped cut deep enough to expose the cambium layer below the bark. The cross-stroke of the 'T' should be furthest from the root and less than 1cm long; the upward cut should be over 2.5cm. Use the flattened end of the knife handle to peel back the two flaps of bark.

**4** Slip the prepared bud, pointing upwards, under the flaps of bark, making sure that the two cambium layers are together.

**5** Trim off any surplus bark from the bud so that it is level with the stroke of the 'T'.

**6** Secure the union with budding strips made of thin rubber. These may be stretched over the bud union and held with an open staple. (If you are old-fashioned like me, you can use raffia instead.)

**7** Once the bud starts to grow, remove the raffia (if you have used a rubber strip, it will perish). In early spring, cut the rootstock above the new bud growth leaving it to flourish and flower that summer.

# saddle grafting

I presume that this takes its name because the scion, which is cut as an inverted 'V', resembles a saddle sitting on the back of a horse. Saddle grafting uses the same principle as the whip and tongue method, and is carried out at the same time – late winter or early spring.

*Deciduous azaleas like this* Rhododendron molle *are usually grafted on to the scented, yellow-flowering* R. luteum.

I recommend it as the best method for grafting rhododendrons, witch hazel, maple and rowan. For best results, make sure the scion and rootstock stems are the same thickness. If one is thicker than the other, line up the rootstock and the scion so that one side of each is in line and touching. If the thinner scion is placed in the centre with neither rim in contact, the graft will not unite to form a bond.

## Basic technique

You can perform a saddle graft either in situ with a planted rootstock, or on a table, in which case you plant the complete graft afterwards.  Using a sharp knife, cut the rootstock close to the ground to form an inverted 'V' or wedge shape. Cut a matching 'V' into the stem of the scion. When the two are joined together, the two cuts should fit exactly without any gaps, and the cambium and bark layers should be touching. If the union leaves gaps, the graft will dry out and fail to bind. Secure and seal as for the whip and tongue technique (see page 83).

**1** For your scion, choose a stem or branch of growth made the previous summer, of similar thickness to your rootstock. Cut an inverted 'V' shape into each piece so that they will lock neatly together.

**2** Fit your graft together, ensuring that there are no gaps between the two pieces of wood and that the cambium and bark layers are touching. Cut the scion down to 2–3 buds.

**3** Seal the graft to keep it in place, to prevent it from drying out and to protect it against disease. First paint the union with pruning paint and then tie it together with rubber strips or raffia as for whip and tongue grafting on page 83.

# bulbs, corms and tubers

There are many gardeners who, in everyday language, refer to corms, rhizomes and tubers as bulbs. We all know what they mean: the swollen, fleshy bits that, when planted, become plants. For the sake of accuracy, I will explain their differences referring to them by their proper name. Thereafter I will lump them all together and call them bulbs.

*Above* Dividing *dahlias every year will result in lots of flowers.*

*Opposite* The *different forms of bulb-like growths – clockwise from top left a begonia tuber, a gladiolus corm, the true bulb of a tulip and a lily-of-the-valley rhizome.*

**A corm,** such as a gladiolus or a crocus, is a thickened, underground stem base covered with scale leaves; a cormel or cormlet is an immature corm that forms round the base of the mature corm. An exception to this rule is crocosmia, where the new corm is formed on top of the old one over the years, resulting in 'strings' of old, hard dead corms.

**A rhizome** is an underground plant stem usually found at, or just below, the soil surface where it spreads horizontally. A good example is the bearded iris, where the rhizomes prefer to be on the surface getting a suntan. Other examples include lily-of-the-valley *(Convallaria* spp.) and elephant's ears *(Bergenia* spp.). Each piece of rhizome that has a bud attached to it will grow into a new plant. The dreaded couch grass weed is an example of a rhizome that roots easily from the smallest piece.

**A tuber** may be either a root tuber, such as a dahlia – where the roots at the base of the stems swell producing growth buds– or a stem tuber, such as a cyclamen or potato. A stem tuber is a modified stem that produces its buds on the surface ('eyes' on potatoes).

**A bulb** is a compressed stem with fleshy leaves known as scales. Unlike a corm, the flower bud is enclosed within the scales of a bulb. Narcissus and tulips have tightly packed scales and are referred to as tunicate, due to the papery outer skin or tunic. Lilies have loosely packed scales without a protective cover and are more prone to damage.

Apart from seed sowing, there are two main methods of propagating bulbs, corms, rhizomes and tubers. Dividing or splitting those that form clumps is easy and without risk, providing the operation is undertaken carefully and at the right time of the year. Cutting or breaking up individual bulbs, corms and tubers is fun, but it is not always 100 per cent successful.

# dividing or splitting bulbs

Large drifts of flowering bulbs are an impressive sight, but the only economical way to achieve such a display is to propagate your own. If you divide existing clumps, they may flower in two or three years – much quicker than growing from seed, which can take between two and seven years.

*Above Clumps of narcissus will benefit from regular splitting and spacing.*

*Below In the garden hyacinths are quite slow to multiply.*

Narcissus (daffodils) and tulips are good examples of plants that readily produce small bulbs called offsets. Others, such as some of the lilies, produce small bulbs (bulbils) at the base of the leaves where they join the stem. Other lilies produce bulblets, which are attached to the plant below ground.

## Basic technique

The best time to split most bulbs is six or seven weeks after they have finished flowering when the foliage has become yellow and the plant has entered its dormant period. However, there are exceptions (see page 91). Long-established clumps of narcissus often become congested and these benefit from being separated and spaced out after dividing them.

Dig up the parent bulb and remove all the young offsets from the sides and base. Store or replant the parent bulb in a permanent position. Plant the offsets individually in a nursery bed or container to gain in size. Use a free-draining, gritty compost or good-quality topsoil, covering them to twice their depth.

After two to three years, the offsets will be at flowering size and may be lifted when the foliage has turned yellow. They can then be stored in a cool, dry, frost-proof position in a shed or garage until autumn when they can be planted out in a permanent position.

*Please propagate lilies, as it is impossible to have too many in the garden. Your success will smell as sweet as the flowers!*

## tips for success with bulbs

- Clumps of snowdrops are best divided every three or four years to prevent them becoming congested. The best time to divide them is when they are still 'in the green', that is straight after the flowers have faded. Dig the clumps up with a garden fork, separate them (retaining the green leaf) and immediately replant individually at the same depth as before.
- Dig up clumps of crocus from summer to autumn while they are dormant, and replant the cormlets in drills or in pots of free-draining compost immediately after they are removed from the parent corm.

- Remove lily bulblets as soon as the dormant bulb is lifted. These form on the stem below soil level. Carefully separate them (sometimes they will already have formed some roots) from the parent and pot them up. They should be sufficiently large to flower within three years. Bulbils of *Lilium lancifolium* and some other lilies need to be removed from the leaf axils in late summer before they drop off. Pot them up straightaway and overwinter them in a garden frame.
- Nerines are an exception. They flower better when the bulbs are congested and should only be divided in order to propagate. To prevent damaging the flower buds, these are best divided in spring before the leaves die down.

# Dividing root tubers

1 Plants with root tubers (here a dahlia) can be divided as long as they are separated with a piece of stem attached to each of the fleshy tubers. The growth buds are located at the base of the stem. Simply cut down through the hard, hollow stem using a sharp knife and pull the tubers apart.

2 Dust any cut surfaces with sulphur powder to reduce the risk of disease.

**3** Pot up or plant out in the open ground when all risk of frost is past. Dahlias prefer a sunny position in a rich, moisture-retentive, free-draining soil. Taller varieties will require staking for support. They will flower from midsummer onwards until the first frost.

# Dividing corms

**1** Lift the clump of corms (here gladioli) in autumn and remove excess soil.

## a tip for gladioli

To encourage lots of gladioli cormlets to form on the parent plant, plant in a shallow hole and cover it with less than 2.5cm of soil. In summer, when the flower spike appears, remove all the flower buds before they open. As a result of this harsh treatment, the plant will divert all its energy into producing masses of cormlets for you to propagate.

**2** You will see that the main corm has produced lots of tiny cormlets.

**3** Carefully remove the cormlets from the parent plant. Overwinter in a frost-proof place and line them out in drills 2.5cm deep in spring. Each year the cormlets will become larger, reaching flowering size after three years.

## Dividing rhizomes

**1** Dig up a clump of rhizomes (here an iris) immediately after flowering and remove excess soil.

**2** Cut off and dump the old, woody part of the rhizome, retaining the young, rooted portions with healthy leaves.

**3** Trim the fan of leaves back to 15cm (trimming the leaves will prevent the young rhizomes from rocking about in the soil in windy weather). Then cut each leaf on a slope to form a mitre, to allow rainwater to run off.

**4** Immediately replant in open ground or pot up, keeping the top of the rhizome 1cm below the surface of the soil. As the soil settles the rain will wash it off the rhizome exposing the upper surface.

## Dividing tunicate bulbs

**1** Simply remove the side bulbs of daffodils and tulips and replant at the same depth as before.

# scaling, scoring and chipping bulbs

Scaling, scoring and chipping bulbs may seem to be little short of vandalism, yet the result is many more bulbs from a single bulb, all identical to the original. These methods are only successful with true bulbs (as opposed to corms and tubers) and my favourites are hyacinth, lily, fritillary, narcissus and snowdrop.

*Scoring is the quickest method of increasing your stock of the snake's head fritillary Fritillaria meleagris.*

Good hygiene is essential with scaling, scoring and chipping because there are a lot of wounds. Avoid propagating from material that is diseased and use methylated spirit to sterilize equipment such as knives after you have worked on each batch of bulbs. To help prevent rot, coat any cut surfaces with sulphur dust, available from the garden centre.

*Scoring snowdrop bulbs will quickly increase your stock.*

**1** In late summer or early autumn, snap off any loose scales from the bulb (here a lily) using your fingers.

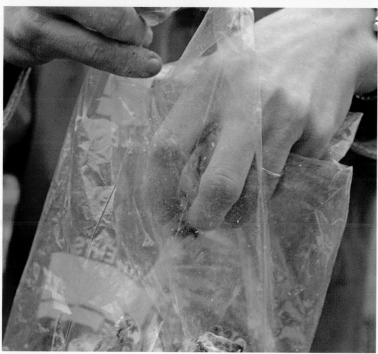

**2** Dust with sulphur and place in a clear polythene bag with a handful of vermiculite. Damp the mixture and seal the bag with as much air as possible.

**3** Store in a dark, warm cupboard until bulblets form at the base of the scale. This may take as long as 8–12 weeks. Pot up the individual scales complete with the tiny bulblet in peat-based compost, lightly covering the bulblet. Keep them in a cool greenhouse. Plant them out the following year, in either spring or autumn. It may take lily bulblets up to five years to flower, but they are worth the wait.

# Scoring

Scoring is a unique way of multiplying your stock of bulbs. Every year I propagate a few hyacinths this way, just for the fun of it.

**1** In late summer, choose a large, healthy bulb. Holding it upside down, cut a shallow groove in the basal plate and another one at right angles, forming a cross.

**2** Dip the base in sulphur. To keep the bulb steady, place it nose down in a container of damp sand with the basal plate showing.

Place it in a warm, dark cupboard. After eight to ten weeks, bulblets will form where the base has been scored. Replant the bulb in peat-based compost, still upside down, and lightly cover the bulblets with compost. Water the compost and leave in a cold frame. The following autumn, separate the small bulbs and pot them up individually. With luck, they will flower within three years.

# Chipping

Chipping works well in late summer with narcissus, nerines (shown here) and alliums.

**1** Remove the outer dry skin of the bulb.

**2** Remove the 'nose' of the bulb using a sharp knife, but leave the basal plate. Cut the bulb into eight sections, each with a piece of the base attached.

**3** Dust the segments with sulphur (wear gloves)...

**4** ...and place in a bag of moist vermiculite, as for scaling (see page 99).

After 10–12 weeks, small bulbs will have formed and these may be potted individually into a peat-based compost. They should be capable of flowering within three years.

# Aftercare

The young, freshly rooted plant will need time to settle down and spread its roots. It is at this stage that a little tender, loving care will ensure success by encouraging the plant to grow away and become established.

Above *Once rooted, young lavender plants will soon reward you with leaf growth and abundant flowers.*

Opposite *Ease seedlings out of the compost without damaging the roots. Hold the leaves rather than the stems, which bruise easily.*

As I may have had occasion to mention before, with gardeners patience is not only a virtue, it is obligatory. Some seeds and cuttings will grow and flower within a season. Others, such as trees propagated from seed and bulbs from division, may take years to reach maturity and during this period watering, feeding and re-potting are ongoing.

## Potting up or transplanting

If the material being propagated shows signs of growing, with new leaves unfurling at the tip, that is a good sign but not a reason to break open the champagne – yet. The potential plant is still very vulnerable. Allow it time to make sufficient root growth to survive a move. Check the base of cuttings in pots to see if there are any roots showing through – this would indicate a good root run. Gently tap the cuttings out of the pot, making sure that the rootball remains intact.

It is more important to have lots of roots than it is to have leaves. Plants grow at different rates and, at this stage, well-rooted fuchsia, lavender and pieris may not show much leaf growth, whereas philadelphus and weigela may have grown 5–10cm with lots of foliage. After 12 months, hardwood cuttings, such as forsythia or blackcurrant, may have become bushy plants ready to go out into the border.

Good hygiene is crucial for the newly rooted plant. When potting up, only use sterilized potting compost and never be tempted to use garden soil, which will be full of disease spores and weed seeds. If possible, use new containers. If you are reusing pots, make sure you scrub them clean in hot water and use a fungicide. Wash your hands before handling seedlings, particularly if you smoke tobacco. Tobacco mosaic virus can be transmitted to tomato plants on your fingers.

The best compost to use for potting up is one designed for the purpose. Unlike seed compost, potting compost will contain some nutrients but only a weak mixture. Too many nutrients will literally 'blow' the plants up, making them leggy and prone to diseases. Always use appropriate compost for the plant. Some plants, such as rhododendrons and pieris, are lime haters and need an ericaceous compost. Others, such as lavender, favour a free-draining mixture with extra grit. For further information on individual plants, see the directory that starts on page 114.

Transplanting and potting up seedlings is quite a fiddly job. Seedlings are very

*Some plants are destined to spend their lives in containers and regular feeding is essential.*

vulnerable to damage and holding the thin stem can cause bruising, so always lift the plant by the leaves. Newly rooted cuttings have brittle roots. Ease them out of the container gently, retaining as much compost around the roots as possible. Pot firmly without compacting the compost around the roots. The rooted cutting should be at the same depth as it was prior to lifting. Seedlings should be planted with the first leaves just above the compost.

Don't be tempted to pot rooted cuttings or seedlings into a large container. Choose a pot that will comfortably hold the roots with some space for root development. In a large pot with lots of compost, the roots will not be able to hold the compost together in a rootball. Root development will be weak and the plant will refuse to make growth.

Transfer the seed or cutting label to its new home and where necessary copy the information to other labels, giving the date of propagation along with the plant's name.

Water using a fine rose on the watering can immediately after potting up to settle the compost around the roots. Young plants prefer water at room temperature, so if possible leave the water in the can for a few hours before use; this takes the chill off it and prevents a sudden shock to the plants.

Stand the young plants in an area where they will be visible. 'Out of sight, out of mind' can be disastrous for container-grown plants during their first summer. Newly potted rooted cuttings and seedlings should be kept away from strong, direct sunlight for a few weeks. Avoid cold exposed sites.

Water your plants regularly, always prior to the compost drying out. In winter and when plants are resting, provide less water than when they are growing strongly. With practice, you should be able to tell from the weight of the pot if water is needed – a plant with dry compost is much lighter. During the growing season, apply a weak liquid feed of a balanced fertilizer at half the manufacturer's recommended strength every 10–14 days to ensure sturdy growth. Allow the newly potted plant a week to settle in and spread its roots before commencing feeding.

## Hardening off

This is an instance when size doesn't matter. A small plant that has been hardened off in preparation for life outdoors is no more vulnerable to adverse weather than a large one. The important thing is to make the plant hardy to your particular climate. The best tip I can give you is to assume the worst. In Northern Ireland we very seldom have serious frost or snow (and any we do have are usually over by early March at the latest), but the year the girl this book is dedicated to was born there was a heavy frost in mid-May, causing lots of damage to plants that both I and they thought were hardy.

Harden the plants off before finally leaving them outside. In spring, it is a good idea to set them out during days when the weather is kind and to bring them back inside before the evening turns cold. After a week, it should be safe to leave them out all night, but cover with a sheet of newspaper to begin with until they are fully acclimatized.

Don't allow your newly potted plants to become pot-bound. Check them on a weekly basis to make sure the roots haven't escaped through the drainage holes in the base of the container into the garden soil. Where this is a problem, set them on hard standing or on a layer of sand spread over a sheet of landscape fabric.

And finally, check for pests and diseases on a regular basis and isolate any plants immediately that appear to be unhealthy with yellow or distorted leaves. Slugs and snails will devour a whole tray of seedlings overnight, so bait the area or smear Vaseline around the rim of the container to act as a barrier. For more information on pests and diseases, see pages 106–111.

*Even hardy polyanthus benefit from a gradual introduction to the outdoor elements.*

# pests and diseases

Hygiene starts before you commence propagating. We have discussed the importance of cleaning pots, using sterilized compost and good housekeeping (see page 8). But despite your best efforts, later on your plants may be subject to pests and diseases that are imported on other plants as well as those that blow, fly and crawl into your garden.

*Outdoor cyclamen are prone to vine weevil attacks, so watch out for any signs of notching in the leaves and treat the soil or compost to kill the larvae.*

If you can ensure that the propagating material is free of pests such as greenfly, then your new plants should be off to a good start. Diseases such as virus are more difficult to spot on young leaves but any plant that looks 'funny' with dead, yellow or mottled foliage should not be considered as a potential source of propagating material.

I am reluctant to mention specific chemicals that will control pests and diseases, not because I don't believe in them or use them myself, but because so many of them have been taken off the garden centre shelves in recent years, and I fear that the list of available products will continue to shrink. It has become too expensive for manufacturers to test and market them and, as a result, perfectly good controls have been withdrawn, leaving gaps in our fight against serious problems.

*Pest-and-disease-free lettuce is a joy to harvest.*

# PESTS AND THEIR CONTROL

## APHIDS

### SYMPTOMS

The common or garden name is greenfly, but they may also be black, yellow, grey, pink or even suntanned! Aphids suck the plant's sap, weakening cuttings and young plants and stunting their growth. As aphids move from one cutting to another, they may also spread virus disease. Greenfly exude sticky honeydew, which falls on the upper surface of the lower leaves. This turns a mouldy black colour, resembling soot.

### CONTROL

There is no way of preventing an attack of aphids in the garden. There are few plants immune to an attack. The best control when propagating is to make sure that every cutting is free of greenfly.

Contact insecticides (which kill on contact) or systemic insecticides (which are absorbed into the plant) are effective, but aphids will build up resistance to them, making it necessary to switch frequently to a different chemical.

Organic treatments include applying soft soap.

Beneficial insects such as the hoverfly and the ladybird devour large numbers of aphids and should be encouraged to visit and eventually reside in your propagating area.

## FUNGUS GNAT

### SYMPTOMS

These tiny, grey-brown flies move quickly over the soil's surface or fly up onto the lower leaves of plants. However, it is the small, black-headed, white maggots that do the damage. While they usually feed on decaying plant material, they will damage softwood cuttings by tunnelling into the base of the stem. They also occasionally eat young seedlings.

### CONTROL

Good hygiene is the best control. Remove all debris and fallen leaves from the surface of the seed or cuttings compost. Cut sticky, yellow fly traps into pieces and place them on the soil's surface to trap the flies.

## MEALY BUG

### SYMPTOMS

Mealy bugs are usually grey-white or pinkish and are mainly a problem for indoor plants, especially cacti and succulents. They spend their lives on the underside of leaves and on the stems close to the leaf axils, where they cover themselves with a protective coat of fluffy white or mealy looking wax.

Mealy bugs suck the sap, weakening the plant, and excrete sticky honeydew which makes the leaves sticky and eventually becomes covered with a black, sooty mould.

### CONTROL

Insecticidal soap is an effective chemical control. Remove infected plants from the propagating area and examine all cuttings prior to propagating.

## RED SPIDER MITE

There are several mites that can be troublesome when propagating from cuttings, the worst being the Conifer red spider mite and the Glasshouse red spider mite. Those that attack fruit trees may be spread by grafting.

### SYMPTOMS

The mites are tiny and best seen through a hand lens. They cause foliage to become speckled yellow and fall prematurely.

Conifer mites are greenish yellow with fine webbing. The eggs are a deep orange colour. Greenhouse mites cause similar webbing and pale yellowish-white leaves on a range of house plants.

Spruce species are most susceptible. Without treatment, the branches towards the centre of the tree become bare of needles.

### CONTROL

Spray with a suitable insecticide every week for three to four weeks during late spring and early summer. Daily spraying with water from a hose will deter a build up of mites.

Only propagate from clean stock. Spraying with insecticidal soap on a regular basis will break the mite's life cycle. Good hygiene is essential, as the mites overwinter in the finest of cracks and on decaying foliage.

## SCALE

### SYMPTOMS

These sap-feeding insects attack the foliage and stems of greenhouse and outdoor plants. They are usually grey or brown-white, flat or domed. Once the young scale finds a suitable leaf or stem, it remains there covering itself with a waxy protective coat. An infestation will result in a weak, unhealthy plant.

### CONTROL

The adult scale insect's waxy coat offers protection from most chemicals, although insecticidal soap will kill young scales before they become covered in wax. Scale insects are vulnerable when young and on the move. Mature scale insects are best removed by pushing them off with your fingernail.

Prevention is better than cure, so make sure that all cutting material is free from infestation. Carefully examine any other plants in the propagating area.

## SLUGS

### SYMPTOMS

Slugs eat irregular holes in the leaves of cuttings. Sometimes they graze the upper surface tissue of the leaf. A sure sign that a slug is around is a silvery slime trail on the cutting, the compost and the container.

### CONTROL

Slugs feed mainly during the hours of darkness, all year round. A nightly inspection with a torch will identify the problem and allow you to dispose of the culprits.

Baiting and trapping slugs is an effective way to limit the damage. I doubt if you will eliminate all the slugs this way, but any reduction is worthwhile. Slugs love beer, milk and the peel of citrus fruit. Special gadgets are available that trap the slug once it has been lured to the bait.

Surrounding cuttings with a copper strip will prevent slugs crawling into the area. A smear of Vaseline on the rim of containers will also deny them access.

Biological control, using a pathogenic nematode, will work, but may be expensive for small batches of cuttings.

Chemical control, using metaldehyde either as poison bait ('slug pellets') or as a spray, is effective, but bear in mind that the chemical is dangerous to pets.

## SNAILS

### SYMPTOMS

Snails cause identical damage to slugs and the controls are the same. They only feed from early spring until late autumn, or early winter if the weather is mild. During the day they hide under debris, pots or trays.

### CONTROL

Keep the propagating area tidy; carry out a daily visual check.

## VINE WEEVIL

### SYMPTOMS

Adult weevils eat irregular notches from the leaf edges. They feed mainly between mid-spring and late autumn and attack almost any leaf, including rhododendron, hydrangea, camellia, viburnum and bergenia (elephant's ears). In severe attacks, all the lower leaves of a shrub will be marked.

Vine weevil larva, which is cream and plump with a pale brown head, remains in the soil. It is most active from late summer through to mid-spring and devours small roots and tubers such as begonia. Bedding plants such as polyanthus suddenly wither and die. When they are lifted for examination, the roots will have been cut through just below soil level. Plants grown in pots are more prone to vine weevil attack.

### CONTROL

Insecticides containing the chemical imidacloprid or thiacloprid are successful at treating this pest. They may be used as a drench or bought already incorporated in the compost. If you suspect that notching has been caused by vine weevils, a late-evening visit with a torch should catch them feeding and they can then be eliminated.

Treating the soil and compost with pathogenic nematodes will kill the larvae, breaking the cycle. After a few treatments, the population of this pest should be well reduced.

## WHITEFLY

### SYMPTOMS

Like greenfly, whitefly is a sap-feeding insect that excretes honeydew onto the lower leaves. When they are disturbed, flies become active – flying around the cuttings. The nymphs (immature whitefly) don't move, and can be found attached to the underside of leaves. Fuchsia cuttings are particularly prone to whitefly attack.

### CONTROL

As with greenfly, prevention is difficult but if the cuttings are examined and any flies or nymphs are removed before they are brought into the propagating area, it may save you a lot of annoyance.

Biological control using a parasitic wasp, *Encarsia formosa*, is very successful. However, it is important that the wasps are introduced to the area before the whitefly population builds up to an uncontrollable level.

Insecticides introduced to treat whitefly will also kill beneficial wasps – and anyway, whitefly quickly build up a resistance to chemicals. Hanging sticky, yellow traps over the cuttings early in the season will eliminate the bulk of the flies; disturbing the foliage will encourage them to fly up into the trap.

## WOOD LICE

### SYMPTOMS

There are worse pests than woodlice. They occasionally damage seedlings, but their mouth parts are too weak to cause harm to cuttings.

### CONTROL

Wood lice are so common in most gardens that it would be pointless in the long term to try and control them. Usually they feed on dead material and are useful for breaking down organic matter. Protect seedlings with a perimeter band of Vaseline.

*This little 'shelter' is just the thing to keep slug pellets dry and safe from birds, but still available to slugs and snails.*

# DISEASES AND THEIR CONTROL

## BLACK LEG

### SYMPTOMS

Black leg is a perfect description for the damage caused by similar soil-borne fungi to those that cause damping off. Before the cutting forms roots, the base of the stem turns black, the leaves turn yellow or brown and fall off.

### CONTROL

As with damping off, hygiene is critical and the same precautions should be taken. Dip the base of the cutting in a rooting hormone that contains a fungicide. Pay special attention to pelargoniums.

## BOTRYTIS

### SYMPTOMS

Also called Grey mould, *Botrytis cinerea* is a fungal disease. It causes infected leaves and stems to produce grey-brown or dull white growth. Prior to this showing, the infected area turns soft, yellow and then brown.

### CONTROL

Botrytis is a common fungus and its spores are widespread in the air, soil and water. Control is therefore difficult, but good hygiene and close attention to the cuttings as they root is the best prevention. Remove all suspect plants before the grey mould appears. Tidy up any dead leaves and spray with a suitable fungicide.

## CANKER

### SYMPTOMS

Various fungal and bacterial organisms cause canker on trees and shrubs. Usually the bark is raised or sunken with cracks or splits. The surface may be rough and, with some types, the bark may peel like tissue paper. Once the disease girdles the branch, the flow of sap is cut off and the branch dies – often retaining the withered leaves.

### CONTROL

When selecting material for hardwood cuttings or grafting, choose healthy, canker-free stems.

## CLUB ROOT

### SYMPTOMS

Club root disease is caused by a slime mould. Infection is usually through infected soil, where the spores can remain active for 20 years without a host to live on. It attacks members of the Cruciferae family, including brassicas such as cabbage and swedes, as well as wallflower, candytuft and stocks. The plant roots become swollen and distorted, resulting in yellow foliage. Plants collapse and die.

### CONTROL

Sow seed and insert cuttings in sterilized soil or compost. Dump infected plants and if handling the roots of diseased plants or the soil in which they were growing, wash and change your clothes before taking cuttings.

## CORAL SPOT

### SYMPTOMS

Bright red (coral) or orange raised pustules appear on dead, woody branches. Dieback occurs, travelling down the stem and eventually killing the whole branch or the plant. The spores of the fungus are spread by air or water, often splashing up onto an open wound caused by pruning.

### CONTROL

When selecting hardwood cuttings of shrubs such as flowering currant (*Ribes* spp.), maple (*Acer* spp.) or elaeagnus, use only healthy stems.

## DAMPING OFF

### SYMPTOMS

Damping off is caused by one of several fungal diseases that are transported by water or soil. Seedlings collapse, usually showing discolouration on the stem at soil level. Within days, patches or even whole batches of seedlings die. A white fungal growth is often apparent on the seedling stems.

### CONTROL

Good hygiene is paramount to prevent damping off. When pots and containers are reused they should first be scrubbed in hot water containing a fungicide. Use sterilized seed and cuttings compost. Water using mains water rather than stored rain water. Dump infected seedlings.

Sow seed thinly to ensure that the seedlings are well spaced.

Some seedlings are more prone to damping off than others, so as a preventative measure, I drench the compost with a copper-based fungicide such as Cheshunt compound immediately after germination.

## MILDEW

### SYMPTOMS

There are two mildews that are troublesome in propagation: downy mildew and powdery mildew. Both are fungal diseases and their spores may be spread by water or by air.

Downy mildew produces yellow blotches on the upper surface of the leaf with a corresponding grey, white or purple fungal growth on the underside. Badly infected leaves wither and die.

Powdery mildew causes white, powdery fungal growth to appear on both surfaces of the leaf. The foliage turns yellow and becomes distorted.

### CONTROL

Examine the stock plants where the cuttings are being taken. If there is any sign of mildew, don't propagate from the plant.

Remove infected leaves from cuttings as soon as they are seen. Where there is a history of mildew, space the cuttings out to allow good air circulation. Open greenhouse vents during the day and raise propagator lids. Avoid watering overhead or wetting the foliage and make sure that the plant's foliage is dry before evening. Spray infected plants with a suitable fungicide.

## ROSE BLACK SPOT

### SYMPTOMS

Purple-black spots appear on the leaves of roses. In some cases, they may become blotches. The leaf yellows and falls off prematurely. Smaller spots appear on the stems. The rose plant becomes weakened after repeated attacks.

### CONTROL

In spring, remove the leaves of any hardwood cuttings that are affected. Collect any leaves that have fallen on the ground to prevent the disease overwintering. Burn the diseased leaves to prevent the spores spreading. Only take cuttings from healthy wood where the stems are free from black spot disease. Regular applications of a suitable fungicide will offer some control.

## RUST

### SYMPTOMS

Bright orange spots appear on the upper leaf surface with corresponding orange spore masses on the underside. In severe cases, defoliation occurs.

### CONTROL

Cutting material and bud grafts should not be taken from infected plants. Where the disease occurs in beds of hardwood cuttings, remove all the infected leaves. Weed between the cuttings to improve the circulation of air around the plants. Spray with a suitable fungicide.

## VIRUS

### SYMPTOMS

Plants may be stunted or the shoots distorted. In many cases the foliage becomes mottled, flecked or streaked with yellow. Flowers such as those of tulips become striped and streaked with various colours.

### CONTROL

There is no control. Take care to propagate from healthy, virus-free plants. Regularly disinfect cutting equipment and wash your hands after handling any suspicious plant material. Burn diseased plants. Control sap-sucking insects such as aphids and whitefly, which spread virus as they move from plant to plant.

# TROUBLESHOOTING

If your best efforts fail to produce new plants, there may be a number of reasons. The following checklist should help you to avoid the same pitfalls next time. Pay particular attention to hygiene (see page 8). With all pests and diseases, prevention is better than cure.

## ▌ SEED

### NO OR POOR GERMINATION

*Seed not viable*  Most seed needs to be stored in a cool, dry place; seed that has not been stored correctly may lose viability. With most seed, the chances of germination are less once it is more than a year old.

*Compost too wet*  The seed may have rotted; be less generous with your watering.

*Seed sown too deep*  The smaller the seed the closer to the surface it is sown (see page 25). If you plant small seed too deep, it won't have the strength to reach up through the compost to the light.

*Lack of moisture*  Keep the compost moist at all times.

### SEEDLINGS DYING

*Damping off disease*  Treat with Cheshunt compound (see page 110).

### SEEDLINGS YELLOW

*Cold compost*  Check the directory (starting on page 114) for instructions on individual plants, but most need to be kept at a temperature of about 19–20°C.

*Wet compost*  Avoid overwatering.

*Lack of nutrients*  Too long growing in seed compost. Seed compost does not contain sufficient nutrients for steady growth and is designed for short-term use only. Transplant into potting compost.

### SEEDLINGS DISAPPEARING

*Mice, wood lice, slugs or snails*  See Pests and Diseases (pages 106–111) for methods of protection.

## ▌ CUTTINGS

### BLACK STEMS

*Fungal disease such as mould or botrytis*  Apply fungicide as prevention (see page 110–111).

### WITHERING

*Lack of moisture*  Keep the compost moist at all times.

*Vine weevil attacking roots*  As a preventative measure next time, use a compost containing the chemical imidacloprid.

### LEAVES FALLING

*Dry compost*  Keep the compost moist at all times.

*Leaf or stem disease*  Before inserting cuttings in the compost, dip them in a rooting hormone that contains a fungicide. Treat the foliage with a fungicidal spray.

### NO ROOTS

*Not a suitable type of cutting*  Check the directory (starting on page 114) for advice on individual plants.

*Dry compost*  Keep it moist at all times.

*Heavy callusing*  Scrape off and reinsert the cutting.

### FLOWERING

*The cutting was taken with flower bud already formed*  Nip out the growing tip of the cutting, thus removing the flower buds.

### YELLOW FOLIAGE

*Cutting losing moisture before roots form*  Use a propagator or cover the plant with a clear polythene bag to maintain humidity. With large-leafed plants such as bergenia, trim off the top half of the leaf to reduce the area available for transpiration.

*Cold atmosphere or compost*  Check the directory (starting on page 114) for instructions on individual plants, but most need to be kept at a temperature of about 19–20°C if they are to grow healthily. Protect from draughts.

*Waterlogged or wet compost*  Be less generous with your watering regime.

### DISEASED FOLIAGE

*Yellow blotches on leaves*  A number of diseases, including virus disease, rose blackspot, black leg, club root disease and powdery mildew, will cause leaves to yellow or to develop yellow blotches. See Pests and Diseases, (pages 106–111).

### DISTORTED FOLIAGE

*Virus disease*  See page 111.

*Contact with a hormone weedkiller*  Keep young plants well away from weedkillers – even the smell of such weedkillers will damage most plants.

## LAYERING

### NO ROOTS
*Requires longer to produce root*
Have patience.
*Layer moving in the wind* Stake the
portion above ground.
*Soil too dry* Apply more water where
the branch meets the ground.

### STEM WITHERING
*Sloping cut made too deep* Start again.
*Roots drying out* Keep compost moist.
*Parent plant dry at roots* Keep watered.

### DEAD BRANCH
*Lack of green fingers* Try again.

## █ GRAFTING

### DEAD PLANT
*Graft didn't take* Try again.

### NO GROWTH
*Dry roots* Keep the plant watered.
*Waterlogged soil* Avoid overwatering.
*Dormant season* Have patience.
*Callus part of the new union* Encourage
growth by feeding. May eventually
callus over completely.

### SUCKER
*Rootstock suckers not wanted* Remove.

## █ DIVISION

Propagating plants by division is usually
trouble-free – provided you plant and
water sensibly!

*If a graft goes well, as with this maple,
you will have a plant to be proud of.*

# directory of plants

Just like every gardener, I have my favourite method of propagation for every plant, but that doesn't mean you can't propagate successfully using other methods – in this directory, I have often included several for you to choose from. My choice may simply reflect the first method I tried with that plant, or one which for some reason works for me. For what it's worth, I have marked my way with a 🇯. If a plant is particularly easy to propagate, I have marked the easiest method with an 🇪. Full details of all the propagation methods are given on pages 19–101. Any terms that I think might be unfamiliar are explained in the glossary on page 251.

I have generally named only one species or cultivar under each genus. This may be the best recognized, the most typical or simply my favourite. However, as a rule, all members of a genus can be propagated using the same techniques. There are, of course, exceptions – notably large genera such as *Iris*, where some species grow from rhizomes and others form clumps, which need to be treated differently – and these are detailed in the entries. Unless otherwise stated, propagated seed, seedlings and cuttings should be kept at a temperature of 19–20°C. Where I have specified a minimum temperature, you should use a heated propagator.

Bupleurum fruticosum (see page 138)

### ABELIA × GRANDIFLORA
Shrub. Semi-evergreen with fragrant, pink-tinged, white summer flowers. Provide shelter from biting cold winds.

🇯 *Softwood cuttings* in late spring under clear polythene or in a heated propagator at 21°C.
*Semi-ripe cuttings* in late summer. These cuttings will not be well rooted by autumn, so leave them undisturbed until growth starts the following spring.

Pot well-rooted plants from either type of cutting into a soil-based compost for the first year. The following autumn they can be planted in their permanent position and will flower after 2 years' growth.

### ABELIOPHYLLUM DISTICHUM
(White forsythia)
Shrub. Deciduous with fragrant, white or pink-tinged flowers in late winter and early spring.

*Semi-ripe cuttings* in summer. They will flower within 2 years.
🇯 *Layer* in early summer. The layer will be well rooted after 15 months. During that time it will flower as a layer and should be pruned after flowering. To check whether the plant is well rooted, ease it up with a fork to examine the root structure. If the roots look well developed and healthy, carefully ease the rooted branch out of the soil and sever the new plant from the parent shrub. Pot up or plant out in a spot where you can enjoy it in winter. For both scent and sight, plant against a red brick wall below an opening window.

### ABIES GRANDIS (Giant fir)
Conifer. Evergreen with shiny, dark green foliage and cones.

*Sow seed* as soon as it is ripe.

Germination is always poor as most seed isn't viable. However, the chances are that you will only require one plant of such a large tree, so sow plenty and you should get one! As soon as the cone opens, shake out the ripe seed. Cover it immediately in moist peat and chill for 4 weeks at 1-2°C, then sow outside or in a compost that is 50 per cent sterilised soil and 50 per cent washed grit in a garden frame.

▯ *Seed* Alternatively, try a spring sowing. Remove the outer coat of the seed and sow only the pale, soft, rubbery embryo in seed compost in a garden frame.

*Saddle graft* cultivars that won't come true from seed. The rootstock that seems to work best is *A. alba*.

---

## ABUTILON VITIFOLIUM

Shrub. Deciduous with soft, grey-green, lobed leaves and large, saucer-like, white, pale mauve or violet flowers in early summer.

▯ *Sow seed* 1cm deep in a propagator at 16°C in spring. To prevent fungal disease attacks, remove all debris and pieces of seed case if storing seed.

*Semi-ripe cuttings* in midsummer. Trim the large leaves to half their length to reduce transpiration. Avoid strong sunlight. If this plant likes you, it will root like a weed and germinate like cress.

---

## ACACIA DEALBATA

(Mimosa, Silver wattle)
Tree or shrub. Evergreen with fern-like foliage and fragrant, yellow flowers in winter and spring.

*Sow seed* in spring at a minimum temperature of 20°C. Prior to sowing, soak the seed in very hot water for 24 hours to speed up germination. Grow for 18 months in a container before planting out into its permanent position.

▯ *Semi-ripe cuttings* in midsummer. After

Abelia x grandiflora

propagation, grow on in a pot for at least a year with winter protection from frost or cold winds. Will flower within 3 years.

## ACAENA MICROPHYLLA
**'COPPER CARPET'** (New Zealand burr)
Evergreen perennial with leaves tinged bronze or purple and small, round flowers followed by red burrs in mid- to late summer.

**Sow seed** in a cold frame in autumn. Pot up the seedlings in spring.
- **Divide** clumps in late autumn or early spring depending on your soil and climate (see page 64).
**Softwood cuttings** in late spring under clear polythene. Cuttings root quickly and may be in flower by the end of the same season.

## ACANTHOLIMON GLUMACEUM
(Prickly heath)
Evergreen perennial with rosettes of spiny, dark green leaves and deep pink flowers in summer.

**Sow seed** immediately after collection in a peat-based compost in a cold frame. Pot up in spring and plant out the same autumn. Flowers in the second year.
- **Softwood cuttings** in spring. Nip out the tip of the shoot to prevent it flowering.

## ACANTHOPANAX SIEBOLDIANUS
syn. Eleutherococcus sieboldianus
Deciduous shrub with cane-like branches and bright green, palmate foliage. Green-white flowers appear during late spring and early summer, followed by black berries.

**Sow seed** outdoors in autumn in rows.
**Softwood cuttings** in early summer under horticultural fleece.
**Root cuttings** with bottom heat in winter in a propagator.

- **Rooted suckers** in late winter. These form at the base of the plant. Pot into soil-based, gritty compost for the first year and leave outside until the sucker develops a good root system. Then plant out in a permanent position.

## ACANTHUS SPINOSUS
(Bear's breeches)
Deciduous perennial with spiny, dark green leaves. The 2-lipped, pure white flowers with spiny, purple bracts appear in late spring and early summer.

**Sow seed** thinly in a cold frame in spring. Transplant seedlings when small, as soon as the first pair of true leaves has appeared. Pot the growing plant on early to prevent roots becoming congested (knock the plant out of the pot to check). Flowers the following spring.
- **Divide** in early spring using the young outer pieces of plant.
**Root cuttings** taken from the outer edge of the clump in mid-winter in a garden frame.

## ACER (Maple)
Deciduous trees and shrubs with palmate leaves, many of which colour beautifully in autumn.

**Sow seed** in early autumn in a garden frame or in trays outdoors in a sheltered corner. Prevent the seed from drying out prior to sowing by storing away from heat in a small, airtight container. The seeds have an appendage known as a wing which should be broken off to make sowing easier. Germination can be erratic and seed viability of most species is low. I can honestly say that over the years I have had more disappointments than brilliant successes with *A. griseum*, but I persist because it is one of my favourite trees and, in spite of my

disappointments, I now have 7 excellent plants of various ages. Acers are hardy and after the seedlings have been potted up they can remain outside as long as they are sheltered from cold winds.

**Softwood cuttings** of the cultivars of *A. palmatum* (Japanese maple) taken in late spring and early summer. Root in a heated propagator, preferably with the aid of a mist propagation unit to prevent the leaves drying out.

**Whip and tongue grafts** outside in late winter and early spring. Use the species for the rootstock and your chosen variety for the scion. *Acer platanoides* (Norway maple) is the ideal rootstock for the beautiful, variegated variety *A. p.* 'Drummondii'.

## ACHILLEA FILIPENDULINA
**'CLOTH OF GOLD'** (Yarrow)
Perennial with light green leaves and corymbs (flat-topped flower clusters) of golden-yellow flowerheads in summer and early autumn.

**Sow seed** outdoors in open ground in late spring or early summer.
**Divide** in early spring.
- **Softwood cuttings** taken in late spring. Use a sharp knife to remove shoots from the outside of the clump close to the crown of the plant. Root in gritty, free-draining compost in a heated propagating frame at 15°C. Pot up when well rooted and keep shaded for a few days. They will flower the same year.

## ACHIMENES GRANDIFLORA
(Cupid's bower)
Tender perennial with dark green, hairy leaves, red flushed on the underside. Reddish-purple flowers with a white eye and purple-dotted throat appear in summer and autumn.

**Softwood cuttings** in spring at 18°C in gritty compost.

▯ **Divide** rhizomes in early spring.

---

### ACONITUM 'BRESSINGHAM SPIRE'
(Monk's hood)
Perennial with glossy, dark green foliage and tall spikes of deep violet flowers from midsummer to mid-autumn. All parts of this plant are poisonous, so use gloves when handling it.

**Sow seed** as soon as it is collected in late summer, outside or in a garden frame. Alternatively, chill the seed in the fridge for 30 days and sow in spring.

▯ **Divide** in early spring. Tease rooted pieces off the side of the clump and plant up as soon as possible. Keep the foliage damp until the plant starts to grow.

Some species of *Aconitum* have tuberous rather than fibrous roots. Propagate these plants by separating the tubers and replanting the larger ones. Small tubers should be grown on for a year in a nursery bed before planting them out in their permanent positions.

---

### ACORUS GRAMINEUS (Japanese rush)
Bog or aquatic, semi-evergreen perennial with fans of glossy, deep green leaves.

**Divide** in late spring. Repot using a peat-based compost and keep in a shaded site for a few days, then position the pots in shallow, 10cm deep water in full sun.

---

### ACTAEA RUBRA (Red baneberry)
Perennial. White flowers in late spring and early summer are followed by spikes of bright, shiny red berries on green stalks. The seeds are poisonous.

**Sow seed** in late autumn in a garden frame. Cover with grit. It will take 2 years for it to flower.

▯ **Divide** in early spring, taking care not to damage the new shoots.

This plant will tend to sulk in dry, impoverished soil.

---

### ACTINIDIA (Kiwi fruit)
*A. deliciosa* is a deciduous climber with large, mid-green, heart-shaped leaves and creamy-white flowers that turn to yellow. Female plants produce greenish-brown fruit (providing you have a male plant nearby).

*A. kolomikta* is a deciduous climber with dark green leaves becoming variegated white and pink on the top half. Fragrant white flowers in summer are followed on female plants by small, greenish-yellow fruit.

**Sow seed** in autumn or spring in a garden frame.

▯ **Semi-ripe cuttings** in late summer in a propagator. Cut the leaves in half to reduce transpiration.

**Hardwood cuttings** in early winter in a greenhouse with bottom heat.

Both species will produce flowers within 3–4 years from either type of cutting. *Actinidia deliciosa* will hopefully also bear fruit.

**Whip and tongue grafts** of cultivars in late summer.

---

### ADIANTUM PEDATUM
(Northern maidenhair fern)
Deciduous fern with pinnate, mid-green fronds carried on shiny black stalks.

Actinidia kolomikta

**Divide** rhizomes in early spring. Repot in orchid compost.

**Sow spores** as soon as they are ripe at 15°C. This plant propagates so easily by division that I would only sow spores to be able to say: 'Been there, done that.'

## ADONIS AMURENSIS
Perennial with mid-green leaflets with pointed lobes. The bowl-shaped, bright yellow flowers appear in late winter and early spring before the leaves.

**Sow seed** in a garden frame as soon as it is ripe in summer. If you sow in spring, germination is slow and erratic with seedlings not appearing until midsummer. Use an ericaceous compost.

**Divide** perennials after flowering but plant a few extras and be prepared for a percentage of deaths. Plant in a moist, acid soil in full shade.

## AEONIUM ARBOREUM 'ZWARTKOP'
Succulent sub-shrub. Rosettes of spoon-shaped, glossy, black-purple leaves with panicles of bright yellow flowers are produced in spring.

**Sow seed** in spring in a propagator at 22°C.

**Semi-ripe cuttings** in summer. Allow the cut stem to dry out for 24 hours after removing it from the parent plant, then insert in moist, open, gritty cutting compost at 18°C until well rooted. This may take 4–5 weeks. Don't water cuttings until they are rooted. Pot up individually and, as the stems become woody and bare of foliage, prune to encourage side shoots.

## AESCHYNANTHUS LOBBIANUS
(Lipstick vine)
Perennial conservatory plant. Trailing stems with deep green leaves margined with purple. Terminal clusters of scarlet flowers with purple calyces are produced during summer and early winter. A terrible shade for a lipstick!

**Softwood cuttings** in spring in a gritty rooting compost in a propagating frame.

**Semi-ripe cuttings** in summer in a propagating frame at 16°C with bottom heat.

For both methods, short cuttings, 2.5–5cm long, will root more easily. Pot up the young plants in a free-draining compost. Keep them in shade for a few days.

## AESCULUS HIPPOCASTANUM
(Horse chestnut)
Deciduous tree with large, palmate, 'fingered', mid-green leaves that are 30cm long. Upright, conical panicles of white flowers with yellow marks appear in late spring and early summer. Pink is added to the flowers as they mature. The familiar, spiny fruit contains the conkers loved by children. The chestnut colour is derived from the shiny seed coat.

**Sow seed** (conkers) outdoors in autumn as soon as the outer shell splits open. *Aesculus × carnea* (red flowers) comes true from seed.

**Whip and tongue grafts** of cultivars in late winter or early spring. Use *A. hippocastanum* for the rootstock.

**Suckers** *Aesculus parviflora* (bottlebrush buckeye) can be propagated by removing the rooted suckers in late autumn or winter. Pot them up for a year in a soil-based compost to allow the roots to become established.

## AETHIONEMA GRANDIFLORUM
Semi-evergreen perennial with small, blue-green leaves and racemes of rose-pink flowers in late spring and early summer.

**Sow seed** in a cold frame in late spring.

**Softwood cuttings** in early summer. Cover with horticultural fleece.

## AGAPANTHUS (African lily)
Evergreen perennial with deep green, strap-like leaves. The umbels of trumpet-shaped, blue or white flowers are carried on tall, strong stems in mid- to late summer.

**Sow seed** in a gritty compost at 15°C in spring. Overwinter the young plants in a frost-proof frame for the first year. They may take 3 years to flower. Colour will probably differ from the parent.

**Divide** clumps in early spring. Treat the fleshy roots carefully and avoid damaging the early new growth.

Containerized plants prefer to be crowded.

## AGAVE (Century plant)
Evergreen perennial with large, broad rosettes of succulent, sharp pointed leaves. Tall panicles of yellow flowers appear in summer.

**Sow seed** in early spring at 20°C.

**Root offsets** in a mixture of equal parts peat and coarse sand. Some offsets may be detached with some root still attached; these can be potted up in free-draining, soil-based compost.

## AGERATUM (Floss flower)
Half-hardy annual with panicles of blue or blue and white flowers from midsummer until the first frosts.

**Sow seed** in early spring at 16°C or sow thinly in autumn and overwinter at 9°C.

## AGROSTEMMA (Corn cockle)
Annual with grey-green foliage and purple flowers in summer.

**Sow seed** as soon as it is ripe in early autumn in open ground or in trays outside.

**Seed** Alternatively, sow in early spring where it is to flower.

## AILANTHUS ALTISSIMA
(Tree of heaven)
Deciduous tree with large, 60cm long, pinnate leaves and terminal panicles of small, green, summer flowers followed by deep red fruit and winged seed.

**Seed** Chill seed as soon as it is ripe in moist peat for 60 days at 3°C. Sow seed in a garden frame.

**Root cuttings** in early winter in a garden frame.

**Rooted suckers** Remove in winter, pot up in a soil-based compost and leave outside for a year. Use a 3-litre pot to accommodate the fast growth.

## AJUGA REPTANS (Bugle)
Evergreen perennial with dark green leaves and spike-like whorls of deep blue flowers in late spring and early summer.

Ajuga reptans

**Lift rooted stems** in autumn or early spring and pot up in soil-based compost.

**Softwood cuttings** in early summer. Shade the cuttings for 5–10 days with horticultural fleece.

## AKEBIA QUINATA (Chocolate vine)
Semi-evergreen climber with dark green leaves that are blue-green on the underside and tinged purple in early autumn. The racemes of brownish-purple, fragrant flowers appear in early spring followed by 10cm long fruit.

**Sow seed** in a garden frame as soon as it is ripe in early autumn.

**Semi-ripe cuttings** in late summer. Use rooting hormone. Pot up the rooted cuttings the following spring.

**Layer** in late summer. Use free-draining compost. The stem should be well rooted by the following autumn.

## ALBIZIA JULIBRISSIN (Silk tree)
Deciduous tree with ferny, mid-green leaves made up of small, sickle-shaped leaflets. The terminal clusters of green-yellow flowers appear in summer.

**Sow seed** in spring at 22°C. Pre-soak the seed for 24 hours in warm water or carefully chip the seed.

**Semi-ripe cuttings** with a 'heel' in a propagator with bottom heat in summer. Use rooting hormone.

**Whip and tongue grafts** of named cultivars such as *A. j. alba* (white flowers) and *A. j. rosea* (my favourite, with pink flowers).

## ALCEA ROSEA (Hollyhock)
Perennial with hairy, rounded, light green leaves. The tall racemes of saucer-shaped flowers appear in early and midsummer.

Alchemilla mollis

**Sow seed** in open ground in midsummer or singly in pots for transplanting in early autumn. Don't save seed from plants suffering from rust disease.

**Seed** Alternatively, sow in early winter at 14°C and the plants will flower the following summer.

## ALCHEMILLA MOLLIS (Lady's mantle)
Perennial with lobed, hairy, pale green leaves and masses of frothy, greenish-yellow flowers throughout summer.

**Sow seed** outdoors in late spring or early summer. Every seed will germinate. Transplant seedlings when young before a strong root system develops. It self-seeds like a weed.

**Divide** in early spring using rooted pieces from the outside of the clump.

### ALISMA PLANTAGO-AQUATICA
(Water plantain)
Aquatic perennial with lance-shaped, dark green leaves and dense panicles of pinkish-white flowers in late summer.

*Sow seed* as early as possible in autumn. Sow thinly in trays of peat-based compost that's half submerged in a tray of water outside; keep protected from animals.

◨ *Divide* swollen rhizomes in late spring.

### ALLIUM (Ornamental onion)
Bulbous perennial with deciduous leaves that are strongly pungent when crushed. The flowers are bell-, cup- or star-shaped and white, pink, red or purple.

*Sow seed* in a container in a garden frame in autumn or outside in spring. They will self-seed freely. Lift the seedlings in the autumn and pot up for a year. Some species will flower in the second year, others will take 3–4 years.

◨ *Remove bulbous offsets* in autumn and plant them out in rows 2.5–5 cm deep in open ground. Alternatively, store them over winter as small bulbs in dry peat or sawdust in a frost-free shed for planting outside in late spring. Some species will flower in the first year; larger-growing species may take 2 years.

### ALNUS CORDATA (Italian alder)
Deciduous tree with attractive, glossy, dark green leaves and yellow-brown, male catkins that open before the leaves appear.

*Sow seed* outside in a seed bed as soon as it is ripe in late autumn. Alternatively, store them in packets or boxes in a dry, frost-proof cupboard , ready for sowing outside in open ground in early spring.

◨ *Hardwood cuttings* in winter.

### ALOCASIA MACRORRHIZA (Giant taro)
Tender perennial with glossy, mid-green, arrow-shaped, 90–120cm long leaves on 2m stalks. Green-yellow spathes, 20cm long, appear throughout the year. The rhizomes and shoots are edible.

*Sow seed* as soon as it is ripe at 23˚C.
*Softwood stem cuttings* in spring.
◨ *Divide* rhizomes in late spring or summer.

### ALOE VARIEGATA
(Partridge-breasted aloe)
Evergreen, succulent perennial with rosettes of fleshy, dark green, V-shaped leaves marked with white cross bands. Racemes of pink or scarlet flowers are carried on 30cm long stems in summer.

*Sow seed* as soon as it is ripe, at 20°C in free-draining compost.
◨ *Root offsets* in cactus potting compost or peat-free compost with added grit and some crushed charcoal. As a boy I had every windowsill lined with plants propagated this way. Then I discovered that they could be sold.
*Separate rooted offsets* in spring or early summer.

### ALOPECURUS PRATENSIS 'AUREOVARIEGATUS' (Foxtail grass)
Perennial grass with leaves attractively striped yellow and green. Its dense, purple, 10cm long panicles appear in late spring and early summer.

*Sow seed* thinly in seed compost in spring at 15°C. Every seed will probably germinate.
◨ *Divide* in late spring, taking care to retain a piece of root on each section of plant. I have found that teasing them apart by hand works better than using implements.

### ALOYSIA TRIPHYLLA (Lemon verbena)
Deciduous shrub with 10cm long, narrow, bright green, lemon-scented leaves. In late summer it produces panicles of small, pale lilac or white flowers.

*Sow seed* in spring in well-drained compost in a garden frame. A lot of the seed will not be viable, so sow plenty to give yourself more chance of success.
◨ *Softwood cuttings* in summer under horticultural fleece. Provide frost protection for the first winter.

### ALPINIA PURPURATA (Red ginger)
Tender, evergreen perennial with lance-shaped, 75cm long, mid-green leaves. Small, pendant, 2.5cm long, white flowers are produced in summer from bright red bracts.

*Sow seed* as soon as it is ripe at 20°C in open, peat-based compost.
◨ *Divide* in spring.

Plantlets may appear among the bracts. These may be removed and potted up as offsets.

### ALSTROEMERIA LIGTU (Peruvian lily)
Tuberous perennial with lance-shaped, mid-green leaves and umbels of funnel-shaped flowers in summer. The flower colour varies from white to pinkish-red.

*Sow seed* as soon as it is ripe in a container in autumn and overwinter in a garden frame. Alternatively, pre-soak the seed for 24 hours in warm water and sow in spring at 20°C. As they have brittle, easily damaged roots, sow thinly in small containers and plant out each pot of seedlings as a clump.
◨ *Divide* clumps in autumn rather than in spring as they come into growth early. Tubers should be planted 15–20cm deep.

Amaranthus caudatus

## ALTHAEA CANNABINA
(False hollyhock)
Perennial with 30cm long, rounded and lobed, hairy, dark green leaves. The 2m high spikes of cup-shaped, deep pink flowers appear during summer and early autumn.

**Sow seed** in open ground in midsummer, transplanting the seedlings in early autumn. Plant in their permanent positions the following spring. I have never had good plants when transplanted into pots.

## ALYSSUM WULFENIANUM
Evergreen perennial with small, grey-green leaves. Masses of pale yellow flowers appear in summer.

**Sow seed** in containers in a garden frame in autumn or mid-spring.

**Softwood cuttings** Root short-stemmed cuttings in early summer.

## AMARANTHUS CAUDATUS
(Love-lies-bleeding)
Hardy annual or short-lived perennial with stems that are green, purple or red and light green leaves. During summer and early autumn the trailing, tassel-like panicles of deep crimson flowers measure up to 60cm long.

**Sow seed** in open ground in mid-spring. Once 3–4 leaves have formed, transplant the seedlings to their flowering position.

## AMARYLLIS BELLADONNA
Bulbous perennial with stout, purple-green stems carrying 6–8 funnel-shaped, pale pink, fragrant flowers. Its fleshy, 30–40cm long, strap-like leaves appear after the flowers.

**Sow seed** as soon as it is ripe at 17°C. Thin the seedlings early and grow under glass for 2 years.

◪ **Remove offsets** in late spring. Grow in a container for 2 years, setting them outside during summer. After this period they can be planted out in a sheltered position in the border and hopefully they will flower that year.

## AMELANCHIER CANADENSIS
(Snowy mespilus, Juneberry)
Deciduous shrub or small tree. Mid-green leaves turn orange-red in early autumn. Erect racemes of small, white flowers appear in spring, followed by edible, blue-black fruit.

**Sow seed** as soon as it is ripe in open ground. Cover the seed with coarse sand. The species tend to hybridize, so your seedlings may be variable.

**Semi-ripe cuttings** in midsummer or early autumn under horticultural fleece. Don't pot the rooted cuttings until the following spring.

◪ **Rooted suckers** in winter. Pot up and stand outside for the first year before planting out.

## AMORPHA FRUTICOSA
(Bastard indigo)
Deciduous shrub with pinnate foliage. The deep purple flowers have deep yellow anthers and are produced in racemes during summer.

**Sow seed** in a garden frame in autumn. Pre-soak the seed for 12 hours in warm water.

◪ **Rooted suckers** in late autumn. Pot up in a soil-based multi-purpose compost for the first year outside in a sheltered position.

## AMPELOPSIS BREVIPEDUNCULATA
Deciduous climber with dark green, palmate leaves. Small, green flowers appear in summer followed by small, pink fruits that ripen to bright blue.

**Sow seed** in a garden frame in late autumn or stratify over winter outside and sow in spring.

◪ **Softwood cuttings** in gritty compost in early summer.

**Hardwood cuttings** in early winter with bottom heat.

**Bud cuttings** in a garden frame in early winter. Although the technique is the same as that described for camellias, this is a deciduous plant so there will be no leaf on the cutting.

## ANACYCLUS PYRETHRUM
**VAR. DEPRESSUS** (Mount Atlas daisy)
Tender perennial with grey-green leaves. During summer white, daisy-like flowers appear. Each flower petal is red on the reverse with a pure white strip.

**Sow seed** in a garden frame in autumn.

◪ **Softwood cuttings** in early summer in free-draining, gritty, soil-based compost.

## ANAGALLIS MONELLII
(Blue pimpernel)
Evergreen perennial with mid-green leaves and deep blue, saucer-shaped flowers in summer.

**Sow seed** in a garden frame in spring.
**Divide** clumps in late spring.

◪ **Softwood cuttings** in early summer. Remove the growing tip of the cutting to prevent flowering. I root them in cactus compost under horticultural fleece.

## ANANAS BRACTEATUS (Red pineapple)
Tender, evergreen perennial with brown-green, spiny leaves 45cm long. The red-yellow flowers with distinctive red bracts appear in summer, followed by green-brown fruit.

**Softwood basal cuttings** in midsummer.

◪ Cut off the leafy rosette at the top of the pineapple fruit. Leave it for 1–2 days for the cut end to callus. Insert the base of

the rosette in cactus compost at 20°C and protect from strong, direct sunlight. Within 6 months the new plant should be well rooted and ready to pot into a humus-rich, free-draining compost with added grit.

## ANAPHALIS NEPALENSIS
(Pearly everlasting)
Perennial with pale, grey-green leaves that are white on the underside. The yellow flowers appear in late summer.

**Sow seed** in a garden frame in spring.

◪ **Softwood basal cuttings** in late spring under clear polythene.

**Divide** clumps in early spring. Make sure the new plants are well watered during the first year.

## ANCHUSA AZUREA (Alkanet)
Perennial with lance-shaped, stiff, hairy, dark green basal leaves. Panicles of gentian-blue, early summer flowers turn blue-purple with age.

**Sow seed** in containers in a garden frame in spring.
**Softwood basal cuttings** in late spring.

◪ **Root cuttings** in winter in soil-based compost in a garden frame.

## ANDROMEDA POLIFOLIA
(Bog rosemary)
Evergreen shrub with leathery, dark green leaves and white or pale pink flowers that appear during spring and early summer.

**Softwood basal cuttings** in midsummer.
**Rooted suckers** potted into an ericaceous compost outside in early winter.

◪ **Layer** in late spring in a mixture of peat and leaf mould. Rooting is slow, so leave undisturbed for 12 months.

### ANDROSACE CARNEA (Rock jasmine)

Evergreen perennial with rosettes of fleshy, mid-green leaves and umbels of pink, yellow-eyed, late spring flowers.

*Sow seed* as soon as it is ripe in a garden frame.

▯ *Root rosette cuttings* in free-draining compost in early summer. Cover with horticultural fleece and water from below. They will flower the following year.

### ANEMONE APENNINA (Windflower)

Perennial with dark green, palmate leaves. The single flowers appear in spring – usually blue, but sometimes white or pink.

*Sow seed* as soon as it is ripe in a container in a cold frame. Woolly-coated seeds need a shave. Place the seeds in a jam jar with some dry sand and shake to remove the hairy surface. I have mixed luck with seed sowing. They always succeed, but they usually take months to germinate with only a few seedlings appearing.

▯ *Divide* the small rhizomes in late spring.

### ANEMONOPSIS MACROPHYLLA

Perennial with glossy, dark green leaves and sharply toothed leaflets. In late summer the racemes of nodding, cup-shaped, lilac-pink flowers are held above the foliage.

*Sow seed* in a garden frame as soon as it is ripe in autumn. Be patient as germination is erratic, with the seedlings appearing over a period of several months.

▯ *Divide* in late spring. The fleshy roots should be replanted immediately in moisture-retentive, acid soil. The new plant may not flower for 15 months.

### ANGELICA ARCHANGELICA (Archangel)

Perennial with 60cm long, mid-green leaves. In early summer large umbels of greenish-white flowers appear on stout, ribbed stems.

*Sow seed* as soon as it is ripe on the surface of the compost in a garden frame or cold greenhouse. Don't cover the seed, as daylight is necessary for germination. Overwinter the seedlings in a garden frame. Transplant seedlings as soon as possible to minimise root disturbance. It will flower within 3 years.

### ANIGOZANTHOS PULCHERRIMUS (Yellow kangaroo paw)

Tender, evergreen perennial with grey-green leaves and panicles of up to 15 bright yellow flowers with yellow hairs during late spring and summer.

▯ *Sow seed* as soon as it is ripe at 16°C.
*Divide* clumps in spring. Pot up the rooted pieces in free-draining compost. They will flower within 2 years.

### ANTENNARIA DIOICA (Pussy-toes)

Semi-evergreen perennial with grey-green, spoon-shaped leaves that are white on the underside. White or pale pink flowerheads are carried on 2cm stems during late spring and early summer.

*Sow seed* thinly in a garden frame in spring. Drench the seedlings with Cheshunt Compound to reduce the risk of damping off disease.

▯ *Lift and pot up rooted stems* in spring. They will flower the following year.

Anemone apennina

## ANTHEMIS TINCTORIA
(Golden marguerite)
Perennial with mid-green leaves that are smaller on the stems than those that are basal. In summer it produces masses of solitary, daisy-like, bright yellow or cream flowerheads.

**Sow seed** in a garden frame in early spring. Plants will flower in the course of the second year.
**Softwood basal cuttings** in early summer.
**Divide** in mid-spring. Even small rooted pieces will quickly form strong plants.

## ANTHERICUM LILIAGO (St Bernard's lily)
Perennial with grass-like, mid-green leaves and racemes of trumpet-shaped, white flowers during late spring and early summer.

**Sow seed** in containers in autumn. Overwinter in a garden frame. From seed they will flower within 3 years.
**Divide** large clumps in early spring as growth commences.

## ANTHRISCUS CEREFOLIUM (Chervil)
Annual herb with pinnate, aniseed-flavoured leaves and umbels of white flowers in midsummer.

**Sow seed** in open ground every 2 weeks from late spring to midsummer to ensure a continuous crop.

The perennial A. sylvestris (Cow parsley, Queen Anne's lace) may be propagated by root cuttings taken in early winter in a garden frame or by seed sown in the autumn. Seed of the purple-leafed A. s. 'Ravenswing' will produce mixed seedlings. Select those with dark-coloured leaves if you want them to match the parent.

## ANTHURIUM ANDRAEANUM
(Flamingo flower)
Perennial house plant with glossy, dark green leaves. The 'flowers', which are in fact waxy, red spathes with yellow spadices, are produced at any time of the year.

**Sow seed** as soon as it is ripe at 24°C. Germination is slow, often taking several months.
**Root softwood cuttings** at 24°C in late spring or summer.

## ANTHYLLIS HERMANNIAE
Deciduous shrub with spiny branches and bright green, palmate leaves. Small, bright yellow flowers are produced in early summer.

**Sow seed** thinly in seed compost in a garden frame in early autumn. Soak seed beforehand for 12 hours in warm water. Plants will flower within 3 years.
**Semi-ripe cuttings** in late summer at 15°C. Leave undisturbed in the rooting compost until spring.

## ANTIRRHINUM MAJUS (Snapdragon)
Perennial normally treated as an annual. Glossy, deep green leaves with upright racemes of 2-lipped flowers in a mixture of colours are produced from early summer to autumn.

**Sow seed** in spring. Alternatively, sow in late autumn and prick out the seedlings (see page 31). Overwinter the seedlings with protection from frost. When grown from seed, the young plants may not be replicas of the parent plant.
**Softwood cuttings** taken in early summer will flower in late spring the following year.

The dwarf shrub A. pulverulentum requires a sheltered site.

Anthurium andraeanum

## APHELANDRA SQUARROSA
(Zebra plant, Saffron-spike)
Tender, evergreen shrub treated as an evergreen house plant. The dark green, 30cm long leaves have white or yellow veins and a mid-rib. The 20cm long, terminal spikes of waxy, yellow flowers with maroon-tinged outer yellow bracts appear throughout the year.

**Softwood cuttings** rooted in open, free-draining compost at 21°C. Encourage side shoots suitable for cutting material by cutting back the stem after flowering to a pair of strong leaves.

## APONOGETON DISTACHYOS
(Water hawthorn)
Aquatic perennial with lance-shaped, bright green leaves. Small, hawthorn-scented, white flowers are held in white spathes above the water during spring and autumn.

- **Sow seed** as soon as it is ripe in small containers of soil-based compost. Immerse the container 5cm deep in water heated to 15°C. Where seed has to be stored, keep it moist in a sealed, waterproof packet.
- **Division** Tease out the rhizomes of large clumps during winter dormancy and pot up in soil-based compost.

## AQUILEGIA VULGARIS
(Columbine, Granny's bonnet)
Perennial with mid-green leaves. Stiff-stemmed racemes of flowers with hooked spurs appear during late spring and early summer in colours ranging from white and pink through blue to deep purple.

- **Sow fresh seed** in late summer in containers in a garden frame. Germination percentages will be less for older, stored seed. Aquilegias readily self-seed becoming weedy in some gardens. Unfortunately most species hybridize freely, the resulting seedlings differing from the parent plant. I don't collect seed, but prefer to buy it from a seed company. Seed of alpine species such as *A. alpina* can take up to 24 months to germinate.
- **Division** Named varieties may be divided in early spring, but avoid damaging the roots which resent being disturbed. Replant the pieces as soon as possible and water regularly until the foliage recovers.

## ARABIS CAUCASICA (Rock cress)
Evergreen perennial with rosettes of grey-green leaves and racemes of fragrant, white flowers in late spring.

- **Sow seed** in a garden frame in early autumn.
- **Softwood cuttings** in midsummer under clear polythene.

## ARALIA ELATA (Japanese angelica tree)
Deciduous tree with thick, spiny stems. The enormous, 120cm long leaves have up to 90 dark green leaflets and turn orange or purple in autumn. Large umbels of tiny, white flowers appear during late summer and autumn, followed by small black fruit.

- **Sow seed** in a garden frame as soon as it is ripe in autumn. Alternatively, stratify the seed outside in sand and sow in spring.
- **Root cuttings** in early winter in a garden frame. For best results, select roots that are of pencil or index finger thickness.
- **Whip and tongue grafts** of variegated varieties in early winter.
- **Rooted suckers** removed in early spring can be potted into a soil-based compost and left outdoors. Plant out in the border in autumn.

## ARAUCARIA ARAUCANA
(Monkey puzzle, Chilean pine)
Evergreen conifer with horizontally ridged, grey-brown bark. The branches are whorled up the trunk. The leathery, dark green leaves are dangerously sharp. Male and female cones are 15cm long. The seed is edible.

- **Sow seed** thinly outdoors in the open ground as soon as it is ripe. If the seed dries out, it is unlikely to germinate – so eat it instead! Germination can be speeded up by mixing the seed with damp peat in a clear polythene bag and storing it at 1–3°C for 4 weeks. Allow the seed to return to room temperature and then chill again for another 20 days. When the seed starts to germinate, sow it in moist compost at 15°C. Growth is slow for the first few years.
- **Semi-ripe cuttings** 10cm long in midsummer in a garden frame. Use only the vertical shoot tips; cuttings taken from side branches never produce an erect tree. Wear tough gloves as the leaves are needle sharp.

## ARBUTUS UNEDO (Strawberry tree)
Evergreen tree with shredding, red-brown bark. The leaves are mid-green and glossy. Pendant panicles of small, pink-tinged, white flowers appear in autumn, followed a year later by strawberry-like, red, warty fruit. This year's flowers and last year's fruit are available at the same time.

- **Sow seed** in containers of ericaceous seed compost in the autumn, as soon as it is ripe. Germination can be slow and erratic.
- **Semi-ripe cuttings** in late summer with bottom heat. Cover with clear polythene.
- I root semi-ripe cuttings in pots of compost covered with clear polythene bags on a hot bed of rotting farmyard manure in a garden frame (see page 17). Pot on in late spring the following year.

## ARCTOTIS FASTUOSA
(Monarch of the veldt)
Tender perennial usually grown as a tender annual. The deeply lobed, silvery-white, woolly haired leaves are 10cm long. The deep orange flowers have deep purple disc-florets and appear in late summer and early autumn.

- **Sow seed** at 18°C in spring or autumn. Sow thinly and pot up the seedlings when small to reduce root disturbance.
- **Softwood cuttings** in spring and summer in peat-based compost.

Arbutus unedo

## ARCTOSTAPHYLOS NEVADENSIS
(Pine-mat manzanita)
Evergreen shrub with sharp pointed, glossy, bright green leaves. Clusters of white or occasionally pink-tinged flowers appear in early summer, followed by reddish-brown fruit.

**Seed** Soften the fruit in water to remove pulp. Dry the fresh seed to ensure the seed coat is free of pulp, then immerse it in boiling water for 10 seconds prior to sowing in a garden frame in autumn. Flowering occurs within 3 years.
**Division** Remove rooted pieces of stem in winter and pot up for a year.
**Semi-ripe cuttings** in peat-based compost in summer.
**Layer** in autumn.

## ARDISIA JAPONICA (Marlberry)
Evergreen shrub with glossy, dark green leaves and clusters of star-shaped, pale pink to white flowers in summer, followed by bright red berries.

**Sow seed** at 13°C in spring.
**Semi-ripe cuttings** in late summer. Take the cuttings with a 'heel'.
**Lift and transplant rooted plantlets** (runners) in early spring.

## ARENARIA BALEARICA
(Corsican sandwort)
Evergreen perennial with shiny leaves. Masses of tiny, star-shaped, white flowers in spring to midsummer.

**Sow seed** thinly in autumn in a garden frame.
**Softwood basal cuttings** in midsummer.
**Divide** in spring, replanting immediately.

## ARGEMONE MEXICANA (Prickly poppy)
Tender annual with deeply lobed, silver-veined, blue-green leaves and solitary, pale to deep yellow, fragrant, poppy-like flowers in late summer and autumn.

**Sow seed** at 20°C in early spring. This plant resents any root disturbance so sow 2 seeds in a small container. Remove one if both germinate. After all risk of frost has passed, plant out with the minimum of root disturbance.

## ARGYRANTHEMUM
Evergreen sub-shrub with mid-green leaves and daisy-like flowers in a range of colours during summer and autumn.

**Softwood cuttings** in spring under clear polythene.
**Semi-ripe cuttings** in summer.

Overwinter the plants with frost protection.

## ARISAEMA CANDIDISSIMUM
Tuberous perennial with 3-palmate leaves that appear in autumn after the pink-striped, white, fragrant, 15cm long summer spathes.

**Sow seed** in seed compost container in autumn or in spring. Transplant the seedlings as early as possible.
**Division** Remove and pot up offsets in late summer. I find that dormant tubers refuse to grow if they are allowed to dry out.

## ARISARUM PROBOSCIDEUM
(Mouse plant)
Perennial with glossy leaves. In spring the long thin tips of the brown, hooded spathes resemble a mouse's tail.

**Sow seed** in a shaded garden frame as soon as it is ripe and cover with grit.
**Divide** clumps of tubers in late autumn or winter.

## ARISTOLOCHIA MACROPHYLLA
(Dutchman's pipe)
Deciduous, twining climber with heart-shaped, dark green leaves. In summer the solitary, mid-green flowers are spotted with brown, yellow and purple.

**Sow seed** as soon as it is ripe in autumn at 15°C. Pot up the seedlings in deep pots until the roots are well established.
**Softwood cuttings** in midsummer under horticultural fleece. Cut back the leaf area by more than half to reduce transpiration.

## ARISTOTELIA CHILENSIS (Macqui)
Tender, evergreen shrub with glossy, dark green leaves. Small, greenish-white flowers appear in summer. The female plants produce small, purple fruit ripening to black.

**Sow seed** in a container in a garden frame in late spring.
**Semi-ripe cuttings** in midsummer. Shorten the leaves to reduce transpiration.

Overwinter with frost protection for the first year.

## ARMERIA MARITIMA (Thrift)
Evergreen perennial with dark green leaves and white, pink or deep red flowers from spring to summer.

**Sow seed** in a garden frame in autumn or spring. Soak the seed overnight in warm water before sowing to soften the outer coat. The resulting plants may differ from the parent.
**Semi-ripe basal cuttings** in midsummer in free-draining, sandy compost.
**Divide** clumps in early spring.

## ARNEBIA PULCHRA (Prophet flower)
Perennial with light green, hairy leaves and yellow, trumpet-shaped flowers in summer.

**Sow seed** in a garden frame as soon as it is ripe.
**Root cuttings** laid horizontally in a tray of peat-based compost in a garden frame in winter.

Aronia melanocarpa

**Sow seed** in a garden frame in spring. Transplant as soon as the seedlings are large enough to handle. Overwinter in a frost-free greenhouse for the first year.

**Stem cuttings** Sections of stem will root in water in midsummer. Pot up rooted stems in moist, peat-based compost.

**Divide** in late spring or early summer.

## ASARUM EUROPAEUM
(Wild ginger, Asarabacca)
Evergreen perennial with glossy, dark green leaves covering the small, greenish-purple to brown, bell-shaped, late spring flowers.

**Sow seed** in a garden frame in early autumn as soon as it is ripe.

**Divide** in early spring.

**Divide** in early spring. Discard the older, centre portion of the clump. Protect from strong sunlight until established.

## ARONIA MELANOCARPA
(Black chokeberry)
Deciduous shrub with glossy, mid-green leaves turning a deep purple-red in autumn. White or pink-tinged flowers appear in late spring and early summer followed by black berries.

**Sow seed** thinly in rows outside in autumn in well-cultivated soil.

**Softwood cuttings** in early summer.

**Rooted suckers** in winter. Pot up in moisture-retaining compost and position outside in a sheltered part of the garden.

## ARTEMISIA ABROTANUM
(Southernwood)
Semi-evergreen shrub with aromatic, grey-green leaves. Dense panicles of grey-green flowers appear in late summer.

**Sow seed** in a container in autumn or in spring in a garden frame.

**Softwood cuttings** in early summer. I find that shoots measuring 5cm long taken with a 'heel' root best.

## ARUM ITALICUM (Lords and ladies)
Tuberous perennial with arrow-shaped, mid-green leaves with white veins during winter and early spring. In summer pale, green-white spathes are followed by spikes of bright orange berries.

**Sow seed** in autumn in a garden frame. Wear gloves to remove the outer, caustic flesh from the seed.

**Divide** clumps of tubers in late summer after flowering.

## ARUNCUS DIOICUS (Goatsbeard)
Perennial with fern-like, mid-green, 1m long leaves. During summer large panicles of creamy-white (male) and greenish-white (female) flowers appear.

**Sow seed** in a garden frame in autumn or spring. Self-seeds readily around the base of the plant.

**Divide** in early spring.

## ARUNDO DONAX (Giant reed)
Perennial with stout stems and mid-green, 60cm long leaves. In late autumn it produces green to purple terminal spikelets.

Asarum europaeum

Asphodeline lutea

### ASCLEPIAS INCARNATA
(Swamp milkweed)
Perennial with mid-green leaves. From midsummer to early autumn clusters of pinkish-purple flowers appear in the leaf axils.

*Sow seed* in a garden frame in early spring.
▯ *Softwood basal cuttings* in spring under clear polythene. Shorten the leaves by half to reduce transpiration.
*Divide* in late spring.

### ASIMINA TRILOBA (Pawpaw)
Deciduous shrub or small tree with 30cm long, mid-green leaves that turn yellow in autumn. The cup-shaped, spring flowers have 6 purple-brown petals, 3 large and 3 small. They are followed in autumn by 10cm long, yellow-brown, edible fruit.

*Seed* Stratify seed in moist sand at 4°C for 3 months. Sow in spring in open ground and cover with coarse grit.
*Layer* in autumn, leaving the layer undisturbed for 12 months.
▯ *Root cuttings* in early winter in a garden frame.

### ASPERULA SUBEROSA (Woodruff)
Evergreen perennial with white-haired, glaucous leaves. In early summer it covers itself with clusters of small, tubular, bright pink flowers.

*Sow seed* in a garden frame in autumn.
▯ *Softwood cuttings* in early summer under horticultural fleece. Plants will be ready for potting within 4–6 weeks and will flower the following summer.
*Divide* in late autumn.

### ASPHODELINE LUTEA
(Yellow asphodel, King's spear)
Perennial with 30cm long, blue-green leaves. Dense racemes of fragrant, bright yellow flowers appear in late spring.

*Sow seed* in a garden frame in late spring. Transplant when 4 leaves have formed.

▯ *Divide* clumps in late autumn by teasing apart the brittle rhizomes. Take care not to damage the tender shoots.

## ASPHODELUS ALBUS (Asphodel)

Perennial with mid-green leaves up to 60cm long. Racemes of star-shaped, white flowers with pink veins appear in late spring.

▯ *Sow seed* in a garden frame in early spring. If the young plants are fed regularly with tomato fertilizer they will flower the following spring.
*Divide* in early spring.

## ASPIDISTRA ELATIOR (Cast iron plant)

Perennial house plant with 30–50cm long, lance-shaped, glossy, dark green leaves. Small, cream, bell-shaped flowers with maroon centres appear on the rhizomes at soil level in early summer.

*Divide* in spring. Tease out the rhizomes, making sure there is a growing point as well as a couple of leaves on each piece.

## ASPLENIUM BULBIFERUM

(Mother spleenwort, Hen and chicken fern) Evergreen fern with dark green, 1.2m long fronds.

*Sow spores* at 15°C as soon as they are ripe.
*Divide* in spring.
▯ *Division* Pot up plantlets when there are 3–4 leaves. I use a potting mixture of equal parts loam, leaf mould and coarse grit. I also add some charcoal to keep the mixture from going stagnant.

Aster x frikartii

## ASTELIA CHATHAMICA

Evergreen perennial with 1.2m long, leathery, silvery, arching leaves. Panicles of tiny, greenish-yellow flowers appear in late spring, followed on female plants by orange berries.

▯ *Sow seed* as soon as it is ripe in a garden frame. Transplant seedlings into peat-based compost. Plants will flower within 30 months.
*Divide* in late spring. Protect young plants from strong, direct sunlight.

## ASTER × FRIKARTII

Perennial with dark green leaves. Light blue, daisy-like flowers with orange centres are produced during late summer and early autumn.

*Sow seed* in containers of seed compost in a garden frame in autumn or spring.
▯ *Divide* large clumps in early spring, using the young, rooted portions from the outside of the clump.
*Softwood basal cuttings* in spring.

## ASTERANTHERA OVATA

Evergreen, climbing shrub with bristly, deep green leaves. During summer deep bright pink, tubular flowers are produced in the leaf axils.

*Sow seed* in a garden frame in autumn. Sow on the surface of the compost.
▯ *Semi-ripe cuttings* in early autumn.
*Layering* Where stems touch the soil they will 'layer' themselves and form roots. Remove rooted portions in late spring and pot up in soil-based compost.

## ASTILBE CHINENSIS

Perennial with hairy leaves and panicles of pinkish-white flowers in late summer.

*Sow seed* on the surface of the compost in a garden frame. Cover the container with cling film or clear polythene to raise humidity. Transplant the seedlings when small.
▯ *Divide* large clumps in winter or in early spring before growth starts. Plant out in the ground or pot up the rooted portions until late autumn.

### ASTILBOIDES TABULARIS

Perennial with sharply lobed, light green leaves and 1.5m high panicles of tiny, creamy-white flowers in early summer.

- *Sow seed* thinly in a garden frame in autumn. Transplant individually into pots until spring before planting out. Do not allow the compost to dry out.
- *Divide* in early spring, taking care not to damage any new growth.

### ASTRANTIA MAJOR (Masterwort)

Perennial with 3–7 lobed basal leaves. In early summer the umbels of small, green, pink or purple flowers are surrounded by green-veined, white bracts.

- *Sow seed* as soon as it is ripe in autumn in a garden frame or chill for 30 days and sow in spring. It will flower within 20 months.
- *Divide* in spring, ensuring each division has sufficient root.

### ATHROTAXIS × LAXIFOLIA
(Tasmanian cedar)

Evergreen conifer with red-brown bark and tiny, glossy, dark green leaves. The cones are bright green, turning yellow and finally brown.

- *Sow seed* in soil-based compost in a garden frame in late winter. Germination is slow.
- *Semi-ripe cuttings* with a 'heel' in late summer. I always root them in pots on a hot bed of decaying farmyard manure in a garden frame.

### ATHYRIUM FILIX-FEMINA (Lady fern)

Deciduous fern with light green, 1m fronds.

- *Sow spores* as soon as they are ripe at 16°C.
- *Divide* clumps in early spring.

### AUBRIETA × CULTORUM 'JOY' (Aubretia)

Perennial with mid-green leaves and double, mauve flowers in spring.

- *Sow seed* thinly in a garden frame in autumn or spring. Seed will germinate readily, but seedlings will seldom be the same as the parent plant.
- *Softwood cuttings* in early summer. Plants will flower the following spring.
- *Semi-ripe cuttings* in midsummer.
- *Division* in autumn is possible but the success rate is low. Try laying the divisions on the surface of moist compost in a garden frame and lightly working damp compost through the foliage. Keep away from strong sunlight until the plants start to grow. Transplant to permanent sites as soon as possible.

### AUCUBA JAPONICA 'CROTONIFOLIA'
(Spotted laurel)

Evergreen shrub with glossy, mid-green leaves liberally speckled with bright yellow. Panicles of small, purple-red flowers appear in spring, followed by bright red berries in autumn.

*Sow seed* in a garden frame in autumn.

*Semi-ripe cuttings* in mid- to late summer. Shorten the leaves by half to reduce transpiration. Trim the cutting as close as possible to the lower leaves.

### AURINIA SAXATILIS (Gold dust)

Evergreen perennial with hairy, grey-green leaves. Dense panicles of bright yellow flowers appear in late spring and early summer.

- *Sow seed* in a garden frame in autumn.
- *Softwood cuttings* in summer. Shorten the leaves to reduce transpiration and cover with horticultural fleece.

### AZARA MICROPHYLLA

Evergreen tree with small, dark green leaves. Tiny, greenish-yellow, vanilla-scented flowers appear at the leaf axils on the undersides of the shoots in late winter and spring.

- *Semi-ripe cuttings* in midsummer. Take the cuttings with a 'heel'. Pot up in late summer and encourage some root growth before late autumn. I have great success using the hot-bed system. The young plants will flower within 3 years.

Azara microphylla

## BABIANA STRICTA

Tender, cormous perennial with lance-shaped, mid-green leaves. Spikes of yellow, blue or purple, scented flowers appear in spring.

***Sow seed*** as soon as it is ripe at 13°C.

☐ ***Offsets*** Lift dormant corms in autumn and remove offsets. Replace the parent corms Store the offsets in a dry, frost-proof place and plant 20 cm deep in spring

## BALLOTA PSEUDODICTAMNUS

Evergreen sub-shrub with grey-green leaves. Small, white flowers, often with a pink tint, appear in late spring and early summer.

***Softwood cuttings*** in late spring.

☐ ***Semi-ripe cuttings*** in early summer with a 'heel'.

In both cases, nip out the growing tip of the cutting to prevent it flowering before it is fully rooted.

## BANKSIA COCCINEA

Tender, evergreen shrub with heart-shaped, deep green leaves, downy-white on the underside. Cylindrical, bright scarlet flowerheads appear in late spring and early summer.

☐ ***Sow seed*** in autumn at 18°C. Sow individually in small pots of loam-based compost with extra grit.

***Semi-ripe cuttings*** in summer with bottom heat. Trim the leaves to reduce transpiration.

## BAPTISIA ALBA (False indigo)

Perennial with palmate, glaucous leaves. In summer it produces racemes of white flowers, occasionally with purple markings, followed by inflated seed pods.

☐ ***Sow seed*** as soon as it is ripe in a garden frame in autumn.

***Divide*** in early spring.

Begonia sutherlandii

## BARBAREA VULGARIS 'VARIEGATA'
(St Barbara's herb)

Short-lived perennial with rosette-forming basal leaves that are deep green splashed with yellow. Racemes of yellow flowers appear from early spring to early summer.

***Seed*** Chip the hard seed coat and soak in water for 24 hours. Sow seed as soon as it is ripe in a garden frame in early autumn. Most seedlings of this variety will come true from seed. Remove and discard seedlings with all green leaves.

☐ ***Softwood cuttings*** in early summer under horticultural fleece.

***Divide*** in spring.

## BEGONIA

For propagation purposes I have divided begonias into groups.

### Ornamental-leafed species such as
***B. rex*** Evergreen perennials with ovate, richly coloured, 20cm long leaves often with a metallic sheen on the upper surface and inconspicuous, single pink flowers in spring.

***Sow seed*** in early autumn as soon as ripe in soil-less compost at 20°C. Plants should flower in the second year after sowing.

☐ ***Divide*** rhizomes into sections in early summer and insert in compost. Protect from strong sunlight.

◻ *Leaf cuttings* in late spring and early summer in a propagating case. Avoid strong sunlight. Water the compost by standing in a dish of water. Keep the leaves dry.

**Cane-stemmed species such as B. aconitifolia** Evergreen perennials with bamboo-like stems with swollen nodules. The leaves are beautifully marked and frequently toothed or lobed. The showy flowers appear in spring and summer.

*Leaf cuttings* in late spring and early summer, as above.
◻ *Softwood cuttings* in a propagating case in midsummer. Reduce the cuttings to 2 leaves. Allow the base of the cutting to dry for an hour before inserting it in the compost.

**Semperflorens species** Evergreen perennials usually with bronze or bright green leaves. The flowers appear in summer in a range of colours from white to pink and red.

*Sow seed* in early spring at 16°C in a propagating frame. Do not cover the seed with compost. Avoid overwatering the compost. They will produce flowers within 3 months.
◻ *Softwood basal cuttings* in late spring. Take short, 3–5cm cuttings. Always use rooting hormone to speed up rooting and reduce the risk of stem rot.
*Divide* plants that have been kept growing over winter in late spring. When overwintering, keep the compost as dry as possible while keeping the plants alive. Store in a frost-proof room with air movement. Apply a fungicide as necessary and remove all decaying foliage and stems.

**Tuberous begonias** Winter dormant perennials with succulent stems and glossy, mid-to dark green leaves. The summer flowers are usually in clusters of 3 with a showy, fully double male and a single female flower of the same colour on each side of the male.

*Sow seed* in spring at 20°C. Don't cover the seed with compost. Avoid strong sunlight. Plants should flower in the second year after sowing.
*Softwood basal cuttings* in early summer in a garden frame.
*Softwood stem cuttings* from side shoots in summer in a garden frame. Space cuttings well to allow air to circulate
*Divide* large tubers in spring, making sure there is at least one growth bud on each piece. Dust the cut section with Flowers of sulphur or fungicide. Pot up in gritty, free-draining compost.

---

**BELLIS PERENNIS 'TASSO' SERIES** (Daisy)
Perennial normally treated as a biennial with spoon-shaped, bright green leaves and red, pink or white double daisy flowers during summer.

◻ *Sow seed* in early spring at 10°C or outside in drills in early summer.
*Divide* after flowering. To be honest, although some people recommend this method, I never bother as after the second year the flowers tend to be small on spindly stems and are seldom worth keeping.

---

**BERBERIDOPSIS CORALLINA** (Coral plant)
Evergreen climber with heart-shaped, dark green leaves with marginal spines. Dark red flowers on long stalks appear in summer and early autumn as terminal racemes and as small clusters from the leaf axils.

*Sow seed* in a garden frame in spring.
◻ *Semi-ripe cuttings* taken with a 'heel' in late summer, under clear polythene.

*Layer* in late autumn. Be patient – the layers will take 18–24 months to become well rooted.

---

**BERBERIS × STENOPHYLLA** (Barberry)
Evergreen shrub with arching branches and small, spine-tipped, dark green leaves. Small racemes of deep yellow flowers are produced along the branches in late spring followed by blue-black fruit.

*Sow seed* outdoors in rows in the open ground in early spring.
◻ *Semi-ripe cuttings* in midsummer with bottom heat.

---

**BERGENIA 'SILBERLICHT'** (Elephant's ears)
Evergreen perennial with broad, 20cm long, mid-green, scalloped leaves and white, spring flowers ageing to pink.

*Sow seed* in seed compost in a garden frame in autumn. Garden-saved seed often produces hybrid plants.
◻ *Divide* rhizomes in autumn or in late spring after flowering and propagate in a garden frame in a tray of moist sand covered with horticultural fleece.

---

**BETULA PAPYRIFERA** (Paper birch)
Deciduous tree with white, peeling bark exposing pale orange-brown new bark. Ovate, dark green leaves turn yellow in autumn. Male catkins in early spring are yellow.

◻ *Sow seed* thinly outdoors in well-cultivated ground in autumn or early spring. Do not cover the seed, as light is necessary for germination. Where possible, use seed from a natural, wild habitat; seed from garden plants usually produces hybrids. The birches are quick-growing trees and it should be possible to produce a 3m high specimen within 4–5 years from seed.

*Softwood cuttings* in summer.
*Whip and tongue graft* named
   varieties in winter.

## BIDENS FERULIFOLIA
Perennial often treated as an annual
with bright green, pinnate leaves
and daisy-like, bright yellow flowers
on 30cm stems during summer and
autumn.

- *Sow seed* at 13°C in spring.
   *Softwood cuttings* in spring under
   horticultural fleece.
   *Divide* in late spring.

Betula papyrifera

## BIGNONIA (Trumpet creeper)
*See Campsis*

## BILLARDIERA LONGIFLORA
(Climbing blueberry)
Tender, evergreen, perennial climber
with small, deep green leaves. Solitary,
bell-shaped, pale green flowers in
summer are followed in autumn by
glossy, deep purple-blue berries.

- *Sow seed* as soon as it is ripe in early
   autumn in ericaceous seed compost at
   13°C. The percentage that germinate
   will be lower if sown in spring. From
   seed, I have had the luck to grow plants
   with white and with deep red berries.
   *Softwood cuttings* in early summer
   with bottom heat.
   *Semi-ripe cuttings* in late summer in
   a garden frame.
- *Layer* in autumn in free-draining, gritty
   soil. This is the quickest way to get a
   good-sized plant, but propagating by
   seed is more fun.

## BILLBERGIA NUTANS (Queen's tears)
Tender, perennial bromeliad with funnel-
shaped rosettes of strap-like, grey-green
leaves. Red-bracted flower stems produce
flowers with green petals edged with blue
and tipped with dark green.

- *Sow seed* as soon as it is ripe at 25°C.
- *Remove offsets* in early summer and root
   in orchid compost with bottom heat.

## BLECHNUM SPICANT (Hard fern)
Hardy, evergreen fern with lance-
shaped, dark green, pinnate fronds that
are sterile. In summer taller, fertile
fronds appear in the centre of the
rosette of sterile fronds.

- *Sow spores* as soon as they are ripe in
   late summer.
   *Divide* in spring. Use an ericaceous
   compost.

## BLETILLA STRIATA
Tender orchid with lance-shaped,
mid-green leaves and flattened
pseudobulbs. In spring and early
summer it produces racemes of small,
bell-shaped, magenta flowers.

- *Divide* rhizomes in early spring. Pot up
   in free-draining, orchid compost.

## BOLAX GUMMIFERA
Evergreen perennial with rosettes of
3-lobed, leathery, blue-green leaves.
Occasionally produces umbels of tiny,
greenish-white flowers in summer but
I have never seen them.

- *Seed* If you can source seed, sow it in a
   garden frame in autumn.
- *Remove offsets* in spring and pot
   up in free-draining compost in a
   garden frame.

## BOMAREA EDULIS
Deciduous climber with pale green
leaves. Umbels of bell-shaped flowers
appear from summer to autumn. They
are pale red on the outside and green-
yellow on the inside.

- *Sow seed* at 15°C in spring.
- *Divide* large clumps in early spring
   before there is a lot of leaf growth. I
   cut mine back to ground level in early
   winter and surface mulch with
   chopped straw.

## BORAGO OFFICINALIS (Borage)
Annual with bristly, matt green leaves
and star-shaped blue flowers in summer.

- *Sow seed* outside in spring in open, well-
   drained ground.

## BOUGAINVILLEA GLABRA
(Paper flower)
Tender, evergreen climber with mid- to
deep green leaves and white, deep pink or
magenta bracts in summer and autumn.

*Softwood cuttings* in early spring with bottom heat. Trim the leaves to half of their length to reduce transpiration.

◨ *Semi-ripe cuttings* with a 'heel' in summer in a propagator.

*Hardwood cuttings* in a garden frame in late autumn.

*Layer* in autumn or early spring.

## BOYKINIA JAMESII

Perennial with rosettes of mid-green leaves and bell-shaped, deep pink flowers with green centres during late spring.

*Sow seed* in a garden frame in late summer.

◨ *Divide* in early spring, replanting in free-draining, acid soil.

## BRACHYGLOTTIS GREYI

(sometimes labelled *Senecio*)
Evergreen shrub with white-haired young leaves turning to dark green on the upper surface. Masses of bright yellow, daisy-like flowers appear during summer and autumn.

*Semi-ripe cuttings* in summer with a 'heel'. Allow the stem to firm well before taking the cuttings. If taken late in the season, leave the rooted cuttings in the compost until spring before potting up.

## BRACHYSCOME IBERIDIFOLIA

(Swan river daisy)
Half-hardy annual with grey-green leaves and fragrant, daisy-like flowers during summer. They are usually deep blue, but may be white or purple-pink.

*Sow seed* at 16°C in spring.

## BRIZA MAXIMA (Greater quaking grass)

Annual with pale green leaves turning golden-yellow. Panicles of heart-shaped, green spikelets tinged red appear throughout the summer, turning yellow when ripe.

*Sow seed* outside in spring.

## BRODIAEA CALIFORNICA

Cormous perennial with long, blue-green leaves that die down before the flowers appear. Umbels of upright, funnel-shaped, lilac or pink flowers appear in early summer.

*Sow seed* in late summer at 13°C. Transplant when the seedlings are small.

◨ *Remove offsets* in summer when dormant. Pot up for a year in free-draining, loam-based compost.

## BROMELIA BALANSAE (Heart of flame)

Tender, evergreen bromeliad with rosettes of spiny, grey-green leaves sometimes tinted red. Cylindrical groupings of violet flowers with white margins appear in summer in the centre of the rosettes.

*Sow seed* at 25°C as soon as it is ripe.

◨ *Divide* in late spring or early summer. Use free-draining orchid compost. Wear protective gloves, as the leaves are spiny.

## BROUSSONETIA PAPYRIFERA

(Paper mulberry)
Deciduous tree with deeply lobed, hairy, grey-green leaves. Male flowers are pendant catkins in spring and early summer. Female flowers are spheres with purple stigmas and become orange, sweet-flavoured, mulberry-like fruit in autumn.

*Sow seed* in early spring in a propagator.

*Semi-ripe cuttings* in late summer. Take with a 'heel' and reduce the leaf size by half to reduce transpiration.

◨ *Hardwood cuttings* in winter.

*Root cuttings* in late winter in a garden frame.

*Rooted suckers* in winter. Pot them into a free-draining, soil-based, multi-purpose compost until the following autumn.

## BRUGMANSIA AUREA

(Angels' trumpets or Datura)
Evergreen shrub with mid-green, 25cm long leaves. Trumpet-shaped, 25cm long, golden-yellow flowers are night scented and appear in summer and autumn.

*Sow seed* at 16°C in spring. Seeds resemble corky pieces of wood. Soak in water for 12 hours before sowing.

*Semi-ripe cuttings* in summer under clear polythene. Shorten the leaves by half to reduce transpiration. All parts of the plant are poisonous. I have always found that these cuttings root like weeds.

## BRUNFELSIA PAUCIFLORA

(Yesterday, today and tomorrow)
Tender, evergreen shrub with leathery, glossy, deep green leaves. Terminal, pansy-like, purple, wavy-edged flowers that age to almost white appear from spring to late summer.

*Softwood cuttings* in late spring or summer under clear polythene. Shorten the leaves by half to reduce transpiration.

## BRUNNERA MACROPHYLLA

Perennial with soft, hairy, deep green leaves. Basal leaves are heart-shaped. Stem leaves are lance-shaped. Panicles of bright blue flowers appear in spring.

*Sow seed* in early spring in a garden frame.

◨ *Divide* in late spring.

*Root cuttings* in early winter taken from the outside of the clump and kept in a garden frame during winter.

*Brugmansia aurea x 'Goldilocks Apricot'*

Buddleja davidii

**BUDDLEJA DAVIDII** (Butterfly bush)
Deciduous shrub with lance-shaped, grey-green leaves and dense panicles of fragrant white, pink, lilac, deep red or purple flowers in summer and autumn.

*Sow seed* if you have nothing better to do. If you have grown every other plant on earth from seed, then by all means have a go, but buddleias are so easy and quick to propagate from cuttings that it is really a waste of time and effort. Mix the tiny seed with talcum powder to make it more visible. Do not cover the seed with compost.

*Semi-ripe cuttings* in summer. Shorten the mature leaves by half to reduce transpiration.

◻ *Hardwood cuttings* in late autumn.

**BULBINELLA HOOKERI**
Tender perennial with long, thin, mid-green leaves and racemes of yellow flowers from spring to summer.

*Sow seed* in early autumn in a garden frame.

◻ *Divide* in autumn. Pot into ericaceous compost with added leaf mould and overwinter in a garden frame.

**BULBOCODIUM VERNUM**
Cormous perennial with pink-purple, funnel-shaped flowers in spring followed by glossy, dark green leaves.

*Sow seed* in autumn or spring in a garden frame.

◻ *Remove offsets* in late summer. Plant out before late autumn.

**BUPHTHALMUM SALICIFOLIUM**
Perennial with thin, willow-like, dark green leaves. Deep yellow, daisy-like flowerheads appear in summer and early autumn.

*Sow seed* in a garden frame in late spring.

◻ *Divide* in early spring.

**BUPLEURUM FRUTICOSUM**
(Shrubby hare's ear)
Evergreen shrub with dark green leaves. Terminal umbels of small, yellow flowers appear from midsummer to mid-autumn.

*Sow seed* in a garden frame in spring.

⏹ *Semi-ripe cuttings* in summer under horticultural fleece. I find that cuttings root better if you cut them immediately below the leaves, rather than with a 'heel'.

## BUTOMUS UMBELLATUS
(Flowering rush)
Aquatic perennial with twisted, narrow, mid-green leaves that become purple and then dark green. Cup-shaped, fragrant, deep pink flowers appear above the water surface in late summer.

*Sow seed* in a pot of moist, peat-based compost stood in a tray of water. After germination, submerge the seedlings so that they are covered with 1cm water.
⏹ *Divide* the dormant rhizomes in spring. *Remove bulbils* that form on the roots in early spring. Pot into sterilized soil and submerge in water.

## BUXUS SEMPERVIRENS (Common box)
Evergreen shrub with glossy, dark green leaves that are notched at the tips.

⏹ *Semi-ripe cuttings* in midsummer taken with a 'heel'.
*Whip and tongue graft* varieties in winter.

## CALADIUM BICOLOR (Angel's wings)
Tender perennial with arrow-shaped, dark green leaves streaked or spotted pink or white. It produces greenish-white spathes in spring.

*Divide* the spherical tubers in spring. Treat the cut surfaces with fungicide. Pot into ericaceous compost with added grit.

## CALAMINTHA NEPETA (Calamint)
Aromatic perennial with hairy, dark green leaves and clusters of mauve flowers in summer.

*Sow seed* in a garden frame in spring.
⏹ *Divide* in mid-spring as new growths are appearing.

## CALANDRINIA UMBELLATA
(Rock purslane)
Evergreen perennial with lance-shaped, hairy, grey-green leaves. The panicles of cup-shaped, magenta flowers appear in summer.

*Sow seed* at 16°C in autumn. Overwinter with frost protection. Avoid wet compost in winter.
⏹ *Softwood cuttings* in late spring.

## CALANTHE DISCOLOR
Tender, evergreen orchid with oblong leaves, 20–30cm long. The racemes of purple-green flowers with pale pink or white lips appear in spring.

*Divide* pseudobulbs (swollen stems above the surface of the compost) in early summer after flowering. Repot in orchid compost.

## CALATHEA ZEBRINA (Zebra plant)
Tender perennial grown as a house plant with dark green leaves, purple-red on the underside. The veins, mid-ribs and margins are pale green. Spikes of small, white flowers sometimes appear in summer.

*Divide* clumps in late spring or early summer. Keep in humid conditions under clear polythene until the new plants are established.

## CALCEOLARIA HERBEOHYBRIDA
Biennial normally grown as a house plant with hairy, mid-green leaves. A mass of slipper-like flowers, with the lower lip pouched, appear during spring and summer. They range in colour from yellow through orange and red; some are bicoloured.

*Sow seed* thinly on the surface of the compost at 18°C in early autumn or in spring. Water from below and watch out for damping off disease. Apply Cheshunt compound as a precaution.

Caladium 'Postman Joyner'

**CALENDULA OFFICINALIS** (Marigold)
Annual with soft, hairy, aromatic leaves and daisy-like, single or double flowers in summer and autumn. Colours include orange, cream, yellow or apricot.

***Sow seed*** in open ground in spring or in a garden frame in autumn.

**CALLA PALUSTRIS** (Bog or Water arum)
Aquatic perennial with glossy, dark green, 20cm long leaves. Tall, 25cm high, white spathes appear in summer, followed in autumn by clusters of red berries.

***Sow seed*** in late summer in a soil-based, peaty compost in a container. Stand the container in water up to the rim of the pot. Germination may be erratic.
🪴 ***Divide*** rhizomes in spring.

**CALLICARPA BODINIERI VAR. GIRALDII 'PROFUSION'** (Beauty berry)
Deciduous shrub. The young leaves are bronze, turning to dark green. The pale pink flowers appear in the leaf axils during summer, followed by clusters of small, deep violet fruit in autumn.

***Sow seed*** in autumn or spring in a garden frame in a loam-based compost with extra grit for good drainage. With me, luck seems to play a part, as germination percentages vary from year to year.
🪴 ***Softwood cuttings*** in spring.
***Semi-ripe cuttings*** in midsummer with bottom heat. Don't pot the rooted cuttings until the following spring.

**CALLIRHOE INVOLUCRATA**
(Prairie poppy mallow)
Perennial with lobed, mid-green leaves and masses of solitary, cerise flowers with white bases in late spring and early summer.

***Sow seed*** in open ground in spring. Transplant the seedlings as early as possible before the tap root becomes too long.
🪴 ***Softwood cuttings*** in early summer.

**CALLISTEMON CITRINUS** (Bottle brush)
Evergreen shrub with arching branches and lance-shaped, dark green leaves. Spikes of brilliant crimson flowers with long stamens appear in spring and summer. The tiny, hard seed capsules remain on the stem for many years.

*Sow seed* on the surface of moist compost in spring at 16°C. Treat with Cheshunt compound to reduce the risk of damping off.

🟦 *Semi-ripe cuttings* taken with a 'heel' in late summer under clear polythene. Pot up the rooted plants the following spring.

### CALLISTEPHUS CHINENSIS
(China aster)
Annual with bushy stems and mid-green leaves. From summer to late autumn they produce chrysanthemum-like, single or double flowerheads in white, yellow, pink, red, blue and mauve.

🟩 *Sow seed* in early spring at 15°C. Alternatively, sow outdoors in a drill in open ground during late spring. Asters were one of the first annuals I ever grew as a boy and I still enjoy the quick results from seed.

### CALLITRICHE HERMAPHRODITICA
(Water starwort)
Submerged aquatic perennial with small, light green leaves on thin branching stems. Minute white flowers form at the leaf axils in summer.

*Softwood cuttings* of terminal shoots, 15cm long, in summer. Form bundles of 4–6 shoots and bind them together using a thin strip of lead, which will help them to sink to the bottom of the pond, where they will root, or insert them in submerged aquatic pots of humus-free soil.

### CALLUNA VULGARIS (Heather, Ling)
Evergreen shrub. Small, mid- to dark green leaves. Racemes of small, bell-shaped or tubular pink, mauve or occasionally white flowers form in midsummer to late autumn.

*Semi-ripe cuttings* in summer.
*Simple layer* in spring.

🟦 *Drop layer* in mid-spring. This is my preferred method because nature does the rooting.

### CALOCEDRUS DECURRENS
(Incense cedar)
Evergreen conifer with 1cm long, glossy, dark green leaves. The small, dirty-yellow, female cones ripen to red-brown.

*Sow seed* in a garden frame in spring. The female cones have 6 scales but only the 2 in the centre are fertile. There are 2 seeds in each scale.

🟦 *Semi-ripe cuttings* with a 'heel' in late summer. I use a hot bed (see page 17) to encourage rooting and pot up the rooted cuttings in spring. Occasionally cuttings will form a 1cm blob of callus. Scrape this off and reinsert the cutting. It will then root.

### CALOCHORTUS BARBATUS
(Fairy lantern)
Bulbous perennial with mid-green, 45cm long leaves. The open, cup-shaped, summer flowers are mustard-yellow with purple hairs and semi-circular nectaries at the base of each petal.

*Sow seed* as soon as it is ripe in a garden frame in autumn.
*Remove offsets* in late summer and plant 10 cm deep in lines in open ground.

🟦 *Remove bulbils* that have formed at the leaf axils and plant in late summer in soil-based compost in a garden frame.

### CALTHA PALUSTRIS (Marsh marigold)
Marginal, aquatic perennial with kidney-shaped, dark green leaves. The waxy, yellow flowers appear in spring on 30–45cm stems.

*Sow seed* as soon as it is ripe in a pot of compost standing in a tray of water in a garden frame.

🟦 *Divide* in early autumn or late winter.

### CALYCANTHUS FLORIDUS (Spice bush)
Deciduous shrub with rough surfaced, dark green leaves that are aromatic when crushed. The fragrant, summer flowers have strap-like, dark red petals, turning brown at the tips.

*Sow seed* in autumn in a garden frame.

🟦 *Softwood cuttings* in early summer. Shorten the leaves by half and cover with horticultural fleece.
*Rooted suckers* in spring can be potted into a soil-based compost or planted out into their permanent positions.
*Layer* in late autumn.

### CAMASSIA QUAMASH (Quamash)
Bulbous perennial with linear, bright green basal leaves. Tall racemes of bright blue flowers appear in late spring.

*Sow seed* in a garden frame in autumn as soon as it is ripe.

🟦 *Remove dormant offsets* in summer and pot up for a year planting 7 cm deep in well-drained, humus-rich compost. Protect from frost during the first winter.

### CAMELLIA JAPONICA
Evergreen shrub with glossy, dark green leaves and red flowers in early spring.

🟦 *Semi-ripe cuttings* from late summer to winter with bottom heat.
🟦 *Leaf bud cuttings* from late summer to winter.
(Yes, they are both my favourite – I love propagating camellias.)

### CAMPANULA CARPATICA (Bellflower)
Perennial with mid-green basal leaves and upturned, solitary, bell-shaped, white, blue or violet flowers in summer.

🟩 *Sow seed* thinly in a garden frame in spring. I bet you every single one will germinate!
*Divide* in autumn.
🟦 *Softwood basal cuttings* in spring.

Calendula officinalis

## CAMPSIS RADICANS
(Trumpet creeper, Trumpet vine)
Deciduous climber with trumpet-shaped, orange-red flowers during late summer and autumn.

*Sow seed* in a garden frame in autumn.
*Leaf bud cuttings* in late spring.
🛈 *Semi-ripe cuttings* in midsummer with a 'heel' under clear polythene.
*Root cuttings* in winter in a garden frame.

## CANNA INDICA (Indian shot)
Tender perennial with dark green, bronze-tinted leaves. Racemes of iris-like, bright red flowers appear from midsummer to autumn.

*Seed* Sow the large seeds at 20°C in autumn or in early spring. Chit the seed before sowing or soak it in warm water for 24 hours. Discard any seed that floats.
🛈 *Divide rhizomes* in spring into 5–7cm lengths, making sure each section has a growth bud or 'eye'. Pot up in free-draining, soil-less compost at 15°C for the first year.

## CANTUA BUXIFOLIA
(Sacred flower of the Incas)
Half-hardy, evergreen shrub with hairy leaves. Long-tubed, pink flowers with red petal tips hang down during spring.

*Sow seed* at 16°C in spring.
🛈 *Semi-ripe cuttings* in midsummer with a 'heel'. If possible, pot up the rooted cuttings before late autumn to encourage new growth before winter.

## CAPSICUM ANNUUM (Chilli pepper)
Tender annual with mid-green leaves and bell-shaped, white or yellow flowers in summer, followed by edible, pendant, twisted, yellow, orange or red fruit.

*Sow seed* at 21°C in late winter or early spring.

## CARAGANA ARBORESCENS (Pea tree)
Deciduous shrub with thorny stems and light green leaves. Small, pale yellow flowers appear in spring.

*Sow seed* in a garden frame as soon as it is ripe. Pre-soak the seed in warm water for 6 hours.
🛈 *Softwood cuttings* in late spring.

## CARDAMINE PRATENSIS (Lady's smock)
Perennial with rosettes of glossy, dark green leaves. Panicles of white, pink or purple flowers appear in spring.

*Sow seed* in a garden frame in autumn or spring.
*Divide* after flowering.
🛈 *Softwood tip cuttings* in midsummer.
*Remove plantlets* from the leaf axils in late summer. Pot into peat-based compost.

## CARDIOCRINUM GIGANTEUM
(Giant lily)
Bulbous perennial with basal rosettes of 45cm long, glossy, dark green leaves and smaller leaves on the thick stems. During summer racemes with up to 20 large, trumpet-shaped, highly fragrant, white flowers with maroon stripes on the inside are held on tall stems.

🛈 *Sow seed* in a garden frame as soon as it is ripe. Keep in shade after germination for a few weeks.
*Remove offsets* after flowering and plant them immediately in a sheltered part of the garden.

Be patient. Flowering from seed takes 7–8 years; from offsets it will still take 4–6 years. They are worth the wait.

## CAREX ELATA 'AUREA'
(Bowles' golden sedge)
Perennial with bright yellow leaves margined with green. Brown, male spikes appear in late spring and early summer.

*Sow seed* in an open frame in autumn.
🛈 *Divide* in late spring or early summer.

## CARMICHAELIA ENYSII
Dwarf shrub without leaves. The shoots are flattened. In summer it produces tiny, fragrant, purple flowers.

🛈 *Sow seed* in a garden frame when ripe. Alternatively, pre-soak the seed in hot water and sow in spring.
*Semi-ripe cuttings* in late summer in gritty, free-draining compost.

## CARPENTERIA CALIFORNICA
Evergreen shrub with glossy, dark green leaves and cup-shaped, fragrant, white flowers with yellow stamens during early summer.

*Sow seed* at 15°C in early spring. Seed-grown plants are generally inferior to those propagated from cuttings.
*Softwood cuttings* in early summer under clear polythene.
🛈 *Semi-ripe cuttings* in late summer under horticultural fleece. Shorten the length of the leaves by half to reduce transpiration.

## CARPINUS BETULUS (Hornbeam)
Deciduous tree with mid-green leaves that turn orange-yellow in autumn. In spring the small, yellow catkins appear. The female catkins, which are 12cm long and green-yellow, are followed by racemes of green fruit that ripen to yellow.

🛈 *Sow seed* while it is still green in open ground in autumn.
*Softwood cuttings* in midsummer.

## CARTHAMUS TINCTORIUS
(False saffron, Safflower)
Annual with grey-green basal leaves. Thistle-like, yellow, orange or red flowers appear in summer and are surrounded by green bracts.

*Sow seed* at 12°C in late spring.

Cardiocrinum giganteum

### CARYA OVATA (Shagbark hickory)

Deciduous tree with peeling, grey-brown bark and mid-green leaves that colour to golden-yellow in early autumn. Male catkins and smaller, female flower spikes appear in early summer, followed by long, thick-shelled, edible nuts.

*Sow seed* in spring in a garden frame after stratifying them there for 60 days. Transplant seedlings when small before they develop a deep tap root.

### CARYOPTERIS × CLANDONENSIS 'KEW BLUE'

Deciduous shrub with dull green leaves that are silvery-grey on the underside. Terminal clusters of dark blue flowers appear in late summer and autumn.

*Sow seed* in autumn in a garden frame.
🗓 *Softwood cuttings* in late spring under horticultural fleece.
*Semi-ripe cuttings* in early summer.

### CASSIOPE LYCOPODIOIDES

Evergreen shrub with tiny leaves. Bell-shaped white flowers in spring have red calyces and pale red flower stems.

*Sow seed* in autumn in a garden frame. Transplant the seedlings into ericaceous compost as soon as possible.
*Softwood cuttings* in early summer.
*Semi-ripe cuttings* in late summer in a propagating frame.
🗓 *Layer* in autumn or spring in ericaceous compost.

### CASTANEA SATIVA (Sweet chestnut)

Deciduous tree with 20cm long, toothed, glossy, dark green leaves. The edible nuts are held within a spiky outer case.

🗓 *Sow seed* as soon as it is ripe in early autumn in open ground.

*Whip and tongue graft* named varieties onto *C. sativa* rootstock in late winter.

## CATALPA BIGNONIOIDES
(Indian bean tree)
Deciduous tree with 25cm long, mid-green leaves. Large, 30cm high panicles of white flowers with yellow and purple blotches appear in mid- to late summer followed by thin, 45cm long seed pods.

**Sow seed** thinly in a garden frame in autumn.

🗓 **Softwood cuttings** in late spring. Shorten leaves by two thirds to reduce transpiration.
**Root cuttings** in winter in a garden frame.
**Whip and tongue graft** in winter.

## CATANANCHE CAERULEA
(Cupid's dart)
Perennial, but best treated as a biennial plant. The grass-like, hairy leaves are 30cm long. Solitary, dark-centred, blue flowers appear from summer through to autumn.

**Sow seed** in a garden frame in early spring or in open ground in late spring.
**Divide** in spring.
🗓 **Root cuttings** in winter in a garden frame.

## CATHARANTHUS ROSEUS
(Madagascar periwinkle)
Tender, evergreen perennial with glossy, dark green leaves. The white, pink or red flowers appear singly during spring and summer.

**Sow seed** at 15°C in early spring.
**Softwood cuttings** in late spring.
🗓 **Semi-ripe cuttings** in midsummer.

## CATTLEYA JOSE MARTI
Tender orchid with club-shaped pseudobulbs and a single 15cm long leaf. The fragrant, white spring flowers have an orange-yellow throat.

**Divide** when the plant pushes itself out of the container.

## CAULOPHYLLUM THALICTROIDES
(Blue cohosh)
Perennial with palmate, mid-green leaves and green or yellowish-brown flowers in spring. The 1cm seeds are bright blue.

🗓 **Sow seed** as soon as it is ripe. Be patient, as germination is erratic and may take 10–12 weeks.
**Division** If the plant ever becomes large enough, divide in early spring.

## CAUTLEYA SPICATA
Perennial with 30cm long, mid-green leaves. Stiff spikes of yellow flowers with maroon bracts appear in late summer or autumn.

**Sow seed** at 16°C in early spring.
**Divide** in late spring as the new shoots start to grow. Trim the leaves by half to reduce transpiration and keep shaded for the first week.

## CEANOTHUS THYRSIFLORUS
**VAR. REPENS** (California lilac)
Evergreen shrub with glossy, mid-green leaves. Panicles of pale and dark blue flowers appear in late spring.

**Sow seed** in autumn in a garden frame. Soak the seed in boiling water and leave in the cooling water for 24 hours before sowing.
🗓 **Semi-ripe cuttings** in late summer taken with a 'heel'.
**Softwood cuttings** of deciduous varieties such as C. 'Gloire de Versailles' in early summer.

## CEDRUS ATLANTICA (Cedar)
Evergreen conifer with sharply pointed, mid-green to glaucous blue leaves. The green, rounded, female cones turn to pale brown in autumn.

**Sow seed** in spring in a free-draining seed compost in a garden frame. Open the cones in hot water just before sowing. Alternatively, chill the seed for 3–4 weeks at minus 1°C and sow in spring.

## CELASTRUS SCANDENS
(American bittersweet)
Deciduous climber with 10cm long, mid-green leaves and terminal panicles of small, green-yellow flowers. These are followed by clusters of orange-yellow fruit with bright red seeds.

**Sow seed** as soon as it is ripe in early autumn in a garden frame.
🗓 **Semi-ripe cuttings** in summer with or without a 'heel'. Shorten the leaf length to reduce transpiration.
**Root cuttings** in winter in a garden frame.

## CELMISIA SPECTABILIS
(New Zealand daisy)
Perennial with 25cm long, leathery, lance-shaped leaves that are covered with grey-green, silky hairs on the upper surface and white hairs on the underside. The large, 7cm wide, white, daisy-like flowerheads with a centre of bright yellow disc florets appear in early summer.

**Sow seed** in a garden frame as soon as it is ripe. Only a small percentage of the seed collected will be viable.
🗓 **Softwood cuttings** in early spring. Pull off the young side rosettes and root in sandy, free-draining, ericaceous compost.
**Divide** large clumps in spring.

## CELOSIA ARGENTEA (Cockscomb)
Perennial usually grown as an annual with pale green leaves and dense spikes of silvery-white, summer flowers.

**Sow seed** at 18°C in mid-spring.

## CELTIS LAEVIGATA
(Nettletree, Sugar hackberry)
Deciduous tree with dark green leaves.
The small, green flowers appear in
spring and are followed by edible, sweet,
orange-red fruit.

***Sow seed*** in open ground or in a garden
frame in autumn.

## CENTAUREA CYANUS (Cornflower)
Annual with lance-shaped, mid-green
leaves and dark blue summer flowers.

***Sow seed*** in open ground in spring. The
seedlings resent disturbance, so
transplant them when they are small.

## CEPHALANTHUS OCCIDENTALIS
(Button bush)
Deciduous shrub with 15cm long, lance-
shaped, glossy, mid-green leaves and
red veins on the undersides. Dense,
rounded flowerheads of fragrant,
tubular, white flowers are produced in
late summer and early autumn.

***Sow seed*** in a garden frame in autumn.
***Semi-ripe cuttings*** in summer. Cut the
leaves in half to reduce transpiration.
🝙 ***Hardwood cuttings*** in winter.

## CENTRANTHUS RUBER (Red valerian)
***Sow seed*** in soil-based compost in a
garden frame in spring.
🝙 ***Divide*** in early spring. Separate the
clump with care to prevent the stems
breaking off without any roots.

## CEPHALARIA GIGANTEA
(Giant scabious)
Perennial with 45cm long basal leaves.
During summer primrose-yellow
flowers appear on long stems.

***Sow seed*** in a garden frame in early
spring.
🝙 ***Divide*** large clumps in late spring.

## CEPHALOTAXUS HARRINGTONII
(Plum yew)
Coniferous shrub with 5cm long, dark
green leaves with 2 white bands on
the underside. Female plants produce
single seeds inside a fleshy, olive-green
covering.

***Sow seed*** in a garden frame in spring
after stratification. Germination may
take over 24 months.
***Softwood cuttings*** of the young growths
at the tips of shoots in early summer.
🝙 ***Semi-ripe cuttings*** from the ends of
mature shoots in autumn. Always
take the cutting with a 'heel' and
trim it carefully before inserting it
in the compost.

## CERASTIUM TOMENTOSUM
(Snow-in summer)
Perennial with small, white or grey
leaves. In late spring and summer the
plant covers itself with star-shaped,
white flowers.

***Sow seed*** in autumn. Overwinter in a
garden frame.
***Divide*** in spring.
🝙 ***Softwood cuttings*** in early summer.
Propagate the cuttings under
horticultural fleece.

## CERATOSTIGMA PLUMBAGINOIDES
Perennial with red stems carrying bright
green, wavy edged leaves that turn
brilliant red in autumn. Clusters of
brilliant blue flowers appear in late
summer and early autumn.

🝙 ***Softwood cuttings*** in spring.
***Semi-ripe cuttings*** in midsummer. With
both types of cutting, overwinter
young plants in frost-free conditions.
***Rooted suckers*** in autumn in a well-
drained multi-purpose compost in a
garden frame.
***Layer*** in late autumn.

## CERCIDIPHYLLUM JAPONICUM
(Katsura tree)
Deciduous tree with mid-green
leaves. They open bronze in spring,
becoming yellow, orange and crimson
in autumn.

***Sow seed*** as soon as it is ripe in a
garden frame in ericaceous compost.
***Softwood basal cuttings*** in late spring.
🝙 ***Semi-ripe cuttings*** in midsummer.

Cercidiphyllum japonicum

**CERCIS SILIQUASTRUM** (Judas tree)
Deciduous tree with heart-shaped leaves that open bronze in spring, turning glaucous, blue-green in summer and butter-yellow in autumn. The tips of the leaves are notched. The magenta, pink or occasionally white flowers are produced in small clusters at the same time as the leaves, or just before them. The flowers often appear directly on the bark of the trunk and main branches.

*Sow seed* in a garden frame as soon as it is ripe.
▯ *Semi-ripe cuttings* in midsummer.

**CESTRUM ROSEUM**
Evergreen shrub with 10cm long, mid-green leaves. The funnel-shaped, deep pink flowers appear in summer.

*Sow seed* in a garden frame in autumn.
▯ *Softwood cuttings* in summer.
*Semi-ripe cuttings* in midsummer.

**CHAENOMELES SPECIOSA**
(Japanese quince)
Deciduous shrub with spiny stems and glossy, dark green leaves. In early spring to early summer it bears clusters of crimson flowers, followed by greenish-yellow, aromatic, edible fruit.

*Sow seed* in autumn, in containers of compost in a garden frame or directly into well-cultivated soil in the garden.
*Semi-ripe cuttings* in summer.
▯ *Layer* in autumn. I find that there are always stems low enough to layer.

**CHAEROPHYLLUM AUREUM**
(Golden chervil)
Perennial with aniseed-flavoured, fern-like, green-yellow leaves and umbels of white flowers in summer.

*Sow seed* in a garden frame in autumn or in spring.

Cercis siliquastrum

## CHAMAECYPARIS LAWSONIANA
(Lawson cypress)
Evergreen conifer with bright green leaves. The tiny male cones are deep red; the female cones are reddish-brown in summer.

*Sow seed* outdoors in spring. A large percentage of seed isn't viable.

**J** *Semi-ripe cuttings* in late summer with a 'heel'. Try the hot bed method in a cold frame for speedy results.

## CHAMAEDAPHNE CALYCULATA
(Leatherleaf)
Evergreen shrub with glossy, dark green, leathery leaves. The small, urn-shaped, white flowers appear in spring.

*Semi-ripe cuttings* with a 'heel' in midsummer. Use ericaceous compost.

## CHAMAEROPS HUMILIS
Tender palm with 60–90cm long, pinnate, greyish-green leaves. The panicles of yellow, late spring flowers are hard to see in the lower leaf axils.

*Sow seed* at 25°C in spring. Alternatively, try germinating some seeds in moist peat at 22°C, transplanting the tiny seedlings to a loam-based, free-draining compost. Germination should take place within 14 days.

**J** *Rooted suckers* in early summer in a loam-based compost in a frost-proof conservatory or greenhouse.

## CHASMANTHE AETHIOPICA
Cormous perennial with 60cm long, basal, mid-green leaves. The one-sided racemes of red or orange tubular flowers appear in late spring and early summer and are striped with yellow and have a deep orange throat.

*Sow seed* at 15°C in early spring.

**J** *Divide* in spring, taking care not to damage the new growths.

## CHEILANTHES FRAGRANS (Lip fern)
Evergreen fern with mid-green fronds.

*Sow spores* at 16°C as soon as they are ripe.

**J** *Divide* small clumps in spring. It dislikes disturbance, so be careful with the roots. Pot in free-draining, alkaline, soil-based compost.

## CHELONE OBLIQUA (Turtlehead)
Perennial with dark green leaves and dark pink or purple flowers from late summer to mid-autumn. Each flower is 2-lipped with a yellow beard on the inside of the lower lip.

*Sow seed* in a peat-based, moisture-retentive compost in containers in a garden frame during early spring.

**J** *Softwood cuttings* in early summer. *Divide* in early spring.

## CHIMONANTHUS PRAECOX
(Wintersweet)
Deciduous shrub with 20cm long, glossy, mid-green leaves and fragrant, sulphur-yellow, winter flowers that are stained purple on the inside.

*Sow seed* in a garden frame as soon as it is ripe. Treat with Cheshunt compound to avoid damping off disease.

**E** *Softwood cuttings* in midsummer.

## CHIONANTHUS VIRGINICUS
(Fringe tree)
Deciduous shrub with 20cm long, glossy, dark green leaves. Fragrant, pendant panicles of white flowers appear in summer, followed by blue-black fruit. The thin flower petals have a 'shredded' appearance.

*Sow seed* in a garden frame in autumn or in spring after stratification. Germination may take 24 months.

**J** *Layer* during late spring and late summer using ericaceous compost.

*Whip and tongue graft* in late winter using common ash (*Fraxinus excelsior*) as a rootstock.

## CHIONODOXA LUCILIAE
(Glory of the snow)
Bulbous perennial with recurved, mid-green leaves and star-shaped, bright blue flowers with white centres in early spring

*Sow seed* as soon as it is ripe in late summer in containers and overwinter in a garden frame.

**J** *Remove bulblets* in early autumn and plant out in open ground.

## CHIRITA SINENSIS
Tender, evergreen perennial with flat rosettes of hairy, dark green, thick leaves. Occasionally produces tubular, white flowers tinged purple with yellow markings.

*Sow seed* at 20–24°C in early spring.

**J** *Leaf cuttings* in summer in a propagator. Use cutting compost with added coarse sand.

## CHLOROPHYTUM COMOSUM 'VARIEGATUM'
Tender, evergreen perennial with 30cm long, narrow, mid-green leaves edged white. Unusually, its racemes of tiny, white flowers also produce plantlets at the ends of the flower stalk.

*Sow seed* at 20°C in spring.

**E** *Remove plantlets* and pot in spring and summer in a cool greenhouse.

Choisya 'Aztec Pearl'

## CHOISYA 'AZTEC PEARL'
(Mexican orange blossom)
Evergreen shrub with aromatic, mid-green leaves. Clusters of fragrant, white flowers appear in late spring and again in early autumn.

- *Semi-ripe cuttings* in summer under clear polythene.

## CHRYSANTHEMUM
Perennial with dark green, lobed leaves. The flowerheads are made up of ray- and disc- florets and are available in many colours and shapes from late summer until the first frosts. When grown in greenhouses they will flower until midwinter.

- *Softwood basal cuttings* in mid- to late winter in a propagator.
  *Divide* in early spring.

## CHRYSOGONUM VIRGINIANUM
Ground-covering perennial with heart-shaped, mid-green leaves. Star-shaped, butter-yellow flowers appear throughout spring, summer and early autumn.

- *Sow seed* thinly as soon as it is ripe in a garden frame.
- *Lift rooted runners* in autumn and pot up in a soil-based compost.

## CHUSQUEA CULEOU
Clump-forming, evergreen bamboo with branched stems of yellow-green canes and mid-green leaves.

- *Divide* clumps in spring. Remove each section of rhizome with a healthy root. Don't trim the root.

## CIMICIFUGA SIMPLEX (Bugbane)
Perennial with light green basal leaves. Tall stems with racemes of white flowers appear during autumn.

- *Sow seed* in a container as soon as it is ripe. Overwinter in a garden frame. Germination will not occur until late spring.
- *Divide* in late spring.

## CIRSIUM RIVULARE
Perennial with lance-shaped, 45cm long, prickly, dark green leaves. Small, deep crimson-purple, pincushion flowers appear in early summer.

- *Sow seed* in a garden frame in spring.
- *Divide* in late autumn.

## CISSUS STRIATA (Ivy of Uruguay)
Half-hardy, evergreen climber with leathery, glossy, mid-green, 5-palmate leaves. The small, green, early summer flowers are followed by shiny, black berries in autumn.

- *Softwood cuttings* with a 'heel' in summer.
  *Hardwood cuttings* in autumn.

Cistus x purpureus

## CISTUS × PURPUREUS (Rock rose)
Evergreen shrub with dark green leaves. Pink flowers with yellow stamens and maroon blotches at the base of the petals appear in early summer.

*Sow seed* in autumn in a garden frame.
*Softwood cuttings* in early summer under clear polythene.
*Semi-ripe cuttings* with a 'heel' in midsummer.

## CITRUS LIMON (Lemon)
Evergreen, spiny tree with light green leaves. From spring to summer the red-tinted buds open to fragrant, white flowers that are 5cm in diameter, followed by ovoid yellow fruit.

*Seed* does not come true but quickly forms a large plant that will be slow to fruit.
*Semi-ripe cuttings* in summer.

## CLADRASTIS LUTEA (Yellow wood)
Deciduous tree. Long, bright, pale green leaves turn yellow in autumn. Pendant panicles of white, yellow-marked, fragrant flowers appear in early summer.

*Sow seed* outside in a seed bed in late autumn. Scarify the seed as soon as it is ripe.
*Root cuttings* in winter. Prepare the cuttings and insert in gritty compost in a garden frame. Leave the new plants undisturbed for 12 months.

## CLARKIA AMOENA (Godetia)
Annual with mid-green leaves and clusters of single or double, pink-lilac flowers during summer.

*Sow seed* thinly where they are to flower in early spring. If sowing in containers, remember that the young plants dislike transplanting, so place two seeds to a small pot. Thin to one seedling and plant out without disturbing the roots.

## CLEMATIS
(Virgin's bower, Old man's beard)
Hardy, deciduous or evergreen climbers and herbaceous perennials. Leaves are mid- to dark green. Depending on the species, single or double flowers appear from late winter to late autumn in a wide range of colours. Some have fragrance and there are species with evergreen foliage.

*Sow seed* of the species in a container as soon as it is ripe and overwinter in a garden frame. Usually, seed of clematis species comes true, but there may be a slight difference between seedlings, so be prepared to select one sufficiently different to merit naming as a new plant!

Take cuttings midway between pairs of leaves:
*Leaf bud cuttings* at 16°C in a propagator in late summer.
*Softwood cuttings* in late spring.
*Semi-ripe cuttings* in early summer.
*Semi-ripe cuttings* of the evergreen *C. armandii* in late autumn.
*Softwood basal cuttings* of herbaceous perennials in late spring.
*Serpentine layer* in late winter.
*Divide* large clumps of herbaceous perennials in mid-spring.

## CLEOME HASSLERIANA (Spider flower)
Annual with mid-green, palmate, hairy leaves and racemes of white, pink or purple, fragrant flowers in summer.

*Sow seed* at 18°C in a propagator in spring. Protect the young plants from late spring frost.

## CLERODENDRUM BUNGEI
(Glory flower)
Deciduous shrub with dark green leaves, tinged purple when young. Panicles of fragrant, dark pink flowers appear in summer and autumn.

Clematis tangutica

*Sow seed* at 16°C in spring.
*Semi-ripe cuttings* with bottom heat in midsummer.
*Rooted suckers* in spring or late autumn in a free-draining, soil-based compost in a garden frame. Plant out the following spring.
*Root cuttings* in late winter in a garden frame.

## CLETHRA ALNIFOLIA
(Sweet pepper bush)
Deciduous shrub with mid-green leaves. During late summer and early autumn it produces racemes of bell-shaped, white flowers with a spicy fragrance.

*Sow seed* in spring or in autumn in a garden frame.
*Softwood cuttings* in early summer.
*Rooted suckers* in late spring in containers of ericaceous compost outside in a sheltered part of the garden.
*Semi-ripe cuttings* of evergreen shrubs such as *C. arborea* in late summer.

### CLEYERA JAPONICA

Evergreen shrub with glossy, dark green leaves. Fragrant, creamy-white flowers are produced in summer followed by small red fruit that ripen to black.

***Semi-ripe cuttings*** in summer. Trim leaves to reduce transpiration.

### CLIANTHUS PUNICEUS

(Glory pea, Lobster claw, Parrot's bill)
Evergreen, climbing shrub with dark green leaves made up of tiny leaflets. Pendant racemes of red, lobster-claw-like flowers in spring and early summer.

***Sow seed*** at 16–18°C in spring.
***Semi-ripe cuttings*** in midsummer.

The short-lived sub-shrub *C. formosus* dislikes waterlogged compost. Where necessary, graft onto seedling *Colutea arborescens* in spring.

Clianthus puniceus

### CLINTONIA ANDREWSIANA

Perennial with 25cm long, glossy, rich green leaves. Umbels of bell-shaped, purple-pink flowers appear in early summer, followed by dark blue berries.

***Sow seed*** in a peat-based compost in a garden frame in early autumn.
***Divide*** in early spring.

### CLIVIA MINIATA

Tender, evergreen perennial with 60cm long, strap-like leaves. Large umbels of up to 20 tubular, yellow, orange or red flowers appear from spring to summer.

***Sow seed*** at 16–20°C as soon as it is ripe. Transplant as early as possible. A quick way to germinate the seed is to remove it from the pod when it has turned orange, peel off the outer membrane and place the clean seed in an airtight container on a layer of wet tissue. Place this on a sunny window ledge. Within a few days the radical (root) will emerge and the seed can be carefully potted up with the root in the soil and the seed on the surface. In a few weeks the first leaf will appear.
***Divide*** in late winter or early spring, using loam-based, free-draining compost and as small a container as possible.

### COBAEA SCANDENS

(Cup and saucer plant)
Tender, evergreen perennial climber, usually grown as an annual. Each bright green leaf has 4 leaflets and a tendril with small hooks. Large, bell-shaped, fragrant flowers appear during late summer and autumn, opening a yellowish-green and ageing to purple.

***Sow seed*** at 18°C in spring. Protect seedlings from late spring frosts.
***Softwood cuttings*** in a propagator in early summer.

### CODIAEUM (Croton)

Tender, evergreen shrub or perennial with 20–30cm long, leathery leaves, often brightly coloured. Occasionally tiny, yellow flowers appear.

***Softwood cuttings*** in a propagator in summer. Dip the base of the stem in fine charcoal to stop the sap 'bleeding'.
***Air layer*** in late spring. Rooting can be slow, often taking 6 months to form a good root system.

### CODONOPSIS LANCEOLATA

(Bonnet bellflower)
Perennial with twining stems of mid-green leaves. In autumn it produces masses of bell-shaped, greenish-white, mauve-tinted flowers with violet spots on the inside.

***Sow seed*** in autumn or spring in ericaceous compost.

### COIX LACRYMA-JOBI (Job's tears)

Annual grass with 60cm long, bright green leaves. In autumn the flowers are divided into male and female spikelets. The seeds are grey-purple when ripe.

***Sow seed*** at 15°C in late winter. Protect seedlings from late spring frosts.

### COLCHICUM

(Autumn crocus, Naked ladies)
Cormous perennial with white, orange, pink or mauve flowers in autumn before the leaves. The strap-like foliage appears in mid- to late winter, lasting through to midsummer.

***Sow seed*** as soon as it is ripe in midsummer, in a container of seed compost with additional grit to ensure good drainage. Overwinter in a garden frame.
***Divide*** corms in summer. Line out the small cormlets in open ground.

Convolvulus cneorum

## COLLETIA PARADOXA

Deciduous shrub. The flat, blue-grey spines make up for the few leaves. Clusters of fragrant, white flowers appear below the spines in autumn.

*Seed* Catch seed before it drops and sow in spring in a gritty, free-draining seed compost at 15°C.

*Semi-ripe cuttings* in late summer in gritty compost in a cool greenhouse. There are few leaves, but the broad, flat spines effectively take their place and will photosynthesize in daylight.

## COLLINSIA BICOLOR (Chinese houses)

Annual with purplish-green leaves and racemes of 2-lobed flowers with a white upper lobe and a deep pink lower lip during summer.

*Sow seed* outside in late spring where it is to flower.

## COLUTEA ARBORESCENS

(Bladder senna)
Deciduous shrub with pale green, pinnate leaves. Racemes of bright yellow, pea-like flowers are produced throughout summer and are followed by translucent, 7cm long seed pods.

*Sow seed* in a garden frame in autumn or in spring.

*Softwood cuttings* in early summer.

## CONVALLARIA MAJALIS

(Lily-of-the-valley)
Rhizomous perennial with pairs of bright green basal leaves. Pendant, bell-shaped, fragrant, waxy, white flowers appear on leafless stems in late spring.

*Sow seed* as soon as it is ripe, in a garden frame. Remove the outer skin before sowing. Alternatively, chill the seed for 3 months, keep it at room temperature for 3 months and chill again for a further 3 months. If you are still interested, then sow the seed.

*Tease out rhizomes* in early autumn and replant in moist soil or compost.

## CONVOLVULUS CNEORUM

Evergreen shrub with silky, silver-green leaves. From late spring to summer, masses of pink buds open to funnel-shaped, white flowers with bright yellow centres.

*Sow seed* at 17°C in spring.
*Softwood cuttings* in late spring.
*Semi-ripe cuttings* in summer taken with a 'heel' and rooted under horticultural fleece.
*Divide* the perennial *C. boissieri* in spring.
*Sow seed* of annuals such as *C. tricolor* in spring where they are to flower.

## COPROSMA 'BEATSON'S GOLD'

Evergreen shrub with bright green leaves splashed with gold in the centre. This variety is female with shiny, red berries in autumn.

*Sow seed* in a garden frame in spring.
- *Semi-ripe cuttings* with a 'heel' in ericaceous compost in late summer.

### CORDYLINE AUSTRALIS
(Cabbage palm)
Evergreen tree with lance-shaped, pale green leaves up to 90cm long. In summer it produces large panicles up to 90cm in length made up of masses of tiny, creamy-white flowers followed by white berries tinted blue.

*Sow seed* at 16°C in late spring.

### COREOPSIS GRANDIFLORA (Tick seed)
Perennial. The lower leaves are lance-shaped or lobed. On flowering stems the leaves are pinnate. The flowers consist of deep yellow ray-florets with ragged outer margins and dark yellow disc-florets.

*Sow seed* outside in mid-spring.
- *Seed* Alternatively, sow seed in late winter at 14°C and the plants will flower the same year.
*Divide* in early spring.
*Softwood cuttings* in late spring.
*Sow seed* of annuals such as *C. tinctoria* in open ground in spring.

### CORIARIA TERMINALIS
Deciduous, arching sub-shrub with mid-green leaves that turn red in autumn. Racemes of small, green flowers appear in late spring and are followed by fleshy, black-red fruit in late summer.

*Sow seed* at 13°C in spring.
*Divide* in spring.
- *Softwood cuttings* in midsummer.

### CORNUS ALBA (Dogwood)
Deciduous shrub with red winter shoots and dark green leaves that turn orange or red in autumn. Small clusters of white flowers in late spring are followed by white fruit, sometimes tinged blue.

*Sow seed* in spring in open ground, having stratified the seed outside in trays of sharp sand over winter.
*Softwood cuttings* in summer.
- *Hardwood cuttings* during winter.

Cortaderia selloana

## COROKIA COTONEASTER
(Wire-netting bush)
Evergreen shrub with a tangled mass of stems carrying small, dark green leaves. Small, fragrant, yellow flowers are produced in spring, followed by red or yellow fruit.

***Softwood cuttings*** in early summer.
🗓 ***Semi-ripe cuttings*** in late summer under horticultural fleece.

## CORONILLA VALENTINA
Evergreen shrub with bright green leaves and umbels of fragrant, bright yellow flowers in late winter, early spring and again in early autumn. The flowers are followed by thin pods.

***Sow seed*** in late spring at 12°C, having first stratified the seed over winter in sharp sand in a sheltered part of the garden. While stratifying, net the area to protect the seed from vermin.
***Softwood cuttings*** in early summer.
🗓 ***Semi-ripe cuttings*** in late summer with a short 'heel'.

## CORREA BACKHOUSEANA
(Australian fuchsia)
Tender, evergreen shrub with dark red stems and dark green leaves that are hairy on the underside. From late autumn to late spring clusters of pale, red-green or cream flowers appear.

***Sow seed*** at 18°C in spring.
🗓 ***Semi-ripe cuttings*** in midsummer under clear polythene.

## CORTADERIA SELLOANA
(Pampas grass)
Evergreen perennial grass with thin, glaucous, mid-green leaves up to 2.5m long. Panicles of silky, silver spikelets appear in late summer.

***Sow seed*** at 15°C in spring.
🗓 ***Divide*** in spring.

## CORTUSA MATTHIOLI
Perennial with deep green leaves surfaced with rust coloured hairs. Pendant, bell-shaped, magenta flowers (sometimes white) are produced on one-sided umbels in late spring and early summer.

***Sow seed*** as soon as it is ripe in early autumn, in a humus-rich compost. Overwinter in a garden frame.
🗓 ***Divide*** in early spring.

## CORYDALIS FLEXUOSA
Summer-dormant perennial with light green leaves sometimes flushed purple. From late spring to early summer it produces slender-tubed, bright blue flowers with white throats.

***Sow seed*** as soon as it is ripe in containers of seed compost in a garden frame. Germination is slow and erratic, with seedlings emerging over a 3-month period.
🗓 ***Divide*** in spring.
***Divide*** spring-flowering *C. bracteata* in autumn.

*Corydalis lutea* self-seeds, becoming weedy if not controlled.

## CORYLOPSIS GLABRESCENS
(Winter hazel)
Deciduous shrub with 10cm long, dark green leaves, blue-green on the underside. Pendant racemes of pale yellow flowers appear in late spring.

***Sow seed*** in a garden frame in autumn.
🗓 ***Softwood cuttings*** in summer. Shorten the leaves by half to reduce transpiration.
***Layer*** in late autumn.

## CORYLUS MAXIMA (Filbert)
Deciduous shrub with yellow catkins in late winter. Edible nuts are contained in tubular husks in autumn.

*Corylus maxima 'Red Zellernut'*

***Sow seed*** as soon as it is ripe in autumn.
***Saddle graft*** in winter.
🗓 ***Layer*** in autumn

## COSMOS BIPINNATUS
Annual with mid-green leaves. Throughout summer it produces saucer-shaped, crimson, pink or white flowers with yellow centres.

🗓 ***Sow seed*** outdoors in late spring. Alternatively, sow at 16°C in early spring.
***Softwood basal cuttings*** of perennial *C. atrosanguineus* in a propagator in early spring.

## COTINUS COGGYGRIA (Smoke bush)
Deciduous shrub or tree with mid-green leaves turning yellow, orange and then red in autumn. The panicles are green, maturing to grey.

***Sow seed*** in a garden frame in autumn.
🗓 ***Softwood cuttings*** in summer.
***Layer*** in late spring.

Crinodendron hookerianum

**Leaf cuttings** in summer in cactus compost.

## CRATAEGUS MONOGYNA
(Common hawthorn, Quickthorn)
Deciduous tree with thorny stems and glossy, dark green, lobed leaves. Clusters of fragrant, white flowers appear in late spring followed by masses of glossy, dark red fruit.

**Sow seed** as soon as it is ripe in a container outside. Remove the outer flesh before sowing.

**Sow seed** in spring outside in containers or in rows in well-cultivated soil. Before sowing, stratify seed in trays of sharp sand outside over winter. Germination can take up to 24 months.

**Saddle graft** in winter.
**Bud graft** in summer.

## CREPIS INCANA (Pink dandelion)
Perennial with rosettes of grey-haired leaves. In late summer masses of bright pink or deep pink flowers are produced.

**Seed** Extract the seed from the berries. Sow seed as soon as it is ripe in well-drained seed compost in a garden frame.

**Root cuttings** in winter in a garden frame. Use lateral roots rather than the main tap root.

## CRINODENDRON HOOKERIANUM
(Lantern tree)
Evergreen shrub or small tree with toothed, 10cm long, dark green leaves. From late spring to late summer it produces lantern-shaped, scarlet flowers.

**Softwood cuttings** in early summer.
**Semi-ripe cutting** with a 'heel' in late summer.

## COTONEASTER FRIGIDUS 'CORNUBIA'
Semi-evergreen tree with 12cm long, dark green leaves. Clusters of white flowers are produced in summer, followed by masses of bright red fruit.

**Sow seed** as soon as possible after collecting it in late autumn, outside in a sheltered part of the garden. First rub the hard seeds on sand paper to allow moisture to penetrate the outer coat. To break the dormancy, mix the seed with moist peat and use the 'warm and cold treatment' – leave the seed for 5 days at room temperature, then keep it in the fridge at 2°C for 5 days.

**Softwood cuttings** of deciduous species in early summer.

**Semi-ripe cuttings** of evergreens in late summer. Shorten the leaves to reduce transpiration.

## CRAMBE CORDIFOLIA
Perennial with kidney-shaped, 30cm wide, bristly, dark green leaves that die down in late summer. The many branched panicles of small, white flowers appear in early summer on 1.5m high stems.

**Sow seed** in autumn or spring.
**Divide** in spring.
**Root cuttings** in winter in a garden frame.

## CRASSULA SARCOCAULIS
Tender, perennial succulent with small, red-tinted, pale green leaves. Small, pink or white, star-shaped flowers appear in summer.

**Sow seed** at 16°C in early spring.
**Softwood cuttings** in late spring in cactus compost.

## CRINUM × POWELLII

Deciduous perennial with 1.5m long, strap-like, arching, mid-green leaves. Umbels of up to 10 trumpet-like, fragrant, mid-pink flowers are produced in late summer and autumn.

***Sow seed*** at 20°C as soon as it is ripe.
- ***Remove offsets*** in spring. Plant in free-draining, fertile compost.

## CROCOSMIA MASONIORUM
(Montbretia)

Cormous perennial with mid-green, lance-shaped leaves up to 60–90cm long. Spikes of upward-facing, bright red flowers appear in midsummer.

***Sow seed*** as soon as it is ripe in autumn in a garden frame.
- ***Divide*** in early spring.

## CROCUS

Cormous perennial with lance-shaped, mid-green leaves, usually with a silvery central stripe. Goblet-shaped flowers

Crinum × powellii

open in autumn or in early spring in a wide range of colours.

***Sow seed*** as soon as it is ripe ( before the capsule splits and drops the seed) in a well-drained compost in a garden frame. Overwinter in a garden frame.
- ***Remove cormlets*** in summer or autumn while the plant is dormant, and line them out for a year in the garden to allow the corm to swell to flowering size.

## CRYPTOMERIA JAPONICA
(Japanese cedar)

Evergreen conifer with a conical shape when mature and deep green leaves. The female cones are brown.

***Sow seed*** in spring in a garden frame or thinly in rows in the open ground.
- ***Softwood cuttings*** with a 'heel' in late summer under horticultural fleece.

## CUNNINGHAMIA LANCEOLATA
(China fir)

Evergreen conifer with lance-shaped, 7cm long, glossy, bright green leaves that have 2 white bands on the underside. The female cones are green-brown.

***Sow seed*** in a garden frame in spring. Cover with coarse sand.
- ***Semi-ripe cuttings*** with a 'heel' in summer under clear polythene.

## CUPHEA IGNEA (Cigar flower)

Tender, evergreen sub-shrub with lance-shaped, glossy, bright green leaves. The slim, deep red flowers have a white rim and 2 deep purple petals at the tip. They are produced from late spring to autumn.

***Sow seed*** at 15°C in early spring.

## × CUPRESSOCYPARIS LEYLANDII
(Leyland cypress)

Evergreen conifer. A fast-growing, tapering tree with pointed, dark green, grey-tinged leaves and dark brown female cones.

***Semi-ripe cuttings*** with a 'heel' in late summer under clear polythene or with bottom heat.

## CUPRESSUS SEMPERVIRENS
(Italian cypress)

Evergreen, columnar conifer with horizontal branches and grey-green leaves. Female cones are prickly brown.

***Sow seed*** in spring in a garden frame.
- ***Semi-ripe cuttings*** in late summer with bottom heat.

## CURCUMA ROSCOEANA

Tender perennial with shiny, mid-green leaves with dark green veins that are 30cm long. Terminal spikes of bright yellow flowers with orange bracts appear in summer.

***Sow seed*** at 20°C in autumn.
- ***Divide*** in spring.

## CYANANTHUS LOBATUS

Perennial with fleshy, matt green, deeply lobed leaves. Bright blue-purple flowers appear in late summer.

***Sow seed*** in a garden frame in free-draining, ericaceous compost in spring.
- ***Softwood cuttings*** in late spring.

## CYCAS REVOLUTA
(Japanese sago palm)

Tender cycad with glossy, dark green, 1–1.5m long, pinnate, arching leaves. The woolly, golden-brown flowers appear on mature plants during summer. The male flowers are 45cm long and pineapple scented; female flowers are 15cm long and followed by small, yellow fruit.

***Sow seed*** at 29°C in late spring.
- ***Rooted suckers*** in spring in seed compost with added grit, leaf mould and charcoal.

## CYCLAMEN PERSICUM

Tender, tuberous perennial with heart-shaped leaves, often with silver markings and purplish undersides. White, pink or red, fragrant flowers appear in late autumn and winter at the same time as the foliage.

- **Sow seed** at 15°C in peat-based compost. Soak the seed beforehand in water for 12 hours. Rinse the seed well and dry with a paper towel before sowing. Sow individually in small pots and cover with coarse, washed grit.
- **Divide** the tubers by cutting them into sections, making sure you have a growth bud on each cut section. Dust the cuts with fungicide and pot them into a loam-based compost with the top of the tuber just above the surface of the compost.
- **Sow seed** of hardy species as soon as it is ripe in a garden frame.

## CYDONIA OBLONGA (Quince)

Deciduous tree with 10cm long, dark green leaves that are downy-grey on the underside. In late spring, single, white to pale pink flowers are produced from the leaf axils, followed in autumn by golden-yellow, aromatic and edible fruit.

- **Sow seed** outside in well-cultivated, free-draining soil in autumn.
- **Softwood cuttings** in early summer.
- **Semi-ripe cuttings** in late summer.
- **Hardwood cuttings** in early winter.
- **Whip and tongue graft** named varieties in late winter onto seedling quince stock.

## CYMBIDIUM

Tender, evergreen orchid with pseudobulbs and linear leaves, 60–90cm long. Racemes of flowers in a range of colours are produced in winter and spring.

- **Divide** in late spring when the pot becomes congested.

## CYNARA SCOLYMUS (Globe artichoke)

Perennial with deeply lobed, 60cm long, grey-green leaves that are covered with white wool on the underside. Large, thistle-like flowerheads, 10–15cm across, appear in summer. The flower buds are eaten as a vegetable.

- **Sow seed** in spring in a garden frame.
- **Divide** in early spring. Reduce the leaves by half. Keep the plant well watered and the foliage moist until growth starts.
- **Root cuttings** in winter in a garden frame.

## CYNOGLOSSUM NERVOSUM

(Hound's tongue)
Perennial with lance-shaped, bright green leaves. Masses of azure-blue flowers are produced from mid-spring to midsummer.

- **Sow seed** in autumn in a garden frame.
- **Divide** in spring.
- **Sow seed** of annuals such as *C. amabile* in mid-spring.

## CYPERUS ALTERNIFOLIUS

(Umbrella plant)
Tender, evergreen perennial. Dark green stems bear a terminal whorl of deep green, leaf-like bracts. Small spikelets of pale yellow-brown flowers are produced in summer and autumn at the top of the stems.

- **Sow seed** in permanently wet compost in spring at 20°C.
- **Divide** in spring.

## CYPHOMANDRA BETACEA

(Tree tomato)
Evergreen shrub or small tree with soft, downy, dark green leaves, 30cm long.

Racemes of bowl-shaped, white or white-tinged pink flowers appear from spring to summer, followed by orange-red, edible fruit.

- **Sow seed** at 18°C in spring.
- **Softwood cuttings** in early summer in a propagator. Reduce the length of the leaves by half to prevent transpiration.

## CYPRIPEDIUM CALCEOLUS

(Lady's slipper orchid)
Hardy orchid with bright green, elliptic leaves and purple-brown, summer flowers with twisted petals and a large, bright yellow lip.

- **Divide** in early spring, retaining some soil on each new plant. Use an alkaline, soil-based compost. Never remove plants from the wild.

## CYRTANTHUS BREVIFLORUS (Fire lily)

Deciduous perennial. The lance-shaped, mid-green leaves are 20cm long. Up to 20 bell-shaped, bright yellow flowers appear at almost any time of the year.

- **Sow seed** at 15°C as soon as it is ripe.
- **Separate offsets** in spring and pot into a loam-based compost with added leaf mould for a year before planting out.

## CYTISUS (Broom)

Deciduous or evergreen shrub with mid- to dark green leaves and numerous, pea-like flowers in a range of colours. Many varieties have fragrant flowers.

- **Sow seed** in a garden frame in spring. Soak seed in boiling water for 24 hours before sowing.
- **Softwood cuttings** in early summer under horticultural fleece.
- **Semi-ripe cuttings** in late summer. Trim the foliage of *C. battandieri* (Pineapple broom) by half and root under horticultural fleece.

Cytisus 'Royal Standard'

## DABOECIA CANTABRICA
(St Dabeoc's Heath)
Evergreen shrub with small, glossy, dark green leaves, silver-haired on the underside. Racemes of urn-shaped, purple-pink flowers are produced from early summer to mid-autumn.

**Semi-ripe cuttings** in summer. Cut with a sharp knife below a leaf, rather than taking with a 'heel'.

## DACTYLIS GLOMERATA 'VARIETATA'
Perennial grass with lance-shaped, 15cm long, white-variegated leaves. During summer one-sided panicles of pale green spikelets are produced.

**Divide** in early spring.

## DACTYLORHIZA FUCHSII
(Spotted orchid)
Hardy, terrestrial orchid with lance-shaped, purple-spotted leaves. The white, pale pink or mauve flowers are marked with deep red and appear in late spring and early summer.

**Divide** in early spring.

## DAHLIA
Tuberous perennial with mid- to dark green, pinnate leaves. Flowers appear from summer to late autumn in a range of colours and in various styles on long stems.

**Sow seed** of bedding dahlias at 15°C in early spring. Plant them out when there is no risk of frost.
**Softwood basal cuttings** in spring in a propagator.
**Divide** tubers into sections, each with a growing shoot, in spring. Dust the cuts with Flowers of sulphur and pot up. Plant out after all risk of frost is over.

## DANAE RACEMOSA (Alexandrian laurel)
Evergreen perennial with glossy, 10cm long, leaf-like stems. Racemes of greenish-yellow flowers are produced in early summer, followed by red berries.

**Sow seed** in a garden frame in autumn.
**Divide** in winter or early spring.

## DAPHNE CNEORUM (Garland flower)
Evergreen shrub with lance-shaped, dark green leaves that are grey-green on the underside. In late spring white or pale to deep pink, fragrant flowers are produced.

**Sow seed** in a garden frame before it is fully ripe.
**Softwood cuttings** in early summer.
**Semi-ripe cuttings** in late summer taken with a 'heel'.
**Layer** in late spring.

## DARMERA PELTATA
Perennial with 2m long leaf stalks and deeply lobed, 60cm long, dark green leaves that turn red in autumn. White or bright pink flowers with 5 petals each are produced in late spring on flower stems 2m high.

**Sow seed** in a garden frame in spring.
**Divide** in spring. Water well until established.

## DAVIDIA INVOLUCRATA
(Handkerchief tree)
Deciduous tree with mid-green leaves, soft and hairy on the underside, and red stalks. In late spring each flower is surrounded by a pair of leafy, white bracts of uneven size. Ridged, greenish-brown, pendant fruit appear in autumn.

**Seed** Strip off the outer flesh, then crack the nut and remove the seed (3–5 seeds per nut). Sow in autumn in containers in a garden frame or in well-cultivated ground outside.

Darmera peltata

There is another method of propagating from seed that I have never tried. Sow the whole fruit in a container of peaty compost and leave outside. Germination may take 2 years. But since it may take another 10-12 years for it to flower, what does another 2 years matter?
**Leaf bud cuttings** in early autumn.
**Hardwood cuttings** in early winter.

## DECAISNEA FARGESII
Deciduous shrub with 90cm long, pinnate, dark green leaves that are mid-green on the underside. Pendant panicles of bell-shaped, green or yellow-green flowers are produced in summer, followed by dull, deep blue, cylindrical fruit 10cm in length.

**Sow seed** in a garden frame in autumn. Transplant seedlings when small. Protect from late spring frosts.

### DECUMARIA BARBARA

Deciduous climber with glossy, dark green 10cm long leaves and corymbs (flat-topped flower clusters) of white summer flowers.

**Semi-ripe cuttings** in early autumn. Cut the leaves in half to reduce transpiration.

### DELPHINIUM BELLADONNA GROUP

Perennial with palmate, mid-green leaves. The branched spikes of mainly blue, cup-shaped, single flowers have spurs appearing in early summer.

**Sow seed** at 14°C in early spring.
**Softwood basal cuttings** in early spring. Use short, 7–10cm, thin cuttings with a solid 'heel'. (Stem cuttings will be hollow and useless.)

### DENDRANTHEMA WEYRICHII

Perennial with fleshy, mid-green leaves. Daisy-like, white or pink ray-florets with yellow disc-florets are produced in autumn.

**Sow seed** in a garden frame in autumn.
**Divide** in late autumn after flowering or in early spring.

### DENDROMECON RIGIDA (Tree poppy)

Evergreen shrub with lance-shaped, leathery, grey-green leaves. Solitary, poppy-like, fragrant flowers appear from spring to autumn.

**Sow seed** in a garden frame in autumn or spring.
**Softwood cuttings** in early summer. Remove the flower buds and shorten the leaves by half to reduce transpiration while rooting takes place.
**Root cuttings** in winter in a garden frame.

### DESCHAMPSIA FLEXUOSA
(Wavy hair grass)

Evergreen grass with thread-like, blue-green leaves that are 20cm long. In early summer it produces silver-tinted, purple spikelets.

**Sow seed** in open ground in spring.
**Divide** in late autumn or early spring.

### DESFONTAINIA SPINOSA

Evergreen shrub with spiny, glossy, dark green leaves. Pendant, yellow-tipped, red flowers are produced from summer to late autumn.

**Semi-ripe cuttings** in summer. Keep the cuttings as small as 5cm, retaining only one pair of leaves.

### DEUTZIA GRACILIS

Deciduous shrub with bright green leaves. Upright racemes of star-shaped, fragrant, white flowers are produced from spring to midsummer.

**Sow seed** in a garden frame in autumn.
**Softwood cuttings** in early summer.
**Hardwood cuttings** in winter.

### DIANTHUS (Carnation, Pink)

Available as annuals, biennials, perennials and evergreen sub-shrubs. The leaves are lance-shaped and often grey-green or blue-grey. Flowers are often fragrant (clove-scented) in a wide range of colours.

**Sow seed** of alpine species such as D. alpinus in free-draining, gritty compost in early spring in a garden frame.
**Sow annuals** at 15°C in early spring.
**Sow biennials** such as D. barbatus (Sweet William) in open ground in late summer or early autumn to flower the following summer.

Take care when handling dianthus seed. It is brittle and occasionally there will be broken seed in a packet.
**Softwood cuttings** of species such as D. gratianopolitanus (Cheddar pink) in summer.
**Softwood cuttings** of Malmaison carnations such as 'Duchess of Westminster' in winter.

Dianthus spp.

Dicentra spectabilis 'Alba'

## DIASCIA RIGESCENS

Perennial with heart-shaped, stalkless, mid-green leaves. Dense racemes of deep pink flowers with downward-pointing spurs are produced during the summer.

*Sow seed* as soon as it is ripe at 15°C.
*Softwood cuttings* in late spring.
🔲 *Semi-ripe cuttings* in summer without flower buds.

## DICENTRA SPECTABILIS

(Bleeding heart)
Perennial with pale green leaves and lobed leaflets. Arching stems produce racemes of flowers with pale-pink outer petals and white inner petals during late spring and early summer.

*Sow seed* in a garden frame as soon it is ripe or chill for 14 days and sow in spring. I find that germination rates are quite low.
*Divide* in early spring or after the leaves have died down in early autumn.
🔲 *Root cuttings* in winter in a garden frame. Use roots of pencil thickness.

Dicksonia antarctica

## DICKSONIA ANTARCTICA
(Man fern, Woolly tree fern)
Fern, evergreen in mild climates. The stem is really an upright rhizome with pale green fronds up to 3m long, ageing to dark green.

**Sow spores** at 16°C as soon as they are ripe.

## DICTAMNUS ALBUS (Burning bush)
Perennial with 30cm long, pinnate, lemon-scented, leathery leaves. In early summer pinkish-white or pure white flowers appear.

**Sow seed** in a garden frame as soon as it is ripe.
**Divide** in late autumn. Old, woody stemmed plants won't survive division.

## DIEFFENBACHIA SEGUINE (Dumb cane)
Tender, evergreen perennial with glossy, dark green leaves with a few, well scattered, white spots and white mid-ribs.

**Softwood tip cuttings** in late spring and early summer.
**Air layering** in early summer.
**Stem sections** (similar to a stem cutting but with no leaves) in late spring, 5–10cm long. Ensure that each section has an active bud, lay it flat on moist compost and cover with clear polythene.

## DIERAMA PULCHERRIMUM
(Wandflower)
Cormous perennial with semi-erect, grey-green leaves up to 1m long. In summer, pendant spikes of bell-shaped, white, pink, magenta or purple-red flowers are produced.

**Sow seed** in a garden frame in spring. Collect the seed before it falls or lift self-sown seedlings when they are very small (the roots are brittle and dislike being disturbed).
**Divide** in early spring.

## DIERVILLA SESSILIFOLIA
(Bush honeysuckle)
Deciduous shrub with mid-green leaves that are bronzed when young. In summer bright yellow flowers are produced.

**Softwood cuttings** in early summer. Shorten the leaves to reduce transpiration.
**Rooted suckers** in winter, potted in multi-purpose compost in a garden frame.

## DIGITALIS FERRUGINEA
(Rusty foxglove)
Perennial with lance-shaped, dark green leaves and racemes of deep yellow-brown flowers in midsummer. The sepals have translucent margins.

**Sow seed** in a garden frame in spring. The common foxglove (*D. purpurea*) may be sown in open ground in spring. It self-seeds like a weed.

## DIMORPHOTHECA PLUVIALIS
(Rain daisy)
Annual with 10cm long, dark green, aromatic leaves. The single, white, summer flowers are blue on the underside and have purple-brown central discs.

**Sow seed** at 16°C in early spring or sow in open ground when all risk of frost is over.

## DIONAEA MUSCIPULA (Venus fly-trap)
Perennial with rosettes of yellowish-green and red leaves. The leaves have 2 hinged lobes, which form the 'traps', with up to 20 spines on each edge. The white flowers appear in early summer.

**Sow seed** at 11°C in late spring. Stand the container in rainwater to ensure the compost remains wet. Germination may take 3–4 months.
**Leaf cuttings** in late spring and early summer.
**Divide** in late spring.

## DIONYSIA INVOLUCRATA
Perennial with tiny, dark green rosetted leaves and deep purple flowers with a white eye in early summer.

**Sow seed** in early autumn in a cold frame in a free-draining compost.
**Semi-ripe cuttings** of single rosettes in a gritty compost in a propagator in summer. Avoid water lying in the rosette by watering from the base of the container.

## DIOSPYROS KAKI (Chinese persimmon)
Deciduous tree with glossy, dark green, 20cm long leaves that turn yellow and purple in autumn. In summer it produces small, bell-shaped, pale yellow flowers. Female flowers produce edible, yellow or orange fruit in autumn.

**Sow seed** in a garden frame as soon as it is ripe.
**Whip and tongue graft** cultivars such as *D. kaki* 'Hachiya' in winter.

## DIPELTA FLORIBUNDA
Deciduous shrub with 10cm long, sharp-pointed, pale green leaves. In late spring and early summer it produces tubular, pale pink flowers with yellow markings.

**Sow seed** outdoors in autumn or in late spring. You may succeed, I never have.
**Softwood cuttings** in midsummer. Cut the leaves in half to reduce transpiration.

Disanthus cercidifolius

**DIPSACUS FULLONUM** (Teasel)
Biennial with a basal rosette of lance-shaped, spiny, dark green leaves. In the second year lance-shaped pairs of leaves are produced on the upright stems. They are joined at the base, forming a 'cup' where the water collects. In mid- to late summer thistle-like, light purple or white flowerheads form with spiny bracts.

*Sow seed* in open ground in autumn or in spring.

Dipsacus fullonum

**DIPTERONIA SINENSIS**
Deciduous tree with 30cm long, pinnate, mid-green leaves. The upright, 30cm long panicles of tiny, greenish-white flowers appear in summer, followed in late autumn by winged, flat, deep brown-red fruit.

*Sow seed* in open ground in autumn.
◻ *Softwood cuttings* in summer under clear polythene. Shorten leaflets to half their size to reduce transpiration.
*Layer* in early summer.

**DIRCA PALUSTRIS** (Leatherwood)
Deciduous shrub with mid-green leaves, blue-green on the underside. Small, pale yellow, funnel-shaped flowers appear in clusters of 3 in spring.

◻ *Sow seed* in a cold frame in autumn.
*Layer* in autumn.

**DISANTHUS CERCIDIFOLIUS**
Deciduous shrub with 10cm long, rounded, glaucous, blue-green leaves that colour beautifully in autumn to yellow, orange and deep red. In mid-autumn it produces masses of spidery, bright, cerise-red flowers with a slight fragrance.

*Sow seed* in open ground in autumn or spring.
◻ *Layer* in spring.

**DISPOROPSIS PERNYI**
Evergreen perennial with glossy, dark green leaves and white, bell-shaped, citrus-scented summer flowers with pale green outer lips.

*Sow seed* in a garden frame in autumn or in spring.
◻ *Divide* rhizomes in spring. Use a compost with lots of added leaf mould.

**DISPORUM SMITHII** (Fairy bells)
Perennial with red-tinged stems and bright green leaves. In late spring umbels of pendant, tubular-shaped, greenish-white flowers appear, followed by orange berries in early autumn.

*Sow seed* in a garden frame in autumn in ericaceous compost.
◻ *Divide* rhizomes before growth commences in spring.

**DISTYLIUM RACEMOSUM**
Evergreen shrub with glossy, dark green, leathery leaves. In late spring and early summer the racemes of small flowers with red calyces and purple stamens without petals appear.

*Sow seed* in a garden frame in late summer.
◻ *Semi-ripe cuttings* in summer.

### DODECATHEON PULCHELLUM
(Shooting stars)
Perennial with rosettes of long-stalked, pale green leaves. Umbels of 3–5 large, bright pink flowers with deep purple anthers are produced in late spring.

*Sow seed* as soon as it is ripe, in seed compost in a container outside. After a few weeks of cold weather, move to a garden frame where it will germinate.

▣ *Divide* in late spring, planting into peat-rich, moisture-retentive compost. Keep the plants shaded for a few weeks.

### DORONICUM PLANTAGINEUM
(Leopard's bane)
Perennial with hairy basal leaves and lance-shaped stem leaves. In late spring it produces golden-yellow, daisy-like flowerheads.

*Sow seed* in a garden frame in spring.

▣ *Divide* in late summer. Discard the old, woody, inner portion of the clump.

### DOROTHEANTHUS BELLIDIFORMIS
(Livingstone daisy)
Annual with succulent, light green leaves and solitary, daisy-like, summer flowers in a wide range of bright colours. The flowers only open when there is good light.

*Sow seed* at 17°C in early spring. Protect seedlings from late spring frosts.

### DRABA MOLLISSIMA (Whitlow grass)
Evergreen perennial with rosettes of hairy, grey-green leaves and racemes of 5–8 tiny, bright yellow flowers during late spring.

*Sow seed* in a container outside in autumn. After a few frosts, move to a garden frame where it will soon germinate. If you are lucky enough to live in a frost-free area, store the seed in the fridge at 2°C for 3–4 days.

Dodecatheon pulchellum

*Softwood cuttings* of individual rosettes in well-drained compost in spring.

## DRACAENA MARGINATA
Tender, evergreen shrub with lance-shaped, 45–60cm long, dark green leaves margined red. The older leaves fall off, leaving a bare trunk. In summer terminal panicles of white flowers are followed by yellow berries.

*Sow seed* at 20°C in spring.
*Semi-ripe cuttings* in summer.
🗍 *Semi-ripe* stem sections, 5–10 cm long, without leaves, in a propagator in summer.

## DRACOCEPHALUM ARGUNENSE
(Dragon's head)
Perennial with mid-green, hairy leaves. The racemes of bluish-purple flowers appear in midsummer among the lance-shaped stem leaves.

*Sow seed* in a garden frame in spring.
🗍 *Softwood basal cuttings* of new shoots in late spring.
*Divide* in spring.

## DRACUNCULUS VULGARIS
(Dragon plant)
Tuberous perennial with 30cm long, dark green basal leaves with deep purple spots. In late spring and early summer, the deep maroon-purple spathes with almost black spadices appear. They are 60–90cm long and smell of rotten meat.

🗍 *Separate offsets* in autumn and replant immediately where they are to flower.

## DREGEA SINENSIS
Evergreen climber with 10cm long, heart-shaped, mid-green leaves and umbels of fragrant, creamy-white flowers that are pink on the inside. These are followed by 7cm long, paired seed pods.

*Sow seed* in a garden frame in spring.
🗍 *Semi-ripe cuttings* in late summer taken with a 'heel'. Keep the cuttings protected from strong sunlight until they root.

## DRIMYS WINTERI (Winter's bark)
Evergreen shrub or small tree with aromatic bark and 20cm long, leathery, dark green leaves that are bluish-white on the underside. It produces large umbels of 10–20 ivory-white, fragrant flowers during spring and early summer.

*Sow seed* in a garden frame in autumn. Transplant the seedlings when small.
🗍 *Semi-ripe cuttings* in midsummer with a 'heel'.

## DROSERA CAPENSIS (Sundew)
Evergreen perennial with basal rosettes of spoon-shaped leaves covered in green or red hairs. From spring to autumn, racemes of rose-pink flowers are produced.

*Sow seed* at 13°C as soon as it is ripe.
🗍 *Leaf cuttings* taken in summer from mature foliage.
*Root cuttings* in mid-winter in permanently moist, peat-based compost in a garden frame.

## DRYAS OCTOPETALA (Mountain avens)
Evergreen sub-shrub with scalloped, oak-like, deep green leaves. The cup-shaped, creamy-white flowers with bright yellow stamens are produced in late spring and early summer.

*Sow seed* in a garden frame as soon as it is ripe.
🗍 *Softwood cuttings* in early summer.
*Layering* Fork up rooted layers in spring and pot up in well-drained, gritty compost for a year before planting out.

## DRYOPTERIS FELIX-MAS (Male fern)
Hardy, deciduous fern with 1–1.2m long, lance-shaped, mid-green fronds.

*Divide* clumps in autumn or early spring.

## ECCREMOCARPUS SCABER
(Chilean glory vine)
Evergreen climber with 4-angled (square) stems and light green, pinnate leaves. Racemes of tubular, orange-red flowers are produced from late spring to autumn.

*Seed* Sow the large, flat, black seeds at 15°C in early spring.
🗍 *Softwood tip cuttings* in a propagator in summer.

## ECHEVERIA ELEGANS
Tender, evergreen succulent with rosettes of spoon-shaped, silvery-blue leaves. During late winter and through to late spring it displays pink flowers tipped yellow and orange-yellow on the inside.

*Sow seed* at 17°C in spring.
*Softwood or leaf cuttings* in free-draining compost in early summer.
🗍 *Remove offsets* in spring and pot up in cactus compost.

## ECHINACEA PURPUREA (Cone flower)
Perennial with hairy basal leaves and lance-shaped, pale green stem leaves. The flowerheads are 10cm across with purple-red ray-florets and cone-shaped, golden-brown disc-florets.

*Sow seed* at 13°C in spring.
🗍 *Divide* carefully in autumn with the minimum of root disturbance.
*Root cuttings* in early winter in a garden frame.

## ECHINOPS RITRO (Globe thistle)

Perennial with stiff, spiny, 20cm long, dark green leaves that are white and downy on the underside. Metallic-blue, spherical flowerheads mature to bright blue during late summer.

***Sow seed*** in open ground in late spring.
🔟 ***Divide*** perennials in late autumn or winter.
***Root cuttings*** in winter in a garden frame. Choose roots that are of pencil thickness.

## ECHIUM PININANA

Evergreen biennial with lance-shaped, hairy leaves. In mid-to late summer it produces a 2–4m high flower spike with masses of funnel-shaped, pale blue flowers.

***Sow seed*** at 15°C in summer and overwinter with frost protection. Self-seeds readily.

## EDGEWORTHIA CHRYSANTHA
(Paper bush)

Deciduous shrub with 15cm long, lance-shaped, dark green leaves. Dense clusters of fragrant, bright yellow flowers covered in silky, silver hairs appear during late winter and spring.

***Sow seed*** as soon as it is ripe. Overwinter the seedlings in a greenhouse protected from late spring frosts.
🔟 ***Semi-ripe cuttings*** in summer with a 'heel'. Shorten the leaves to reduce transpiration.

## EDRAIANTHUS PUMILIO (Grassy bells)

Perennial with tiny, linear, silvery-green leaves and bell-shaped, violet-blue, upturned flowers in summer.

***Sow seed*** in a garden frame in autumn.
🔟 ***Softwood cuttings*** of side shoots without flower buds in early summer.

## ELAEAGNUS PUNGENS

Evergreen shrub with spiny branches and 10cm long, glossy, dark green, wavy-edged leaves that are white on the underside. Pendant silvery-white flowers appear in autumn, followed by red fruit.

***Sow seed*** in a garden frame in autumn.
***Softwood cuttings*** in early summer.
🔟 ***Semi-ripe cuttings*** in late summer. Make the cut immediately below a leaf rather than with a 'heel'.
***Semi-ripe cuttings*** of deciduous species such as *E. commutata* in midsummer.
***Saddle graft*** cultivars in winter.
***Rooted suckers*** in autumn. Pot them up for a year in a soil-based compost. Stand the pots outside in a sheltered part of the garden.

Echinops ritro 'Veitch's Blue'

### ELSHOLTZIA STAUNTONII
Deciduous sub-shrub with 15cm long, mid-green, mint-scented leaves that turn red in autumn. Terminal racemes of tiny, pink-purple flowers are produced in late summer and autumn.

*Sow seed* at 12°C in autumn.
🔟 *Softwood cuttings* in summer. Reduce the leaf length by half and cover with horticultural fleece.

### EMBOTHRIUM COCCINEUM
(Chilean fire bush)
Evergreen tree or shrub with lance-shaped, deep green, 12cm long leaves. The racemes of scarlet flowers are produced during late spring and early summer.

*Sow seed* at 15°C in spring in moist, ericaceous compost.
🔟 *Softwood cuttings* in early summer.
*Semi-ripe cuttings* in late summer in a propagator.
*Root cuttings* in late winter in a garden frame.
*Rooted suckers* in winter. Take great care when removing suckers. Select short suckers and make sure that some roots are attached. Pot up and keep in a sheltered and shaded area for a few weeks.

### ENKIANTHUS CAMPANULATUS
Deciduous shrub with dull green leaves clustered at the tips of the stems. They turn orange and red in early autumn. In late spring and early summer it produces pendant racemes of bell-shaped, cream flowers with pink veins.

*Sow seed* at 20°C in early spring. Do not cover the seeds.
🔟 *Semi-ripe cuttings* in midsummer in ericaceous compost.
*Layer* in early autumn.

### EOMECON CHIONANTHA (Snow poppy)
Perennial with 10cm long, leathery, dull greyish-green, heart-shaped leaves. The loose panicles of glistening, pure white flowers that are 5cm across appear in late spring and early summer.

*Sow seed* in a garden frame in spring.
*Divide* in early spring.
🔟 *Irishman's cutting* Tease out rooted plantlets in late spring.

### EPACRIS IMPRESSA (Australian heath)
Tender, evergreen shrub with deep green leaves with pointed tips. The cylindrical, white, pink or red flowers are pendant and appear in spring and summer.

*Sow seed* on the surface of well-drained compost at 16°C in spring. Germination may take 3–6 months.
🔟 *Semi-ripe cuttings* in summer with bottom heat.

### EPILOBIUM ANGUSTIFOLIUM F. ALBUM
(Willow herb)
Perennial with lance-shaped, willow-like, mid-green leaves. The racemes of saucer-shaped, white flowers with pale green sepals appear in summer and early autumn.

Before you propagate, bear in mind that this plant quickly becomes an invasive weed.
🔟 *Divide* in spring.
*Softwood cuttings* from side shoots in late spring.

### EPIMEDIUM GRANDIFLORUM
(Barrenwort)
Perennial with 30cm long, spiny-edged, light green leaflets. When they first open, the young leaves are bronze. The pendant, white, yellow, pink or mauve flowers have long spurs and are produced in mid- to late spring.

*Sow seed* in a garden frame as soon as it is ripe.
*Divide* after flowering in early summer.
🔟 *Divide* rhizomes in autumn and root in a propagator.

### EPIPHYLLUM CRENATUM
(Orchid cactus)
Tender cactus with leaf-like, green-grey, 10cm wide branches. The funnel-shaped, 20cm long, fragrant, summer flowers are creamy-yellow with pink or greenish-yellow outer segments.

*Sow seed* at 20°C in late spring in cactus compost.
🔟 *Softwood stem cuttings* in early summer. Allow the wound to dry for a day before inserting the cutting in cactus compost.

### EPIPREMNUM PICTUM 'ARGYRAEUM'
Tender evergreen climber with smooth, deep green leaves marked with silver spots; the undersides are pale green and unmarked.

🔟 *Softwood tip cuttings* in a propagator in summer.
*Layer* in summer.

### ERANTHIS HYEMALIS (Winter aconite)
Tuberous perennial with a cluster of bright green leaves during late winter and early spring. A single bright, butter-yellow flower is produced in the centre of each group of leaves in late winter and early spring. Thrives in alkaline soil.

*Sow seed* in a garden frame in late spring.
🔟 *Divide* tubers in late spring after flowering.

### EREMURUS ROBUSTUS (Foxtail lily)
Perennial with strap-shaped, bluish-green, 1.2m long leaves. Tall, 60–120cm high racemes of pale pink flowers with yellow stamens are produced in early summer.

**Sow seed** in a garden frame in autumn but don't hang around waiting for the seedlings to flower – they may take 5–6 years.

🔲 **Divide** after flowering and when the leaves have died down.

## ERICA CARNEA (Heath, Heather)
Evergreen shrub with linear, dark green leaves and small, urn-shaped, dark pink flowers in late winter and early spring.

**Semi-ripe cuttings** in midsummer.

🔲 **Drop layer** in late spring.

## ERIGERON ALPINUS (Flea bane)
Perennial with spoon-shaped, hairy, mid-green leaves. Red-mauve to lilac flowers with pale yellow disc-florets are produced in summer.

**Sow seed** in a garden frame in late spring.

🔲 **Softwood basal cuttings** in spring.
**Divide** in early spring.

Eremurus robustus

## ERINACEA ANTHYLLIS
(Hedgehog broom)
Evergreen sub-shrub with spine-tipped stems and palmate, dark grey-green leaves. In late spring and early summer it produces clusters of pink-blue flowers with white-marked, standard petals.

**Sow seed** in a garden frame in autumn.

🔲 **Softwood cuttings** in early summer, taken with a 'heel', work for me.

## ERINUS ALPINUS (Fairy foxglove)
Semi-evergreen perennial with rosettes of wedge-shaped, sticky, dark green leaves. Racemes of small, white, pink or purple flowers are produced in late spring and early summer.

**Sow seed** in a garden frame in autumn.

🔲 **Softwood cuttings** of rosettes in spring in well-drained compost.

## ERIOBOTRYA JAPONICA (Loquat)
Evergreen shrub or tree with 30cm long, deeply veined, glossy, dark green leaves. Large panicles of fragrant, white flowers are produced from autumn to winter, followed by pear-shaped, orange-yellow, edible fruit.

**Sow seed** at 13°C in spring.

🔲 **Semi-ripe cuttings** in summer. Shorten the leaves by three-quarters to reduce transpiration. Cover the cuttings with clear polythene.

## ERIOGONUM GRACILIPES
(Sulphur flower)
Perennial with green-grey, white-woolly leaves with the margins rolled downwards. Tiny umbels of pink-tinted, white flowers are produced in early summer.

**Sow seed** in a garden frame in autumn.

🔲 **Softwood cuttings** in early summer. Water from below to avoid damaging the leaves.

## ERIOPHYLLUM LANATUM
(Golden yarrow)
Perennial with white-woolly, silver-grey leaves. Basal leaves are spoon-shaped. Masses of bright-yellow, daisy-like flowerheads are produced from late spring to late autumn.

**Sow seed** in a garden frame in autumn. Transplant seedlings when small.

🔲 **Divide** in spring.

## ERITRICHIUM NANUM
(Alpine forget-me-not)
Perennial with rosettes of tiny, silvery-grey-green leaves. The pale blue, tubular flowers have bright yellow eyes and are produced in late spring and early summer.

**Sow seed** in a garden frame in autumn.

🔲 **Softwood basal cuttings** in midsummer. Small, 2–5cm long cuttings are easier to root.

For either method, use an infertile, free-draining cactus compost.

## ERODIUM CHRYSANTHUM
(Stork's bill)
Perennial with silvery-green, lance-shaped leaflets. Umbels of saucer-shaped, pale yellow flowers are produced during summer.

**Sow seed** as soon as it is ripe in early autumn in a garden frame.

🔲 **Softwood basal cuttings** in early summer.
**Divide** in early spring.

## ERYNGIUM GIGANTEUM
(Miss Willmott's ghost, Sea holly)
Perennial with dark green, heart-shaped basal leaves and spiny stem leaves. During summer, cylindrical umbels of prickly, pale green flowers mature to steel-blue with sharp-toothed, silvery-blue bracts.

**Sow seed** outside in the garden or in an open garden frame as soon as it is ripe and allow the compost to become frosted. Overwinter in a garden frame. Plant out the young seedlings before the tap root forms.
- **Root cuttings** in late winter in a garden frame.
  **Divide** in spring and grow in a pot of well-drained, soil-based compost for a year.

## ERYSIMUM 'BOWLES' MAUVE'
(Wallflower)
Evergreen, woody perennial with lance-shaped, grey-green leaves and racemes of mauve flowers from mid-winter to late summer. Others of this genus may be annuals or biennials.

- **Sow seed** in a garden frame in spring. With biennials, sow in early summer in open ground. Transplant to flowering position in late autumn.
- **Softwood cuttings** with a 'heel' in late spring and summer.

## ERYTHRINA CRISTA-GALLI
(Common coral tree)
Tender, deciduous tree with spiny branches and leathery, light green, 30cm long leaves comprising 3 leaflets. Terminal racemes, 30–60cm long, of deep red flowers appear during summer and autumn. In cooler climates this tree can be grown as a woody-based perennial.

- **Sow seed** in spring at 24°C.
- **Softwood cuttings** in early summer in a propagator.
  **Semi-ripe cuttings** in early autumn with bottom heat.

## ERYTHRONIUM DENS-CANIS
(Dog's tooth violet, Trout lily)
Perennial with 10–15cm long, mid-green leaves blotched purple-brown. The solitary, white, pink or purple flowers have purple anthers and are produced in spring.

**Sow seed** as soon as it is ripe, in a garden frame.
- **Divide** congested clumps after flowering in early summer.

## ESCALLONIA 'PRIDE OF DONARD'
Evergreen shrub with glossy, dark green leaves and short racemes of bright, carmine-red flowers in summer.

- **Softwood cuttings** in early summer. **Semi-ripe cuttings** in late summer. **Hardwood cuttings** in late autumn and winter.
  **Layer** in late spring.

## ESCHSCHOLZIA CALIFORNICA
(Californian poppy)
Annual with lance-shaped, blue-green leaves 15–20cm long. The bright, summer flowers are mainly orange but can be white, yellow or red. They are followed by long, thin seed pods.

**Sow seed** in mid-spring in open ground where it is to flower. To extend the flowering period, sow every 14 days. Don't penny-pinch by saving your own seed for more than a couple of years, as the plants will all revert to orange.

## EUCALYPTUS GUNNII (Cider gum)
Evergreen tree with green-white bark that peels to reveal yellow-grey new bark. The juvenile leaves are glaucous, mid-green and rounded. Adult leaves are lance-shaped, 5–8cm long and grey-green. In summer and autumn it produces masses of creamy-white flowers.

**Sow seed** at 15°C in early summer. Do not cover with compost. Germination may be speeded up by storing the freshly collected seed (harvested in spring) at room temperature for 2 weeks. If you are using bought seed, check the packet to make sure it is from trees grown at a high altitude, so that your seedlings will be hardy.

## EUCHARIS × GRANDIFLORA
(Amazon lily)
Tender, bulbous, evergreen perennial with wavy, deep green leaves 30cm long. In early summer it produces 4–6 pendant, white flowers with long stamens on a stem 60cm high.

- **Remove offsets** in late summer after flowering. Pot up and grow at 15°C until well established.

## EUCOMIS BICOLOR (Pineapple flower)
Bulbous perennial with 30–50cm long, strap-shaped, light green leaves. The flower stems are maroon and speckled; the racemes of light green flowers have purple-margined petals.

**Sow seed** at 15°C in autumn and it will be in flower within 3 years.
- **Remove offsets** in late spring and plant in well-drained soil in a sheltered part of the garden.

## EUCRYPHIA LUCIDA
Evergreen tree with a columnar habit and glossy, dark green leaves, glaucous on the underside. It produces pure white, saucer-shaped flowers in early and midsummer.

**Sow seed** in a garden frame as soon as it is ripe.
- **Semi-ripe cuttings** in midsummer under clear polythene.

## EUONYMUS FORTUNEI (Spindle)
Evergreen shrub with leathery, dark green, 5cm long leaves. Small, greenish-white flowers are followed in autumn by small, white fruit that split to reveal seed with red arils.

**Sow seed** in a garden frame as soon as it is ripe. Germination will take place the following spring.
- **Semi-ripe cuttings** in summer.

Eschscholzia californica

**Softwood cuttings** of deciduous species such as *E. europaeus* 'Red Cascade' in early summer.

## EUPATORIUM CANNABINUM
(Hemp agrimony)
Perennial with thin, red stems and 10cm wide, dark green leaves. Panicles of white, pink or purple flowers appear during summer and autumn.

▢ **Sow seed** in a garden frame in spring. **Divide** in late spring.

Euphorbia characias

## EUPHORBIA CHARACIAS (Spurge)
Evergreen shrub with woolly, purple-tinged stems and grey-green leaves that are 10cm long. Green involucres (rings of bracts) surround the masses of green-yellow cyathia (the name given to the flowerlike growths of the spurges), each with purple-brown nectar glands.

**Sow seed** of perennials in a garden frame in early spring to allow the young plants to become sufficiently large to withstand the winter. Small plants should be overwintered in a garden frame.
**Softwood tip cuttings** in early summer in a propagator.
**Divide** in early spring.
▢ **Softwood basal cuttings** in early summer. Dip the cut surface in warm water or in powdered charcoal to prevent bleeding.
**Stem sections** (similar to a stem cutting but with no leaves): root 5–7.5cm long sections of stems of tender succulents in gritty compost in spring.

## EURYOPS ACRAEUS
Evergreen shrub with leathery, silvery-grey, flattened leaves and deep yellow flowers in late spring and early summer.

**Sow seed** in spring at 15°C.
▢ **Softwood cuttings** in late spring under horticultural fleece.
**Semi-ripe cuttings** with a 'heel' in late summer.

## EXACUM AFFINE (Persian violet)
Evergreen perennial usually grown as an annual, with 4-angled (square) stems and shiny, dark green leaves. In summer it produces blue, pink or white, fragrant flowers with conspicuous stamens.

**Sow seed** at 17°C in early spring. Seedlings are subject to damping off caused by bad drainage and disease. Water with Cheshunt compound, using tap water rather than rainwater. Plant out when all risk of frost has passed.

## EXOCHORDA × MACRANTHA 'THE BRIDE' (Pearl bush)
Deciduous shrub with 8cm long, mid-green leaves. In late spring and early summer it produces racemes of saucer-shaped, pure white flowers on arching stems.

**Sow seed** in open ground in autumn.
▢ **Softwood cuttings** with a 'heel' in midsummer.

## FABIANA IMBRICATA
Evergreen shrub with tiny, needle-like, deep green leaves. Tubular, white to pale mauve flowers are produced in summer.

**Sow seed** in a garden frame in autumn or in late spring.
▢ **Softwood cuttings** in early summer under horticultural fleece.
**Semi-ripe cuttings** in late summer. Space the cuttings 5cm apart to allow air to circulate.

## FAGUS SYLVATICA (Common beech)
Deciduous tree. The silky, hairy, pale green, 10cm long leaves turn glossy, dark green in early summer with autumn shades of yellow and orange-brown. In autumn the segmented capsules contain the nuts.

▣ **Sow seed** thinly in open ground in autumn.
**Saddle graft** cultivars in winter.

## FALLOPIA BALDSCHUANICUM
(Mile-a-minute, Russian vine)
Deciduous climber with heart-shaped, 10cm long, dark green leaves. The panicles of tiny, pink-tinged, white flowers appear in late summer and autumn, followed by pinkish-white fruit.

**Sow seed** in spring in a garden frame.
**Semi-ripe cuttings** in midsummer.

J **Hardwood cuttings** in autumn. A word of warning, though: do remember to transplant them after 12 months. A few years ago, I inserted 6 hardwood cuttings for a friend and forgot about them for 18 months. Such a mess. They were everywhere and one had had the cheek to layer itself!

## FARGESIA NITIDA (Fountain bamboo)
Evergreen bamboo with purple-green canes and narrow, lance-shaped, dark green leaves.

**Divide** clumps in spring.
J **Cut rhizomes** into 15cm lengths in spring and root in seed compost with added leaf mould. Don't let them dry out during the first year.

## FASCICULARIA PITCAIRNIIFOLIA
Evergreen perennial with glaucous, mid-green leaves edged with spines. The inner rosettes turn bright red in summer with the bright blue flowers in the centre.

**Sow seed** at 25°C in late winter or early spring. Germination may be erratic.
J **Remove rooted offsets** in late spring and pot into free-draining compost. Make sure you wear gloves to protect your hands from the spines along the leaf edges.

## × FATSHEDERA LIZEI
(Tree ivy, Aralia ivy)
Evergreen shrub with large, palmate, glossy, dark green leaves and panicles of sterile, greenish-white flowers in autumn.

J **Softwood cuttings** in summer or early autumn, taken with a 'heel'. Shorten the leaves to reduce the risk of transpiration. Softwood cuttings taken earlier in summer will need to be kept in a propagator.

Fatsia japonica

## FATSIA JAPONICA (Japanese aralia)
Evergreen, suckering shrub with large, palmate, glossy, dark green leaves that are 15–45cm long. In autumn it produces umbels of creamy-white flowers followed by small black fruit.

**Sow seed** at 20°C as soon as it is ripe in spring.
J **Softwood cuttings** in early summer.
**Air layer** in spring. Support the layer with a bamboo cane to stop it blowing about in the wind.

## FELICIA AMELLOIDES (Blue daisy)
Tender, evergreen sub-shrub often grown as an annual with deep green leaves and deep blue, daisy-like flowers from summer to autumn.

**Sow seed** of annuals at 15°C in spring.
J **Semi-ripe tip cuttings** in late summer. Remove any flower buds as they show. Overwinter with frost protection.

## FERULA COMMUNIS (Giant fennel)
Perennial with pinnate leaves that are 20–45cm long. Large umbels of bright yellow flowers appear in early and midsummer.

**Sow seed** as soon as it is ripe in a garden frame. Transplant seedlings early before the long tap root develops. Practically every seed will germinate, so sow thinly.

## FESTUCA GLAUCA (Blue fescue)
Evergreen, perennial grass with smooth, inward-curling blue-green leaves. In early summer it bears panicles with spikelets of blue-green flowers.

**Sow seed** in autumn or spring in a garden frame.
J **Divide** in late spring.

### FICUS CARICA (Fig)
Deciduous tree with 3–5 lobed, bright green leaves. The single, green, edible fruit matures to purple or dark green.

🌙 *Hardwood cuttings* in mid-winter in a propagator.
*Layer* in summer.

### FICUS ELASTICA (Rubber tree)
Tender evergreen tree with leathery, glossy, dark green leaves that are 30–45cm long and occasionally tinted red. Small, yellow fruit are produced in autumn on mature trees.

*Sow seed* at 20°C in spring.
🌙 *Leaf bud cuttings* in summer in a propagator. Instead of cutting the leaf, roll it along the main vein and secure with an elastic band. This will reduce transpiration and take up less space.
*Air layer* in late summer.

### FILIPENDULA PALMATA
(Meadowsweet)
Perennial with long, palmate, mid-green leaves, white and woolly on the underside. Corymbs (flat-topped flower clusters) of feathery, deep pink flowers appear in summer and early autumn.

*Sow seed* in autumn in a garden frame or in spring at 12°C.
🌙 *Divide* in autumn or early spring.
*Root cuttings* in early spring laid horizontally on free-draining compost in a garden frame and covered with 1cm deep compost.

### FITTONIA VERSCHAFFELTII GROUP
(Nerve plant)
Tender, evergreen perennial with olive-green leaves and sunken red veins.

*Softwood tip cuttings* in late spring. Shorten leaves by half. Use free-draining compost.
🌙 *Layer* in summer.

### FOENICULUM VULGARE (Fennel)
Perennial with long, aniseed-flavoured, mid-green leaves. Umbels of tiny, yellow flowers are produced in mid- to late summer followed by aromatic seeds.

🌙 *Sow seed* in open ground in spring and thin out the seedlings. Don't try transplanting them, unless, like me, you dislike fennel – they will wither and die!
*Divide* in early spring, replanting small portions.

### FORSYTHIA SUSPENSA (Golden bells)
Deciduous shrub with 10cm long, mid-green leaves and clusters of bright yellow flowers in early to mid-spring.

*Softwood cuttings* in early summer.
*Semi-ripe cuttings* in late summer.
🌙 *Hardwood cuttings* in winter.

Forsythia roots like a weed by any method.

### FOTHERGILLA MAJOR
Deciduous shrub with glossy, dark green leaves that turn yellow, orange and red in autumn. Terminal spikes of fragrant, white or pink-tinged flowers appear in late spring before the leaves.

*Sow seed* in a garden frame in autumn. Germination will take 18 months.
*Semi-ripe cuttings* in late summer in a propagator. The secret of my success is to 'wound' the side of the cutting by removing a sliver of bark, about 2cm long, from the base up.
🌙 *Layer* in late summer.

### FRAGARIA (Strawberry)
Perennial with 3-palmate, bright green leaves. Clusters of white or pink flowers appear in late spring followed by bright red, edible fruit in summer.

*Remove rooted plantlets (runners)* and transplant in late summer, resulting in lots of well-rooted young plants and worthwhile fruit the following summer.

### FRANCOA SONCHIFOLIA
(Bridal wreath)
Evergreen perennial with deeply lobed basal leaves. Racemes of deep pink buds open in midsummer to pink flowers with deeper pink markings.

*Sow seed* at 16°C in spring.
🌙 *Divide* in spring.

### FRANKLINIA ALATAMAHA
Deciduous tree with 15cm long, glossy, dark green leaves that turn red in autumn. In late summer and autumn, cup-shaped, fragrant, white flowers with yellow stamens are produced followed by woody, spherical fruit.

*Foeniculum vulgare*

*Sow seed* as soon as it is ripe at 16°C.
*Softwood cuttings* in summer in a
propagator.
◪ *Hardwood cuttings* in early winter.
I have better success when I set the
base of the cuttings on a deep, 5cm
layer of coarse grit.

### FRAXINUS EXCELSIOR (Ash)
Deciduous tree with black winter
growth buds and pinnate, dark green
leaves that turn yellow in autumn.
The flowers are insignificant and
are followed by clusters of single
winged seeds.

◪ *Seed* Store seed in a refrigerator for
8–10 weeks before sowing in a garden
frame or outside in the open ground.
Alternatively, sow in a garden frame
immediately the seed is ripe. Self-
sown seedlings can become a weed
problem, so dig them up as soon as
you notice them.
*Saddle graft* cultivars in spring on
rootstocks of the species.

### FREESIA
Cormous perennial with lance-shaped
basal leaves. Racemes of brightly
coloured, frequently fragrant, funnel-
shaped flowers are produced in late
summer and autumn.

◪ *Seed* Chip the seed or soak in hot water
(not boiling) for 12 hours; discard any
seeds that float. Sow at 18°C in
autumn. Keep the compost moist.
*Remove offsets* in autumn and sow
immediately in containers of multi-
purpose compost in a garden frame.

### FREMONTODENDRON
### CALIFORNICUM (Flannel bush)
Evergreen shrub with rounded, lobed,
dark green leaves. Saucer-shaped, bright
yellow flowers are produced from late
spring to late autumn.

Fremontodendron californicum

*Sow seed* at 18°C in spring. Plants raised
from seed are inferior to the species.

Wear gloves when handling cuttings: the
leaves and stems may irritate the skin.
◪ *Softwood cuttings* in early summer.
Remove any flower buds. Overwinter
the cuttings in a garden frame.
*Semi-ripe cuttings* in late summer.

### FRITILLARIA MELEAGRIS
(Snake's head fritillary)
Bulbous perennial with linear, grey-
green leaves. In spring pendant, bell-
shaped, white, pink or pink-purple
flowers with deep purple markings are
produced.

◪ *Sow seed* in autumn in a container
without protection. After germination
in spring, move to a garden frame.
Grow on in a container for 2 years.
*Divide offsets* in late summer and plant
them in a soil-based compost with
added leaf mould in a garden frame.
Grow them in pots for 2 years, then
plant out in the garden where they will
flower the following year.

### FUCHSIA MAGELLANICA
Deciduous shrub with toothed, mid-
green leaves. In summer it produces
pendant flowers with red tubes, wide
spreading sepals and purple corollas,
followed by red-purple fruit.

*Sow seed* at 16°C in spring.
◪ *Softwood cuttings* in spring. Small,
2–4cm long cuttings will root quickly.
Nip out any flower buds.
*Semi-ripe cuttings* in late summer in
a propagator.

### GAILLARDIA ARISTATA (Blanket flower)
Perennial with 20cm long, grey-green
leaves. In summer and autumn it
produces flowers with yellow ray-florets
and red-orange disc-florets.

*Sow seed* at 16°C in early spring.
(Although they are classed as
perennials, many species will flower in
their first year from an early sowing.)
◪ *Divide* in spring.
*Root cuttings* in winter in a garden
frame.

**GALANTHUS NIVALIS** (Snowdrop)
Bulbous perennial with narrow, glaucous leaves. In winter it produces pendant, pure white, fragrant flowers with an inverted V-shaped green mark on the tip of each inner tepal (petal).

*Sow seed* from species as soon as it is ripe in containers outside. With luck they will flower within 3 years.
E *Divide* clumps of bulbs as soon as the flowers fade, while the leaves are still green. Remove the flower stems to prevent seeds forming.

**GALEGA ORIENTALIS** (Goat's rue)
Perennial with soft green leaves that have sharp tips. It produces racemes of blue-violet flowers in late spring and early summer.

*Sow seed* in a garden frame in spring. Soak the seed in tepid water for 12 hours before sowing.
꘎ *Divide* in late autumn or spring.

**GALIUM ODORATUM** (Sweet woodruff)
Perennial with lance-shaped, bright green leaves. Scented, white, star-shaped flowers appear in late spring and early summer.

*Sow seed* in a garden frame as soon as it is ripe.
꘎ *Divide* rhizomes in autumn. Protect foliage from strong sunlight.

**GALTONIA CANDICANS**
(Summer hyacinth)
Bulbous perennial with lance-shaped, 50–90cm long, grey-green leaves. In late summer it produces tall racemes of fragrant, white flowers with a hint of green at the base.

*Sow seed* in a garden frame as soon as it is ripe or wait until late spring. Keep the young plants in containers for 2–3 years with protection from frost.
꘎ *Separate offsets* in early spring and replant immediately.

**GARDENIA AUGUSTA** (Cape jasmine)
Tender, evergreen shrub with whorls of 3 glossy, 10cm long, deep green leaves. Ivory-white flowers are produced from summer to autumn.

*Sow seed* at 24°C in spring.
*Softwood cuttings* in late spring or early summer. I strike small cuttings with 4 leaves and remove the bottom pair. To water, stand the container in a saucer of rainwater. Cover the container with clear polythene.
꘎ *Semi-ripe cuttings* in late summer in a propagator.

**GARRYA ELLIPTICA** (Silk tassel bush)
Evergreen shrub with wavy-edged, grey-green leaves that are matt or glossy. Pendant, grey-green, male catkins with yellow anthers, 15–20cm long, are produced in late winter and spring.

*Garrya elliptica*

*Sow seed* in a garden frame in spring.
꘎ *Semi-ripe cuttings* in summer with a 'heel'. Don't pot the rooted cuttings until the following spring.

**GASTERIA CARINATA VAR. VERRUCOSA**
Tender, perennial succulent with opposite, 3-angled (triangular in section), lance-shaped, grey-green leaves with white markings. Racemes of reddish-yellow flowers appear in late spring and summer.

*Sow seed* at 20°C in spring or summer.
꘎ *Remove offsets* and root in cactus compost during summer and early autumn.
*Leaf cuttings* in cactus compost in summer.

**GAULTHERIA MUCRONATA SYN. PERNETTYA MUCRONATA**
Evergreen shrub with small, dark green, glossy leaves with spine tips. Urn-shaped, white flowers appear in spring. Female plants produce white, rose-pink, crimson or purple fruit in autumn.

*Sow seed* in a garden frame in spring, in ericaceous compost.
꘎ *Semi-ripe cuttings* in summer.
*Rooted suckers* in spring. If the sucker is straggly, reduce its height by half. Pot up in ericaceous compost and stand outside in the garden.

**GAURA LINDHEIMERI**
Perennial with lance-shaped, dark green leaves. From spring to late summer the panicles of pinkish-white buds open early in the morning to pure white flowers.

*Sow seed* in a garden frame in late spring.
*Softwood cuttings* in spring.
꘎ *Semi-ripe cuttings* in summer. Propagate from basal cuttings taken with a 'heel'.
*Divide* in early spring.

### GAZANIA CHANSONETTE SERIES

Tender, evergreen perennial with glossy, dark green leaves that are silky-haired on the underside. The solitary flowerheads are various colours including yellow, orange, bronze or rose-pink, zoned in a contrasting colour during late summer and autumn.

*Sow seed* at 20°C in late winter or early spring.

🗓 *Softwood basal cuttings* in late summer. Shorten the length of the leaves to reduce transpiration. Overwinter with frost protection and pot the rooted cuttings in late spring.

### GENISTA HISPANICA (Spanish gorse)

Deciduous shrub with spiny branches and mid-green leaves that are silky on the underside. The leaves are only present on the flowering stems. The clusters of golden-yellow flowers appear in late spring and early summer.

*Sow seed* in a garden frame in spring.

🗓 *Semi-ripe cuttings* in summer. Try to keep the cuttings growing and get them potted before late autumn.

### GENTIANA ACAULIS (Trumpet gentian)

Evergreen perennial with rosettes of lance-shaped, glossy, dark green leaves. Deep blue, trumpet-shaped flowers with green spots on the inside are produced in late spring and early summer.

*Sow seed* as soon as it is ripe, in containers in an open garden frame to allow frost to penetrate the compost. Do not cover the seed, as it benefits from daylight.

🗓 *Remove offsets* in spring and root in gritty compost.

*Divide* large clumps carefully in early spring.

### GERANIUM PRATENSE

(Meadow cranesbill)

Perennial with lobed, 20cm long, dull green basal leaves. Saucer-shaped, white, blue or violet flowers with coloured veins are produced in early summer.

*Sow hardy species* outdoors in containers in spring.

*Sow tender species* such as *G. maderense* at 18°C in spring.

🗓 *Softwood basal cuttings* in early spring in a propagator.

*Divide* in early spring, taking care not to damage the young shoots.

### GERBERA JAMESONII (Barberton daisy)

Tender perennial with deeply-lobed, lance-shaped, 20–45cm long, dark green leaves, woolly on the underside. Daisy-like, solitary, orange-red flowers with yellow centres are produced in summer.

*Sow seed* at 18°C in early spring.

🗓 *Softwood basal cuttings* in midsummer under horticultural fleece. Reduce the length of the leaves to prevent transpiration.

*Divide* in early spring. As it resents transplanting, replant in containers of free-draining compost until autumn to allow the plants to recover, make roots and start growing.

### GEUM CHILOENSE (Avens)

Perennial with pinnate, 15–30cm long basal leaves and toothed and lobed stem leaves. During summer it produces saucer-shaped, scarlet flowers.

*Sow seed* in a garden frame in autumn or spring.

🗓 *Divide* in autumn or spring.

Gaultheria mucronata

Ginkgo biloba 'Fastigiata'

## GILIA CAPITATA
(Queen Anne's thimbles)
Annual with feathery, bright green leaves and pincushion flowerheads consisting of masses of small, lavender-blue flowers during summer.

*Sow seed* outside in open ground in autumn or late spring.

## GILLENIA TRIFOLIATA (Indian physic)
Perennial with red-tinted stems and deeply veined, bronze-green leaves. In late spring and early summer it produces star-shaped, white or pinkish-white flowers.

*Sow seed* in a garden frame in autumn or spring.
⬛ *Divide* in late spring.

## GINKGO BILOBA (Maidenhair tree)
Deciduous conifer with flat, yellow-green, fan-shaped, 7–12cm across leaves that colour to butter-yellow in autumn. The clusters of male flowers are pendulous, catkin-like and yellow. Female flowers are solitary and produce green-yellow fruit in autumn that gives off a bad smell as it rots. The large nuts are edible.

*Seed* As soon as the fruit falls, soak the seed in boiling water and leave in the cooling water for 24 hours. Sow the seed at 20°C. Alternatively, sow the seed in a garden frame. Germination can take up to 6 months, no matter which method you use, so be patient.
⬛ *Semi-ripe cuttings* in summer.

## GLADIOLUS
Cormous perennial with erect, basal fans of lance-shaped, mid-green leaves. The flower spikes appear in spring or summer with funnel-shaped flowers in a wide range of colours. The flowers open from the bottom of the spike upwards with the old flowers dying as the new buds open.

*Sow seed* of hardy species in containers in a garden frame in spring.
🅔 *Divide cormlets* when the plant is dormant and sow immediately. The cormlets will become flowering corms within 3–4 years.

## GLAUCIDIUM PALMATUM
Perennial with lobed, light green, crinkly surfaced leaves that are 20–30cm long. In late spring and early summer it produces pink or mauve tepals with golden stamens.

*Sow seed* in a garden frame in spring.
⬛ *Divide* clumps in late winter. Take care not to damage the young roots. Dump the old centre of the plant.

## GLAUCIUM FLAVUM (Horned poppy)
Perennial usually grown as a biennial with rough, glaucous, blue-green leaves that are 15–30cm long. In summer it produces grey stems of bright yellow or orange flowers.

*Sow seed* in open ground in spring.

## GLECHOMA HEDERACEA 'VARIEGATA'
(Variegated ground ivy)
Evergreen perennial with trailing stems of soft green leaves marbled with pure white. Whorls of lilac-mauve flowers are produced in summer.

*Softwood cuttings* in late spring.
⬛ *Divide* in autumn.

## GLEDITSIA TRIACANTHOS
(Honey locust)
Deciduous tree with spiny stems and glossy, dark green, pinnate leaves that turn yellow in autumn. Racemes of greenish-white, spring flowers are followed by pendant, sickle-shaped, twisted seed pods.

⬛ *Seed* Sow scarified seed in a garden frame in autumn. Alternatively, soak in boiling water and allow to cool for 24 hours and sow in spring.
*Whip and tongue graft* cultivars in late winter.

## GLOBULARIA REPENS (Globe daisy)
Evergreen perennial with spoon-shaped, glossy, dark green leaves. In summer it produces lavender-blue flowers.

⬛ *Sow seed* in a garden frame in autumn.
*Softwood rosettes* in late spring or early summer in free-draining, alkaline compost. Water from the base of the container, keeping the rosettes dry.

## GLORIOSA SUPERBA

Climbing perennial with lance-shaped, glossy, bright green leaves that taper to form tip tendrils. During summer and autumn flowers form in the upper leaf axils. They comprise 6 wavy-edged, orange-red or red-purple petals, sometimes margined in yellow, with extended stamens.

*Sow seed* at 22°C in spring.
- *Divide* the long, thin tubers in spring. Don't allow the tubers to dry out.

## GLYCERIA MAXIMA 'VARIEGATA'

Aquatic, perennial grass with white, cream and green-striped leaves that are 30–60cm long. Panicles of purple-green spikelets appear in late summer.

*Divide* in late spring.

## GLYCYRRHIZA GLABRA (Liquorice)

Perennial with pinnate, mid-green, sticky leaves. Panicles of blue and white, pea-like flowers are produced in late summer. Its roots are the source of liquorice.

*Sow seed* in containers outside in spring.
- *Hardwood cuttings,* 15cm long, of the hard, horizontal stolons in spring. Ensure each piece has a growth bud.

## GOMPHRENA GLOBOSA

(Globe amaranth)
Annual with oblong, 15cm long, hairy leaves. From summer to autumn it produces white, pink or purple flowers.

*Sow seed* at 15°C in early spring. Transplant seedlings when young.

## GREVILLEA 'CANBERRA GEM'

Evergreen shrub with lance-shaped, grey-green to deep green leaves that are silky and downy on the underside. From late winter to late summer it produces racemes of waxy, pinkish-red flowers.

*Sow seed* at 16°C in spring. Pre-soak for 24 hours. Germination is erratic.
- *Semi-ripe cuttings* in midsummer. I thin out the clusters of thin leaves and cover the cuttings with horticultural fleece. Overwinter in a garden frame for the first winter.
*Saddle graft* in late summer.

## GRISELINIA LITTORALIS

Evergreen shrub with glossy, leathery, bright green, 10cm long leaves. In late spring it produces greenish-white flowers followed, after pollination, by purple fruit.

*Sow seed* at 16°C in spring.
- *Semi-ripe cuttings* in summer with a 'heel'. Nip out the growing tip.

## GUNNERA MANICATA

Perennial with prickly stalks and kidney-shaped, lobed and deeply veined, dark green leaves up to 1.8m across. In early summer it produces panicles of tiny, greenish-red flowers, up to 90cm high, followed by tiny, green-red fruit.

*Sow seed* as soon as it is ripe on the surface of the compost in a garden frame. Don't cover the seed with compost. Germination is slow and can be erratic. Don't store seed because it loses viability.

- Large sections layer themselves where they touch the ground. Cut through the thick stem with a spade and lift the rooted piece without damaging the fleshy roots.

## GUZMANIA LINGULATA

Bromeliad with rosettes of lance-shaped, 45cm long, deep green leaves often striped with red and purple. In summer it produces erect stems of pink, orange or bright red bracts surrounding tubular, white-yellow flowers.

*Sow seed* at 25°C in spring or early summer in an open, free-draining compost.

- *Remove offsets* in late spring and pot into an orchid compost. Keep in a shaded position at 15°C for 2–3 weeks, then move to better light.

## GYMNOCLADUS DIOICA

(Kentucky coffee tree)
Deciduous tree with large, 2-pinnate, dark green, 90cm long leaves that are pink-tinged when young and yellow in autumn. In early summer it produces large panicles of small, star-shaped, creamy-white flowers followed, on female plants, by 30cm long seed pods.

*Sow seed* in a garden frame in spring. Pre-soak the seed for 24 hours. Seed is toxic if ingested.
- *Root cuttings* in mid-winter in a garden frame. Choose sections of root that are slightly thicker than a pencil.

## GYPSOPHILA PANICULATA

(Baby's breath)
Perennial with lance-shaped, glaucous leaves. In mid- to late summer it produces panicles consisting of masses of tiny, trumpet-shaped, white flowers.

*Sow seed* at 18°C in winter. Alternatively, sow seed in a garden frame in spring.
- *Root cuttings* in late winter in a container in a garden frame.

Grevillea 'Canberra Gem'

### HABERLEA RHODOPENSIS

Evergreen perennial with rosettes of dark green, soft and hairy, scalloped leaves. Umbels of trumpet-shaped, pale blue flowers are produced in spring and early summer.

**Sow seed** at 16°C in spring.
- **Leaf cuttings** in early summer.
**Divide** in late spring.

### HABRANTHUS ROBUSTUS

Tender perennial. The deep green, 15–20cm long basal leaves appear in summer just before the funnel-shaped, solitary, pale pink flowers.

**Sow seed** at 16°C as soon as it is ripe.
- **Remove offsets** in early winter and pot up in well-drained, loam-based compost. Protect from frost.

### HACQUETIA EPIPACTIS

Perennial with glossy, evergreen leaves that expand after flowering. The umbels of tiny, bright yellow flowers appear in late winter and early spring and are surrounded by bright green bracts.

**Sow seed** as soon as it is ripe in a garden frame or wait until autumn.
**Root cuttings** in winter in a garden frame.
- **Divide** in early spring.

### HAKEA LISSOSPERMA

(Mountain hakea)
Tender, evergreen shrub or small tree. The 15cm long, grey-green leaves are leathery with spiny tips. Racemes of small, white, tubular flowers appear during spring and early summer followed by dark brown seed pods.

**Sow seed** singly in pots at 16°C as soon as it is ripe.
- **Semi-ripe cuttings** in summer in a propagator. Avoid unnecessary root disturbance.

Hacquetia epipactis 'Thor'

## HAKONECHLOA MACRA 'AUREOLA'
Perennial grass. The 20cm long, arching leaves are striped yellow and green with some red in autumn. Panicles of pale green spikelets appear in late summer.

- *Divide* in late spring.

## HALESIA MONTICOLA (Snowdrop tree)
Deciduous tree with downy, mid-green leaves that turn yellow in autumn. Clusters of pendant, bell-shaped, pure white flowers are produced in spring, usually before the leaves, and these are followed by 4-winged, green fruit.

- *Sow seed* at 18°C in autumn. After 8 weeks, move the container to a garden frame.
- *Softwood cuttings* in summer in a gritty, free-draining compost.
  *Layer* in spring, mounding up with ericaceous compost.

## X HALIMIOCISTUS SAHUCII
Evergreen shrub with lance-shaped, dark green leaves. In summer it produces saucer-shaped, white flowers with bright yellow centres.

- *Semi-ripe cuttings* in late summer with a 'heel'.

## HALIMIUM UMBELLATUM
Evergreen shrub with glossy, dark green leaves that are covered with white hairs on the underside. Racemes of red buds open in early summer to white flowers stained yellow at the base.

- *Sow seed* at 20°C in spring.
- *Semi-ripe cuttings* in late summer.

## HALIMODENDRON HALODENDRON
(Salt tree)
Deciduous shrub with spiny stems and spine-tipped, pinnate, silver-grey leaves. Purple-pink, pea-like flowers appear in midsummer.

Hakonechloa macra 'Aureola'

- *Sow seed* in a garden frame in spring or autumn in very well-drained, gritty compost.
- *Root cuttings* in early winter in a garden frame.
  *Layer* in autumn into well-drained, alkaline soil.
  *Whip and tongue graft* onto laburnum in early spring.

## HAMAMELIS MOLLIS
(Chinese witch hazel)
Deciduous shrub with oval, mid-green, soft and hairy leaves turning butter-yellow in autumn. The fragrant, golden-yellow flowers appear on the bare branches in mid- to late winter.

- *Sow seed* in a garden frame as soon as it is ripe. I have had great success over the years with home-saved seed.
  *Saddle graft* in late winter.

## HEBE 'AMY'
Also listed as H. 'Purple Queen'
Evergreen shrub. The dark green, 8cm long leaves are bronze-purple when young. The 5cm long spikes of violet-blue flowers appear in late summer.

- *Sow seed* in a garden frame as soon as it is ripe. The seedlings will be variable; select those with dark leaves.
- *Softwood cuttings* in early summer under clear polythene. They will be well rooted within 3–4 weeks.
  *Semi-ripe cuttings* in late summer or early autumn with bottom heat.

## HEDERA HELIX (English ivy)
Evergreen, self-clinging climber with glossy, dark green leaves. Umbels of yellowish-green flowers appear in autumn, followed by black fruits.

- *Semi-ripe cuttings* of juvenile foliage to produce trailing plants.
  *Semi-ripe cuttings* of adult growth to produce plants with a more upright, tree-ivy habit.
  *Layer* at any time of the year.

## HEDYCHIUM FORRESTII (Ginger lily)
Perennial with lance-shaped, mid-green, 30–50cm long, clearly veined leaves. Racemes of white flowers appear in late summer and early autumn.

- *Sow seed* at 20°C as soon as it is ripe.
- *Divide* rhizomes in spring. Don't allow the rhizomes to dry out.

Helleborus orientalis

## HEDYSARUM CORONARIUM
(French honeysuckle)
Perennial with pinnate, mid-green leaves. Racemes of fragrant, pea-like, dark red flowers are produced in spring.

***Sow seed*** in a garden frame as soon as it is ripe.
∎ ***Divide*** young plants in early spring and pot up. Avoid unnecessary root disturbance.

## HELENIUM AUTUMNALE
(Sneezeweed)
Perennial with lance-shaped, toothed, mid-green leaves that are 10–15cm long. The yellow ray-florets with brown disc-florets appear in late summer and autumn.

***Sow seed*** in a garden frame in spring.
***Softwood basal cuttings*** of H. 'Bressingham Gold' in a garden frame in spring.
∎ ***Divide*** in late autumn or early spring.

## HELIANTHEMUM APENNINUM
(Rock rose)
Evergreen shrub with grey-green leaves. The single white flowers have conspicuous bright yellow anthers and appear in late spring and early summer.

***Sow seed*** in a garden frame in spring.
∎ ***Softwood cuttings*** in late spring under horticultural fleece.

## HELIANTHUS ANNUUS (Sunflower)
Annual with hairy, mid- to dark green leaves. Large, daisy-like flowerheads up to 30cm across are produced during summer. The ray-florets are pale yellow with purple disc-florets. This is my favourite of the genus, but there are perennial species too, including H. 'Loddon Gold' and H. × multiflorus.

***Sow seed*** at 16°C in late winter or in open ground in late spring. Where children are sowing the seed for giant plants, show them how to sow a single seed per pot. Repot the young plants into soil-based compost to encourage them to form a strong rootball before planting out.
***Sow perennials*** such as H. × multiflorus in a garden frame in spring.
***Softwood basal cuttings*** of perennials in spring.
***Divide*** perennials in spring.

## HELICHRYSUM PETIOLARE
Tender, evergreen shrub with leaves that are densely covered with grey wool on the upper surface. The creamy-white flowers appear in late summer and autumn.

***Sow seed*** at 16°C in a garden frame in spring.
∎ ***Semi-ripe cuttings*** with a 'heel' in midsummer under horticultural fleece. Don't pot on until the following spring.

## HELICTOTRICHON SEMPERVIRENS
(Blue oat grass)
Evergreen perennial grass forming a mound of tightly rolled, grey-blue, 20cm long leaves. The panicles of pale yellow, purple-tinged spikelets appear in early summer.

***Sow seed*** in a garden frame in spring.
∎ ***Divide*** clumps in late spring.

## HELIOPSIS HELIANTHOIDES (Oxeye)
Perennial with 15cm long, mid-green leaves. The long-stalked, single or double, deep yellow flowerheads appear in midsummer and early autumn.

***Sow seed*** in a garden frame in spring.
∎ ***Softwood basal cuttings*** in spring.
***Divide*** in autumn.

## HELIOTROPIUM ARBORESCENS
(Heliotrope, Cherry pie)
Short-lived shrub usually grown as an annual. The mid- to dark green leaves are wrinkled and are often tinged with purple. Dense heads of lavender-blue, tubular, highly fragrant flowers appear in summer.

***Sow seed*** at 16°C in spring.
∎ ***Softwood cuttings*** in summer. Use the tips of new growth.

## HELLEBORUS ORIENTALIS (Lenten rose)
Perennial with leathery, dark green leaves in winter. The saucer-shaped, white or greenish-white flowers are produced in late winter and early spring on tall, stout stems.

***Sow seed*** on the surface of the compost in a garden frame as soon as it is ripe. Seed falls immediately it is ripe in early summer, so be ready for it. If there is no sign of germination after 4–5 months, leave the container of seed outside under a hedge until the following year. It is sufficiently contrary to germinate in its own time.

◧ *Divide* clumps after flowering or in late summer. (*H. foetidus* and *H. argutifolius* do not form a clump, so can't be divided.)

### HEMEROCALLIS 'NOVA' (Day lily)
Evergreen perennial with strap-like, dark green, 60cm long leaves and star-shaped, lemon-yellow, fragrant flowers in early summer.

*Seed* Chill seed for 30 days and sow in autumn or spring in a garden frame. The seed of cultivars such as 'Nova' will not come true, but who knows – you may grow a winner.

◧ *Divide* in spring, taking care not to damage the shoots that are produced early in the year.

Hepatica nobilis

### HEPATICA NOBILIS
Semi-evergreen perennial with kidney-shaped, mid-green leaves that are covered with silky hairs on the underside. Deep, saucer-shaped, white, pink, blue or purple flowers appear in spring before most of the leaves.

*Sow seed* in a garden frame in autumn.

◧ *Divide* in spring. Keep in light shade until established.

### HERMODACTYLUS TUBEROSUS (Widow iris)
Perennial with 20cm long, bluish-green leaves. The greenish-yellow flowers with dark, purple-brown outer parts appear in spring.

*Divide* in early summer after the leaves wither. Take care not to damage the tubers.

### HESPERIS MATRONALIS (Sweet rocket)
Biennial with hairy, dark green leaves and panicles of purple, lilac or occasionally white flowers in late spring and early summer.

*Sow seed* in open ground in spring.

◧ *Softwood basal cuttings* in spring.

### HEUCHERA 'PALACE PURPLE' (Coral flower)
Evergreen perennial with shiny, bronze-red, sharply edged leaves. The panicles of small, greenish-white flowers with red anthers are produced in summer followed by deep pink seed heads.

*Sow seed* in spring in a garden frame. The tiny seed may be mixed with talcum powder to make sowing easier. Do not cover the seed with compost. Plants raised from seed seldom retain the deep leaf colour.

◧ *Divide* in autumn.

### × HEUCHERALLA ALBA 'BRIDGET BLOOM'
Evergreen perennial with mid-green leaves and brown veins. Erect panicles of tiny, white flowers with pink calyces are produced from late spring to early autumn.

*Divide* in spring.

### HIBISCUS SYRIACUS
Deciduous shrub with 3-lobed, 10cm long, dark green leaves. The trumpet-shaped, dark pink flowers with dark red centres and yellow anthers are produced in late summer and autumn.

*Sow seed* at 18°C in spring.

*Softwood cuttings* in late spring.

◧ *Semi-ripe cuttings* in summer.

*Layer* in late spring or summer in well-drained, alkaline soil. Leave undisturbed until the autumn of the following year.

### HIERACIUM VILLOSUM (Hawkweed)
Perennial with lance-shaped, grey-green, 10cm long leaves covered with white hairs. The pale yellow flowers appear in summer.

*Sow seed* in a garden frame in spring.

◧ *Divide* in spring.

### HIPPEASTRUM × ACRAMANNII
Bulbous perennial with bright green, 30–60cm long leaves, which appear at the same time as, or just after, the flowers. The tall umbels of 3 funnel-shaped, red flowers with white margins and greenish-white centres appear in late winter.

*Sow seed* at 16°C as soon as it is ripe. Keep seedlings growing for 18 months before allowing the foliage to die down, leaving a small bulb for starting into growth in a frost-free room.

**Remove offsets** in autumn and plant in containers of loam-based, multi-purpose compost with the shoulders of the bulbs above the surface of the compost.

## HIPPOPHAE RHAMNOIDES
(Sea buckthorn)
Deciduous shrub or small tree with spiny stems and grey-green leaves with silvery scales on both surfaces. Racemes of tiny, green-yellow flowers appear in spring, followed, on female plants, by masses of bright orange fruit.

**Seed** Stratify seed in a garden frame for 12 weeks prior to sowing, or place in a container of moist peat and chill in the refrigerator at 3°C. Sow in spring.
**Semi-ripe cuttings** in midsummer.
**Hardwood cuttings** in early winter.
**Layer** in autumn.

## HOHERIA GLABRATA (Ribbonwood)
Deciduous tree with dark green leaves that turn yellow in autumn. Masses of fragrant, white flowers with purple stamens are produced in summer.

**Sow seed** in a garden frame in autumn. Seedlings will produce lobed and shiny leaves for up to 2 years.
**Semi-ripe cuttings** in early autumn. They can be slow to root and are best left undisturbed until the following summer when the plants should be making growth.

## HOLBOELLIA CORIACEA
Evergreen climber with 15cm long, dark green leaves made up of 3 leaflets. In spring the male flowers are tinged purple and the female flowers are pale green. Occasionally sausage-shaped, purple fruit are produced.

**Sow seed** in a garden frame in spring.
**Semi-ripe cuttings** in early autumn. Shorten the leaves to reduce transpiration.
**Layer** in autumn.

## HOLCUS MOLLIS 'ALBOVARIEGATUS'
Perennial grass with blue-green, creamy-white margined leaves. Panicles of pale green spikelets appear in summer.

**Divide** in late spring.

## HOLODISCUS DISCOLOR (Ocean spray)
Deciduous shrub with grey-green leaves that are covered with white hairs on the underside. Plume-like, pendant panicles with masses of tiny, creamy-white flowers appear in midsummer.

**Sow seed** in a garden frame in late autumn.
**Semi-ripe cuttings** in summer.
**Layer** in summer.

## HORMINUM PYRENAICUM
(Dragon's mouth)
Perennial with glossy, dark green, 7cm long, toothed leaves. The tubular, 2-lipped, dark blue flowers have prominent stamens and flower throughout summer. They don't really look like a dragon's mouth!

**Sow seed** in a garden frame in autumn.
**Divide** in spring.

## HOSTA (Plantain lily)
Perennial with large, heart- or lance-shaped leaves that can be glaucous, blue-green or variegated. The racemes of funnel-shaped, pale blue or white flowers appear in summer.

**Seed** seldom comes true.
**Divide** in early spring or late autumn, retaining at least one bud on each portion of root. Plant at the same depth as before and watch out for slugs and snails.

Hippophae rhamnoides as a backdrop to Clematis 'Royal Velours'

Houttuynia cordata 'Chameleon'

**HOWEA FORSTERIANA** (Kentia palm)
Tender palm with 2–3m long, pinnate leaves made up of lance-shaped, dark green, pendulous leaflets. During summer the pale brown, male flowers together with the star-shaped, green, female flowers make up a 90cm high spike.

***Sow seed*** at 26°C as soon as it is ripe.

**HOYA CARNOSA** (Wax flower)
Evergreen climber with succulent, fleshy, dark green leaves. The night-scented umbels of up to 20 star-like, waxy, pure white flowers have red coronas and are produced from late spring to autumn.

***Sow seed*** at 20°C in spring.
[J] ***Semi-ripe cuttings*** in a propagator in late summer.
***Layer*** in summer. I have successfully layered pot-grown conservatory plants into containers of wet peat. Don't allow the compost to dry out.

**HUMULUS LUPULUS** (Hop)
Climbing perennial with 15cm long, light green leaves. The fragrant, green, female flowers appear in summer, turning straw-coloured as they fade.

***Sow seed*** at 16°C in spring. Germination is usually poor.
***Softwood cuttings*** in spring.
[J] ***Semi-ripe cuttings*** in midsummer.

**HYACINTHOIDES NON-SCRIPTA**
(English bluebell)
Bulbous perennial with lance-shaped, glossy, dark green leaves. In spring it produces 6–12 bell-shaped, fragrant, pendant, mid-blue, but occasionally white, flowers with cream anthers. It differs from the Spanish bluebell because it has all the flowers on one side of the raceme, which is pendant at the top.

***Sow seed*** in a garden frame as soon as it is ripe.
[E] ***Remove offsets*** in summer and plant in rows in a sheltered part of the garden for 1 year before planting out in their permanent positions

**HYACINTHUS ORIENTALIS** (Hyacinth)
Bulbous perennial with lance-shaped, bright green leaves with a central channel. Erect racemes of up to 40 bell-shaped, waxy, fragrant, pale blue flowers with white tips are produced in early spring.

***Remove offsets*** in summer. Pot them up in multi-purpose compost, then repot in the second year. They will flower the following year.

**HYDRANGEA**
Deciduous shrub or deciduous or evergreen climber. Leaves can be broad or ovate, glossy or velvety and mid- to dark green. The summer and autumn flowerheads are usually made up of fertile and sterile flowers in a range of colours, from white through pink and red to deep mauve. Flower colour can be changed depending on the acidity or alkalinity of the soil.

***Sow seed*** in a garden frame in spring.
[J] ***Softwood cuttings*** of deciduous species in early summer.
[E] ***Semi-ripe cuttings*** of evergreens in summer.
***Hardwood cuttings*** of deciduous species in winter.

With cuttings, cut the leaves in half to reduce transpiration and wilting.

**HYDROCHARIS MORSUS-RANAE**
(Frogbit)
Aquatic perennial with floating rosettes of rounded, glossy, bright green leaves. The white, summer flowers are bowl-shaped with a yellow spot at the base of each of the 3 petals.

**HOTTONIA PALUSTRIS** (Water violet)
Submerged perennial with pinnate, light green leaves. The lilac or white flowers have yellow throats and are carried above the water during spring.

***Sow seed*** in trays submerged in water to rim level, in spring, in a garden frame.
[J] ***Softwood cuttings*** in spring, pushed into the bottom mud or allowed to float in the water.
***Divide*** in spring and plant in the base of the pond.

**HOUTTUYNIA CORDATA 'CHAMELEON'**
Perennial with variegated leaves in red or pale yellow and red. The small flowers appear in spring and are surrounded by white bracts.

***Sow seed*** as soon as it is ripe, in a garden frame.
***Softwood cuttings*** in late spring.
[J] ***Divide*** in early spring.

**Sow seed** in a saucer of water as soon as it is ripe. When germinated, move the seedlings to the pond, making sure the water is sufficiently shallow to allow the stolons to root into the bottom mud and the leaves to float.

🔲 **Pull off pieces of stolon** and float them on the pond surface in late spring.

---

## HYMENOCALLIS × FESTALIS (Spider lily)

Evergreen, bulbous perennial with 90cm long, mid-green basal leaves. The umbels of fragrant, white flowers have long, thin petals and wide cups and are produced in spring and summer.

**Sow seed** at 20°C as soon as it is ripe.

🔲 **Remove offsets** in spring and pot up immediately.

---

## HYPERICUM 'EASTLEIGH GOLD'

Semi-evergreen shrub with lance-shaped, mid-green leaves. Large, cup-shaped, deep yellow flowers are produced in summer.

**Sow seed** in a garden frame in autumn.
**Softwood cuttings** in early summer under horticultural fleece.

🔲 **Semi-ripe cuttings** in midsummer.
**Divide** perennials such as *H. orientale* in spring.

---

## HYPOESTES PHYLLOSTACHYA

(Polka dot plant)
Tender sub-shrub with dark green leaves spotted with deep reddish-pink. Spikes of tiny, magenta flowers appear in late summer and autumn.

**Sow seed** at 16°C in spring.

🔲 **Softwood cuttings** in late spring. Avoid strong sunlight while they are rooting. Water through the base of the pot; don't overwater.

---

## HYPOXIS ANGUSTIFOLIA (Star flower)

Tender, cormous perennial with grass-like, basal, mid-green leaves. In summer the bright yellow flowers face the sky.

**Sow seed** at 16°C in spring.

🔲 **Remove offsets** in autumn and pot up in multi-purpose compost with added grit for drainage in a garden frame.

---

## IBERIS SEMPERVIRENS

Evergreen sub-shrub with spoon-shaped, dark green leaves and clusters of fragrant, white flowers in late winter and early spring.

**Sow seed** in a garden frame in autumn.

🔲 **Softwood cuttings** in late spring.
**Semi-ripe cuttings** in summer.

---

## IDESIA POLYCARPA

Deciduous tree with sharply pointed, 20cm long, glossy, dark green leaves that are tinged purple when young. The small, yellowish-green, fragrant flowers are without petals and appear in large, drooping panicles during summer. Female plants produce red berries.

**Sow seed** in a garden frame in autumn.
**Softwood cuttings** in late spring. Reduce the leaf size to prevent transpiration.

🔲 **Semi-ripe cuttings** in late summer.

---

## ILEX AQUIFOLIUM (English holly)

Evergreen tree with glossy, dark green, spiny leaves. Tiny, white summer flowers are followed in autumn by red, orange or yellow berries. There are also a number of variegated forms.

**Sow seed** in a garden frame in autumn. Germination may take 36 months.

🔲 **Semi-ripe cuttings** in late summer with a 'heel'. Don't disturb the rooted cuttings until late spring.

---

## ILLICIUM ANISATUM (Anise tree)

Evergreen tree or small shrub with blunt-tipped, glossy, dark green, 10cm long leaves. In spring it produces fragrant, star-shaped, pale green flowers that age to creamy-white.

🔲 **Semi-ripe cuttings** in summer. Shorten the leaves and take with a 'heel'.
**Layer** in late summer.

---

## IMPATIENS WALLERIANA (Busy Lizzy)

Perennial treated as an annual with green or bronze-tinged leaves and flattened summer flowers in a wide range of colours.

🔲 **Sow seed** on the surface of seed compost at 16°C in early spring. Don't let the seed dry out. I find them tricky to germinate. My most successful attempts have been when I have sprinkled fine sand to just cover the seed and covered the tray with horticultural fleece. After germination, I have used more fine sand to cover the roots.
**Softwood cuttings** in late spring.

---

## INCARVILLEA DELAVAYI

Perennial with basal rosettes of pinnate, light green, 25cm long leaves. In early summer it produces racemes of trumpet-shaped, deep rose-pink flowers with bright yellow throats.

**Sow seed** in a garden frame in spring. Seed is slow to germinate.

🔲 **Softwood basal cuttings** in spring.
**Divide** in early spring. They are difficult to separate because the root is tough with few lateral roots.

---

## INDIGOFERA DECORA (Indigo)

Deciduous shrub with glossy, dark green, pinnate leaves. Spike-like racemes of pea-like, cerise-pink flowers appear in mid- to late summer.

**Sow seed** in a garden frame in autumn.
**Softwood cuttings** in late spring.
**Softwood basal cuttings** in spring.

🔲 **Semi-ripe cuttings** in early summer.

*Ilex aquifolium 'Gold Flash'*

## INULA HELENIUM (Elecampane)

Perennial with basal rosettes of mid-green, wavy-margined, 75cm long leaves that are woolly on the underside. Bright yellow, thin-petalled flowers, 7cm across, appear during summer.

*Sow seed* in a garden frame in autumn.

🟦 *Divide* in late autumn or early spring.

## IPHEION UNIFLORUM

Bulbous perennial with strap-like, 25cm long, blue-green leaves. Upward-pointing, fragrant, star-shaped, silvery-blue flowers are produced in spring.

*Sow seed* in a garden frame as soon as it is ripe.

🟦 *Divide* in summer.

## IPOMOEA QUAMOCLIT (Star glory)

Tender, climbing annual with deep green leaves. The clusters of small, scarlet flowers (sometimes white) appear during summer.

*Sow seed* in spring at 18°C. Soak the seed for 12 hours before sowing or chip the outer coat. Seed is highly toxic.

## IPOMOEA TRICOLOR (Morning glory)

Tender, twining perennial, usually treated as an annual, with heart-shaped, mid-green leaves. The sky-blue or mauve, funnel-shaped flowers have white tubes and appear in late summer and autumn.

*Sow seed* at 18°C in spring. Chip or soak the seed for 24 hours before sowing.

## IRESINE HERBSTII (Beefsteak plant)

Annual or short-lived perennial with waxy, 8cm long, multi-coloured leaves in orange, yellow or scarlet. The colour of the veins often contrasts with the leaf colour.

*Softwood tip cuttings* at any time. Overwinter in a heated greenhouse.

## IRIS

Rhizomes, bulbs or fleshy-rooted perennials with evergreen or deciduous, lance-shaped, mid- to dark green leaves. The flowers appear in late winter, spring or summer.

*Sow seed* in an open garden frame in late autumn and winter and allow to become frosted.

🟦 *Divide rhizomes* of bearded iris in summer immediately after they have finished flowering.

🟦 *Divide clumps* in early autumn.

🟦 *Remove offsets* in summer and plant out in the garden in a sheltered position before planting in their permanent beds.

## ISATIS TINCTORIA (Woad)

Perennial with basal rosettes of lance-shaped, grey-green leaves. Branched panicles of small, yellow flowers appear in summer.

*Sow seed* in spring at 16°C. Alternatively, sow in a garden frame in early autumn.

🟦 *Divide* in spring.

## ITEA ILICIFOLIA

Evergreen shrub with spiny-toothed, glossy, dark green leaves turning purple in autumn. Pendant racemes of greenish-white flowers appear in late summer and autumn.

*Sow seed* as soon as it is ripe, in a garden frame.

🟦 *Softwood cuttings* in spring. Cut the leaves in half to reduce transpiration.

*Semi-ripe cuttings* with a 'heel', in a propagator in summer.

## IXIA VIRIDIFLORA (Corn lily)

Tender, cormous perennial with 45cm long, bright green, linear leaves. The tall spikes of bluish-green flowers, with black centres edged with crimson, are produced in spring and early summer.

Itea ilicifolia

*Sow seed* as soon as it is ripe, in a garden frame.

🟦 *Remove offsets* in late summer and pot up in soil-based, multi-purpose compost in a garden frame.

## JACARANDA MIMOSIFOLIA

Tender, deciduous tree with 2-pinnate, soft and hairy, mid-green leaves. White-throated, purple-blue flowers appear before or with the emerging leaves in pyramidal panicles from spring to early summer. The seed pods are disc-shaped.

*Sow seed* at 20°C in spring.

🟦 *Semi-ripe cuttings* in summer in a propagator. Transplant the cuttings into loam-based soil as soon as they are well rooted. Position the plants in full light.

Iris 'Elizabeth Poldark'

### JASIONE LAEVIS (Sheep's bit scabious)
Perennial with rosettes of 10cm long, dull green leaves. Spiky, lilac-blue flowerheads appear in summer.

*Sow seed* in a garden frame as soon as it is ripe.
*Divide* in spring.

### JASMINUM NUDIFLORUM
(Winter jasmine)
Deciduous shrub with bright green shoots and pinnate, dark green leaves. Bright yellow flowers are produced in winter and early spring.

*Semi-ripe cuttings* with a 'heel', under horticultural fleece in summer.
*Layer* in late autumn.

### JEFFERSONIA DUBIA
Perennial with 2-lobed, purple-tinted, blue-green, 10cm long leaves. Solitary, cup-shaped, lavender-blue flowers are produced in early summer.

*Sow seed* as soon as it is ripe in a garden frame.
*Divide* in late spring.

### JOVELLANA VIOLACEA
Semi-evergreen sub-shrub with deep green leaves. Panicles of pale, purple-blue flowers with small, purple spots and yellow throats appear in summer.

*Semi-ripe cuttings* taken with a 'heel' in late summer. Cover with horticultural fleece.
*Rooted suckers* in spring planted outside in the garden.

### JUGLANS REGIA (Common walnut)
Deciduous tree with pinnate, 30cm long, glossy, mid-green, aromatic leaves that are bronze-purple when they open. The trailing catkins are green and are followed by spherical fruit containing the edible nut.

*Sow seed* as soon as it is ripe or stratify and sow the following spring.
*Whip and tongue graft* cultivars on to *J. regia* stock.

### JUNCUS EFFUSUS f. SPIRALIS
(Rush, Bog rush)
Leafless perennial grass with spiralled, dark green stems. Small, brown flowers are produced on the stems in summer.

*Divide* in late spring.

### JUNIPERUS CHINENSIS (Juniper)
Evergreen conifer with sharp pointed, dark green, juvenile leaves. Adult leaves are aromatic and scale-like.

*Sow seed* in a garden frame as soon as it is ripe. Germination may take up to 50 months.
*Semi-ripe cuttings* in early autumn with a 'heel'.

### JUSTICIA CARNEA
(Flamingo plant)
Tender, evergreen shrub with 4-angled stems (square) and mid-green leaves that are 20cm long. Spikes of rose-pink flowers with green bracts appear in summer and autumn.

*Sow seed* at 16°C in spring.
*Softwood cuttings* in late spring in a propagator.
*Semi-ripe cuttings* in summer in a propagator.

To reduce transpiration, trim the leaves when taking cuttings.

### KALANCHOE BLOSSFELDIANA
Perennial succulent with glossy, dark green leaves. Panicles of tubular, bright red flowers are produced in early spring.

*Sow seed* at 20°C in spring.
*Stem cuttings* in spring or early summer. Use cactus compost or seed compost with added grit.

### KALMIA LATIFOLIA (Calico bush)
Evergreen shrub with glossy, dark green leaves. In late spring and early summer the tightly crimped, pink or red buds open to saucer-shaped, white, pale pink or red flowers.

*Sow seed* at 10°C in spring.
*Softwood cuttings* in late spring.
*Semi-ripe cuttings* in midsummer. Pot on into ericaceous compost when well rooted.
*Layer* in autumn.

### KALMIOPSIS LEACHIANA
Evergreen shrub with bright green leaves. Racemes of saucer-shaped, deep pink flowers are produced in spring.

*Sow seed* in peat-based compost at 10°C in spring.
*Semi-ripe cuttings* in late summer. Pot the rooted cuttings the following spring.

### KALOPANAX SEPTEMLOBUS
also named Kalopanax pictus
Deciduous tree with spiny branches. The dark green, 30cm wide leaves are variable, some deeply lobed and hairy on the underside. The large, umbel-like panicles of tiny, white flowers are produced in late summer, followed by small, blue-black fruit.

*Sow seed* in a garden frame in autumn.
*Softwood cuttings* in early summer.

### KERRIA JAPONICA (Jew's mallow)
Deciduous shrub with green shoots and bright green, toothed leaves. The golden-yellow flowers appear in late spring.

*Softwood cuttings* in summer.
*Rooted suckers* in late autumn. Prune the suckers back to 30cm long and either pot up in a soil-based compost or plant outside in the garden.

Kerria japonica

### KNIPHOFIA ENSIFOLIA
(Red hot poker, Torch lily)
Evergreen perennial with 15cm long, strap-like, arching, glaucous leaves. Racemes of greenish-white flowers open from orange-red buds during late summer and early autumn.

- **Sow seed** in a cold frame in spring. Cultivars won't come true from seed.
- **Divide** in late spring.

There is an easy way to bulk up your stock of woody-based kniphofias. Cut the whole crown of leaves off in late spring. Numerous offshoots will form. These can be removed and rooted as softwood basal cuttings. Alternatively, leave them attached to the parent plant to form roots and remove them 12 months later.

### KOELREUTERIA PANICULATA
(Golden-rain tree)
Deciduous tree with 45cm long, pinnate leaves that emerge as pinkish-bronze and turn to mid-green and finally deep yellow in late autumn. Large pyramidal panicles of small, sulphur-yellow flowers are produced in late summer followed by 5cm long, bladder-like, pink seed pods in late autumn.

- **Sow seed** in a garden frame in spring. Scarify the seed beforehand using sandpaper.
- **Root cuttings** in late winter in a garden frame.

### KOLKWITZIA AMABILIS (Beauty bush)
Deciduous shrub with dark green leaves. In late spring and early summer the plant covers itself with bell-shaped, light pink to deep pink flowers with yellow throats.

- **Sow seed** in spring at 20°C after cold treatment at 1°C for 30 days.
- **Softwood cuttings** in early summer. **Rooted suckers** in spring potted into a multi-purpose compost. Stand them outside until autumn and then plant out.

### KIRENGESHOMA PALMATA
Perennial with pale green, lobed, sycamore-like leaves with 3 tubular, pale yellow flowers per stem during late summer and early autumn.

- **Sow seed** in a garden frame as soon as it is ripe. Germination will be erratic.
- **Divide** in spring, taking care not to damage early shoot growth.

### KNAUTIA MACEDONICA
Perennial with mid-green basal leaves with a terminal lobe. The purple-red flowerheads are produced in late summer and early autumn.

- **Sow seed** in a garden frame in spring. **Softwood basal cuttings** in spring. Provide good ventilation as they are prone to grey mould disease.

Knautia macedonica

**LABLAB PURPUREUS** (Egyptian bean)
Tender, fast-growing, perennial climber
with 3-palmate, dark green leaves. The
20–45cm long racemes of fragrant,
purple or white flowers appear in
summer and autumn. They are followed
by edible, 10cm long, green pods,
occasionally flushed purple, which
contain the reddish-brown or black seeds.

*Sow seed* at 24°C in spring.

**+ LABURNOCYTISUS 'ADAMII'**
Deciduous tree with 3-palmate, dark
green leaves. The small, pea-like flowers
appear in late spring and early summer
in 3 separate colours: purple, yellow and
pinkish-purple with a pale yellow flush.

Not my favourite plant, but some people
may want to propagate it!
*Whip and tongue graft* in winter onto
laburnum seedlings.

**LABURNUM ALPINUM**
(Scotch laburnum, Golden-rain tree)
Deciduous tree with glossy, dark green
leaves that are hairy on the underside.
Dense, pendulous racemes of bright
yellow flowers appear in late spring and
early summer. The seed is poisonous.

**◻ *Seed*** Chip the outer seed coat and
sow in a garden frame in autumn.
*Whip and tongue graft* in winter.
*Bud graft* in summer.

**LACHENALIA ALOIDES** (Cape cowslip)
Tender perennial with strap-shaped,
glaucous, mid-green basal leaves with
purple spots. In late winter or early spring
it produces racemes of up to 18 tubular,
pendant, yellow flowers with scarlet tips
held on purple spotted, green stems.

*Sow seed* at 16°C as soon as it is ripe.
**◻ *Separate bulblets*** in late summer and
replant immediately.

**LAGERSTROEMIA INDICA**
(Crepe myrtle)
Deciduous tree or large shrub with
peeling grey and brown bark. The dark
green leaves are bronze when young.
Large, 20cm high panicles of white,
pink, scarlet or purple flowers are
produced in summer and early autumn.

*Sow seed* at 12°C in late spring.
*Softwood cuttings* in late spring.
**◻ *Semi-ripe cuttings*** in a propagator in
summer.

**LAGURUS OVATUS** (Hare's tail)
Annual grass with flat, lance-shaped,
pale green leaves. Panicles of pale green
spikelets mature to creamy-brown in
late summer.

*Sow seed* in open ground in spring.

**LAMIUM MACULATUM** (Deadnettle)
Perennial with matt, mid-green leaves
that are often marked with silver.
Whorls of pink or red-purple flowers
appear in summer.

Lagurus ovatus

Sow seed in a garden frame in autumn or spring.
**Divide** in spring.
**Plant up rooted stolons** in spring.

---

## LAMPRANTHUS SPECTABILIS
Tender, perennial succulent with cylindrical, mid-green leaves tinged with red. White or red-purple flowers appear in summer and early autumn.

**Sow seed** at 20°C in spring.
**Softwood cuttings** in spring and summer.

---

## LANTANA CAMARA
Evergreen shrub with deep green leaves. The flowerheads are produced from late spring to autumn, in colours ranging from white and yellow to peach-pink and red-purple.

**Sow seed** at 18°C in spring.
**Semi-ripe cuttings** in summer in a propagator. Watch out for whitefly.

---

## LAPAGERIA ROSEA (Chilean bell flower)
Evergreen climber with dark green, 10cm long leaves. Pink or red, tubular flowers with fleshy petals appear during summer and late autumn.

*Lantana camara*

**Sow seed** at 16°C in spring in ericaceous compost. Pre-soak the seed for 48 hours. Alternatively, provide a chill period of 60 days in the refrigerator. Keep the seedlings under clear polythene for a few weeks before transplanting them to encourage growth, as they are inclined to sulk.
**Semi-ripe cuttings** in late summer in ericaceous compost.
**Layer** in autumn.

---

## LARIX DECIDUA (European larch)
Deciduous conifer with pale green, linear leaves in spring, becoming mid-green in summer and turning butter-yellow in autumn. The small, dark brown, female cones have protruding bracts.

**Sow seed** in open ground in spring.
**Semi-ripe cuttings** in summer, if you have a mist propagator. I have never managed to root a cutting, so it may only be a rumour!

---

## LATHYRUS GRANDIFLORUS
(Everlasting sweet pea)
Herbaceous perennial climber with mid-green leaves. Racemes of 2–4 pink-purple or red flowers are produced during summer.

**Sow seed** in a garden frame in spring. Pre-soak the seed in warm water for 2 hours or chip the outer coat (see page 23). Annual sweet peas (*L. odoratus*) can be sown in autumn in a garden frame or in open ground in spring.
**Divide** clumps carefully in spring and replant immediately.

---

## LAURUS NOBILIS (Sweet bay, Bay laurel)
Evergreen shrub or small tree with glossy, dark green, aromatic, 10cm long leaves. Clusters of greenish-yellow flowers are produced in spring, followed, on female plants, by black berries.

*Laurus nobilis*

**Sow seed** in a garden frame in autumn. Remove the flesh first. If sowing in spring, soak the clean seed in warm water for 12 hours before sowing.

J **Semi-ripe cuttings** in summer with a 'heel'. Cut the leaves in half to reduce transpiration.

**Rooted suckers** in early spring. Plant in a multi-purpose compost and grow on for a year outside before planting out.

## LAVANDULA ANGUSTIFOLIA
(Lavender)
Evergreen shrub with linear, grey-green, aromatic leaves. Dense spikes of pale to deep purple, fragrant flowers are carried on long stalks during summer.

**Sow seed** in a garden frame in late spring.

E **Semi-ripe cuttings** with a 'heel', in summer under horticultural fleece. Space the cuttings to reduce the risk of botrytis disease.

## LAVATERA × CLEMENTII 'BARNSLEY'
(Mallow)
Evergreen sub-shrub with 10cm long, lobed, grey-green leaves. Funnel-shaped, white flowers with red centres and deeply notched petals mature to soft pink during summer.

**Softwood cuttings** in early summer.

## LEDUM GROENLANDICUM
(Labrador tea)
Evergreen shrub with dark green, 5cm long leaves that are pale brown and felted on the underside. Rounded clusters of pure white flowers are produced in late spring.

**Sow seed** at 12°C in spring. Sow on the surface of the compost.

J **Semi-ripe cuttings** in late summer in ericaceous compost.

**Layer** in autumn.

Lavatera × clementii 'Barnsley'

## LEIOPHYLLUM BUXIFOLIUM
(Sand myrtle)
Evergreen shrub with small, glossy, dark green leaves that turn bronze in winter. In late spring and early summer clusters of pink buds open to white flowers.

**Sow seed** on the surface of ericaceous compost in a garden frame in spring.

**Softwood cuttings** in early summer.

J **Rooted suckers** in early spring. Pot them into ericaceous compost to form a good root system until the following spring. Then plant them outside.

## LEONOTIS LEONURUS (Lion's ear)
Tender, semi-evergreen shrub with lance-shaped, deep green leaves. Whorls of tubular, orange-red flowers appear during autumn and early winter.

**Sow seed** at 16°C in spring.

J **Softwood cuttings** in late spring and early summer.

## LEONTOPODIUM ALPINUM
(Edelweiss)
Perennial with lance-shaped, grey-green basal leaves. In late spring and early summer the pale yellow-white flowers are surrounded by star-shaped, grey-white bracts.

**Sow seed** as soon as it is ripe in a garden frame.

J **Divide** in early spring.

## LEPTOSPERMUM SCOPARIUM
(New Zealand tea tree)
Evergreen shrub with tiny, aromatic, dark green leaves. Saucer-shaped, white or pink-tinged white flowers are produced in late spring and early summer.

**Sow seed** at 16°C in autumn or early spring.

J **Semi-ripe cuttings** taken with a 'heel' in summer in a propagator.

## LESPEDEZA THUNBERGII (Bush clover)

Deciduous sub-shrub with 3-palmate, blue-green leaves. Terminal racemes of purple-pink flowers are produced in autumn.

*Sow seed* in spring in containers of seed compost, in a garden frame.

▯ *Softwood cuttings* in summer.
*Divide* in spring. Take great care because the stems tend to separate from the crown.

## LEUCANTHEMELLA SEROTINA

Perennial with lance-shaped, toothed, mid-green leaves. White, chrysanthemum-like flowers with greenish-yellow centres are produced in autumn.

▯ *Softwood basal cuttings* in spring.
*Divide* in early spring.

## LEUCOCORYNE IXIOIDES

(Glory of the sun)
Tender, bulbous perennial with narrow, grass-like, 45cm long, garlic-scented basal leaves. Umbels of scented, funnel-shaped, white flowers with deep blue veins (or sometimes pale blue with white throats) are produced in spring as the leaves wither.

*Sow seed* at 20°C as soon as it is ripe.

▯ *Remove offsets* in autumn. Replant immediately in free-draining, loam-based compost.

## LEUCOJUM AESTIVUM

(Summer snowflake)
Bulbous perennial with strap-like, glossy, 45cm long, dark green leaves. Bell-shaped, chocolate-scented, pure white flowers with green tips to the petals appear in spring.

*Sow seed* in a garden frame in autumn.

▯ *Remove offsets* once the leaves have yellowed. Store the offsets until autumn and plant in containers of multi-purpose compost.

## LEUCOTHOE FONTANESIANA 'RAINBOW'

Evergreen shrub with lance-shaped, dark green leaves streaked with pink and cream. Small, urn-shaped, ivory-white flowers are produced in spring.

*Semi-ripe cuttings* in a propagator in summer.

▯ *Rooted suckers* in early spring. Shorten the shoot to 45cm and pot up for a year in multi-purpose compost. Stand the containers outside.

## LEVISTICUM OFFICINALE (Lovage)

Perennial with hollow, ribbed stems and 60cm long, dark green leaves with toothed leaflets. Umbels of greenish-yellow, star-shaped flowers appear in summer, followed by winged, green fruit.

Lewisia cotyledon

*Sow seed* in open ground as soon as it is ripe.

▯ *Divide* in early spring.

## LEWISIA COTYLEDON

Evergreen perennial with rosettes of thick, wavy-margined, dark green leaves. Panicles of funnel-shaped flowers in a range of pastel shades, including yellow, orange, rose-pink and magenta, appear in late spring and summer.

*Sow seed* in a garden frame in autumn. The seedlings are unlikely to come true for colour.

▯ *Remove offsets* in summer and root under horticultural fleece.

## LEYCESTERIA FORMOSA

(Himalayan honeysuckle)
Deciduous shrub with bamboo-like, sea-green stems in the first year and dark green, 15cm long leaves. Pendant spikes of white flowers with purple-red bracts are produced during summer and autumn, followed by red-purple berries.

Leucojum aestivum

**Sow seed** in a garden frame in spring. Self-seeds readily.

◨ **Softwood cuttings** in summer.

---

**LIATRIS SPICATA** (Gayfeather)
Perennial with lance-shaped, mid-green, 30cm long basal leaves. Dense, upright spikes of long-lasting, deep pink flowers (occasionally white) are produced in late summer and autumn. The flowers open from the top of the spike downwards.

**Sow seed** in a garden frame in autumn.

◨ **Divide** in spring.

---

**LIBERTIA GRANDIFLORA**
Perennial with leathery, 30–60cm long, mid-green leaves. Long panicles of clustered white flowers with deep green keels are produced in late spring and early summer.

◨ **Sow seed** as soon as it is ripe in containers outside.
**Divide** in spring.

---

**LIGULARIA DENTATA** (Golden groundsel)
Perennial with kidney-shaped, toothed, mid-green, 30cm long leaves. Orange-yellow, brown-centred flowerheads carried on red stalks are produced in summer and early autumn.

**Sow seed** in autumn or spring in a garden frame.

◨ **Divide** in spring or late summer. Provide slug and snail protection for young plants.

---

**LIGUSTRUM OVALIFOLIUM** (Privet)
Evergreen or semi-evergreen shrub with oval, bright green leaves. The panicles of heavily scented, white flowers are produced in summer, followed by shiny, black fruit.

**Sow seed** in a garden frame in spring or autumn.
**Semi-ripe cuttings** in summer.

◨ **Hardwood cuttings** in winter.

Ligularia dentata 'Desdemona'

### LILIUM (Lily)

Bulbous perennial with lance-shaped, glossy, mid- to dark green leaves. The summer flowers are often very fragrant and come in a variety of shapes and positions. Most colours are available, with the exception of blue.

*Sow seed* as soon as it is ripe: hardy lilies in a garden frame; tender species at 16°C. Don't be like me and get caught out by *Lilium martagon*. This plant produces its first leaf the second spring; a bulbil forms below ground the first year.

🄴 *Divide offsets, bulblets or scales* as soon as the foliage turns yellow. Grow the young plants for 2 years in containers in a garden frame before planting outside.

🄹 *Sow bulbils* in early autumn in a garden frame.

Liquidambar styraciflua

Limnanthes douglasii

### LIMNANTHES DOUGLASII
(Poached egg plant)

Annual with glossy, bright yellow-green, fleshy leaves. In summer and autumn it produces masses of saucer-shaped, yellow flowers with each petal margined white.

*Sow seed* outdoors in spring.

### LIMONIUM LATIFOLIUM
(Sea lavender, Statice)

Perennial with rosettes of spoon-shaped, 30cm long, mid- to dark green leaves. Panicles of tubular, lavender-blue flowers with white calyces appear in late summer and early autumn.

*Sow seed* in containers outside in early spring.

🄹 *Divide* in spring.

### LINARIA ALPINA (Toadflax)

Perennial with lance-shaped, blue-green leaves. The upper leaves are alternate on the stem with the lower leaves whorled round the stem. Racemes of deep yellow and violet flowers appear in summer.

*Sow seed* in a garden frame in early spring. Transplant when small.

🄹 *Softwood cuttings* in spring. Remove the growing tip.

*Divide* in early spring.

### LINDERA BENZOIN (Spice bush)

Deciduous shrub with aromatic, bright green, 12cm long leaves that turn bright yellow in autumn. Umbels of star-shaped, yellowish-green flowers appear in mid-spring followed, on female plants, by shiny, deep red berries.

*Sow seed* in a garden frame in autumn.

🄹 *Softwood cuttings* in early summer. Shorten the leaves to reduce transpiration. Take cuttings from male and female plants to ensure pollination.

### LINUM FLAVUM (Golden flax)

Perennial with lance-shaped, dark green leaves. Funnel-shaped, golden-yellow, upward-facing flowers are produced during summer but they only fully open in sunlight.

*Sow seed* in a garden frame in autumn.

🄹 *Softwood cuttings* in early summer. Use the tips of the stems.

### LIQUIDAMBAR STYRACIFLUA
(Sweet gum)

Deciduous tree with 15cm long, maple-like, palmate-lobed, glossy, bright green leaves that colour in autumn to shades of orange, deep red and purple.

Inconspicuous, tiny, greenish-yellow flowers appear in late spring. Female flowers produce spiky, spherical seed heads in autumn.

J **Sow seed** in a garden frame in autumn. **Softwood cuttings** in summer. I find them tricky to root without bottom heat.

## LIRIODENDRON TULIPIFERA
(Tulip tree)
Deciduous tree with 15cm long, dark green leaves that turn yellow in autumn. The leaves appear to have the tips removed, leaving 2 short side lobes. Cup-shaped, pale green flowers with an orange band at the base are produced in summer on mature trees.

J **Sow seed** in a garden frame in autumn. For a spring sowing, store the seed at 1°C for 30 days before sowing. **Bud graft** in late summer.

## LIRIOPE MUSCARI (Lilyturf)
Evergreen perennial with dense clumps of strap-shaped, long, dark green leaves. Dense spikes of violet-mauve flowers are produced on purple-green stems during autumn.

**Sow seed** in containers in spring in a garden frame.
J **Divide** in spring.

Liriope muscari

## LITHOCARPUS DENSIFLORUS
(Tanbark oak)
Evergreen tree with leathery, dark green, deeply veined leaves. Spikes of tiny white flowers are produced in summer, occasionally followed by small acorns.

**Sow seed** in a garden frame in autumn.

## LITHODORA DIFFUSA 'HEAVENLY BLUE'
Evergreen shrub with elliptic, deep green, hairy leaves. Masses of deep azure-blue flowers are produced in late spring and summer.

**Semi-ripe cuttings** in summer under horticultural fleece. Avoid watering with limy water.

## LITHOPS (Living stones)
Succulent perennial with thick, fleshy, pebble-like leaves. On the surface of each leaf is a translucent panel. Daisy-like flowers emerge from the fissure between the leaves during summer or autumn, followed by fleshy seed pods.

**Sow seed** at 20°C in late spring.
J **Remove offsets** in early summer and root in cactus compost.

## LOBELIA CARDINALIS (Cardinal flower)
Perennial with reddish-purple stems and lance-shaped, toothed, glossy, bright green leaves. Racemes of tubular, bright scarlet flowers with deep red bracts appear in summer and early autumn.

**Sow seed** as soon as it is ripe at 16°C.
J **Divide** in early summer.
**Bud cuttings** in midsummer.

## LOBULARIA MARITIMA
(Sweet alyssum)
Annual with grey-green leaves. Racemes of tiny, cross-shaped, fragrant, white flowers appear in summer.

**Sow seed** in open ground in spring.

## LOMATIA FERRUGINEA
Evergreen tree with felted, light brown shoots with 2-pinnate, 50cm long, dark green leaves that are fawn-coloured and felted on the underside. Racemes of yellow and red flowers appear in summer.

**Softwood cuttings** in early summer.
J **Semi-ripe cuttings** in midsummer. Trim the leaves, keeping only a pair of leaflets. Roots quickly on a hot bed.

## LONICERA JAPONICA
(Japanese honeysuckle)
Evergreen climber with dark green leaves. Very fragrant pairs of tubular, purple-flushed, white, spring flowers mature to deep yellow in summer and are followed by blue-black berries in autumn.

**Sow seed** in a garden frame in spring.
**Softwood cuttings** in early summer.
**Semi-ripe cuttings** in summer.
J **Hardwood cuttings** in late autumn.

## LOROPETALUM CHINENSE
Evergreen shrub with oval, mid-green leaves, rough on the upper surface. Fragrant, spider-like, white flowers appear in late winter and spring.

**Sow seed** in a garden frame as soon as it is ripe.
J **Semi-ripe cuttings** in summer in a propagator.

## LOTUS BERTHELOTII (Parrot's beak)
Tender, evergreen sub-shrub with palmate, silver-grey leaves. Scarlet, black-centred pairs of flowers resembling lobster claws (or parrot beaks!) are produced in spring and early summer.

**Sow seed** at 20°C in spring.
J **Semi-ripe cuttings** in summer. With me, the rooted plants need winter protection in a cold greenhouse.

Lotus berthelotii

### LUMA APICULATA

Evergreen shrub or small tree with peeling, cinnamon-brown and creamy-white bark. The glossy, dark green leaves are aromatic. The white flowers appear in midsummer and autumn and are followed by purple berries.

- **Sow seed** in a garden frame in spring. Seedlings can normally be found under mature trees.
  **Semi-ripe cuttings** in late summer with a 'heel'.

### LUNARIA ANNUA (Honesty)

Biennial with coarse, mid- to dark green, 15cm long leaves. Racemes of white to pale purple flowers appear in late spring and summer, followed by flat, silvery, translucent seed pods.

**Sow seed** in early summer in open ground.

### LUPINUS (Lupin)

Annual, perennial or sub-shrub with soft and hairy, mid-green, palmate leaves. Spikes of pea-like flowers are produced in a range of colours during early and midsummer.

**Seed** Soak seed for 24 hours or abrade with sandpaper to weaken the tough seed coat. If you are an impatient gardener, sow seed of the tree lupin (*Lupinus arboreus*); it will germinate within 24 hours.

- **Sow seed** of annuals and perennials in autumn or spring in open ground.
  **Sow alpines** in a garden frame in spring.
  **Softwood basal cuttings** of named cultivars in spring.

### LUZULA SYLVATICA (Woodrush)

Evergreen perennial with linear, 30cm long, glossy, dark green leaves. Panicles of small, deep brown flowers are produced during mid-spring and early summer.

**Sow seed** in containers outside in autumn or spring.
- **Divide** in late spring.

Lysimachia clethroides

Lupinus spp.

**LYCHNIS CORONARIA** (Dusty miller)
Short-lived perennial with lance-shaped, silver-grey leaves up to 10cm long. Purple-red flowers, carried on long stalks, open one at a time throughout late summer and early autumn.

***Sow seed*** in a garden frame as soon as it is ripe. Self-seeds freely.

J ***Softwood basal cuttings*** in spring.

***Divide*** in early spring. Clumps older than 3–4 years become woody and are difficult to divide.

**LYCIUM BARBARUM**
(Chinese box thorn)
Deciduous shrub with mid- to dark green leaves. Clusters of small, funnel-shaped, pink or purple flowers are produced in late spring and early summer followed by yellow or deep orange berries.

***Sow seed*** in containers outside in autumn.

***Softwood cuttings*** in early summer.

J ***Hardwood cuttings*** in winter.

**LYCORIS AUREA** (Golden spider lily)
Bulbous perennial with strap-like, 60cm long, fleshy, glaucous, mid-green leaves that appear after the flowers. Between 5 and 6 tubular, wavy-edged, yellow flowers up to 10cm in diameter, with protruding stamens, are produced during spring and summer.

***Sow seed*** at 12°C as soon as it is ripe.

J ***Divide offsets*** after flowering and immediately pot up in a loam-based compost with the neck of the bulb above the compost. Overwinter in a cold frame.

**LYSICHITON AMERICANUS**
(Yellow skunk cabbage)
Marginal, aquatic perennial with rosettes of 60–120cm long, leathery, glossy, mid-green leaves. Ovate, 40cm long, bright yellow spathes are produced in early spring.

***Sow seed*** in a garden frame on wet soil as soon as it is ripe.

J ***Remove offsets*** from around the base of the plant in spring or early summer

and pot up in a moisture-retentive, multi-purpose compost. Overwinter in a garden frame.

**LYSIMACHIA CLETHROIDES**
(Loosestrife)
Perennial with lance-shaped, pointed, mid-green leaves that are paler green on the underside. Racemes of saucer-shaped, white flowers are produced during summer.

***Sow seed*** in spring in containers outside.

E ***Divide*** in autumn or wait until spring in cold areas.

**LYTHRUM SALICARIA**
(Purple loosestrife)
Perennial with lance-shaped, downy green, 10cm long leaves. Spike-like racemes of purple-red flowers appear in midsummer and autumn.

***Sow seed*** at 15°C in spring.

***Softwood basal cuttings*** in spring or early summer.

J ***Divide*** in spring.

### MAACKIA CHINENSIS
Deciduous tree with dark green, 20cm long, pinnate leaves that emerge silvery-blue. Panicles of ivory-white, pea-like flowers appear in late summer, followed by 7cm long seed pods.

**Sow seed** outdoors in containers or in the open ground in autumn.

◻ **Softwood cuttings** in early summer. Shorten the leaves and root in ericaceous compost with extra grit under horticultural fleece.

### MACLEAYA CORDATA (Plume poppy)
Perennial with lobed, grey-green leaves that are downy-white on the underside. Large, plume-like panicles of pendant, off-white flowers with numerous stamens are produced in late summer.

**Sow seed** in a garden frame in spring.
**Divide** the rhizomes in late autumn when dormant.

◻ **Root cuttings** in winter in a garden frame.

### MACLURA POMIFERA (Osage orange)
Deciduous tree with thorny stems and dark green, 10cm long, pointed leaves turning yellow in autumn. Tiny, green-yellow flowers are produced in early summer. Male flowers form spherical clusters; female flowers form racemes. The female plants produce 12cm diameter fruit with wrinkled, greenish-yellow skin.

**Sow seed** in a garden frame as soon as it is ripe. Alternatively, sow in spring after soaking for 24 hours.

◻ **Semi-ripe cuttings** with a 'heel' in summer in a propagator. Where excess callus forms instead of roots, scrape off most of it and re-insert the cutting.

**Root cuttings** in winter in a garden frame.

Macleaya cordata

## MAGNOLIA

Deciduous or evergreen trees and shrubs with mid- to dark green, glossy or matt leaves. Flowers are cup-, saucer- or star-shaped, often fragrant. Colours include white, white flushed with pink or purple, purple, yellow and greenish-yellow. Cone-like fruits are produced in autumn, often with red-coated seed.

**Sow seed** as soon as it is ripe, in individual pots in a garden frame or outside in a sheltered area of the garden. Leave the seeds to dry in the sun before sowing and the red pulp will fall away from the seed. Packets of bought seed should be stored at 1°C for 20 days prior to sowing.

**Semi-ripe cuttings** of evergreen and deciduous species in late summer. Evergreens will root well into autumn.

**Softwood cuttings** of deciduous species in early summer.

**Layer** in late winter. Guaranteed success given a suitably placed branch.

**Saddle graft** in winter.

## MAHONIA AQUIFOLIUM

(Oregon grape)

Evergreen shrub with pinnate, 30cm long, bright green leaves made up of up to 9 sharp-toothed leaflets. The leaves often turn deep red-purple in winter. Racemes of fragrant, deep yellow flowers are produced in spring, followed by blue-black berries.

**Sow seed** in containers outside as soon as it is ripe. Stratification improves germination.

**Semi-ripe cuttings** in late summer.

**Leaf bud cuttings** in late summer or autumn. Cut the large leaf in half to reduce transpiration, but don't split the stem.

**Plant rooted suckers** in winter in a multi-purpose compost in a garden frame.

## MALCOLMIA MARITIMA

(Virginian stock)

Annual with 5cm long, grey-green leaves. Spikes with masses of fragrant red or purple flowers appear from summer to autumn.

**Sow seed** in open ground from late spring until summer for a succession of colour.

## MALOPE TRIFIDA (Annual mallow)

Annual with mid-green, 10cm long, hairy leaves. Trumpet-shaped, pale to dark purple flowers are produced during summer and autumn. The petals have prominent dark purple veins.

**Sow seed** in open ground in late spring.

## MALUS (Apple, Crab apple)

Deciduous tree with oval-shaped, mid- to dark green or purple leaves. The often fragrant, spring flowers are saucer-shaped and may be semi-double or double. Colours include white, pink-flushed white, pink or deep red. In autumn the dessert, culinary or small crab apples are green, yellow, yellow-flushed red or bright red.

**Sow seed** as soon as it is ripe in autumn in a garden frame. Seedlings will be inferior to the named variety.

**Whip and tongue graft** in mid-winter. A great way of rejuvenating an old but canker-free tree.

**Bud graft** in late summer.

## MALVA ALCEA (Mallow)

Perennial with heart-shaped, light green lower leaves. Upper leaves are deeply cut and 15cm long. Racemes of funnel-shaped, deep pink flowers are produced from early summer to mid-autumn.

**Sow seed** in containers in early summer.

**Softwood basal cuttings** in spring.

## MANDEVILLA LAXA (Chilean jasmine)

Deciduous climber with bright, rich green leaves that are purple or grey-green on the underside. Racemes of highly fragrant, tubular, white or creamy-white flowers are produced in summer and early autumn.

*Sow seed* at 20°C in spring.

🔲 *Softwood cuttings* in late spring. Wipe off the milky sap before inserting in the compost. The sap is a skin irritant. *Semi-ripe cuttings* in summer in a propagator.

## MANETTIA CORDIFOLIA
(Firecracker vine)
Tender, evergreen climber with bright green, heart-shaped leaves that are paler green on the underside. Single flowers or loose panicles of tubular, bright red or orange-red flowers with yellow tips are produced from spring to late summer.

*Sow seed* at 16°C in spring.

🔲 *Softwood cuttings* in early summer. Take small tip cuttings, no longer than 5cm.

## MARANTA LEUCONEURA (Prayer plant)
Tender, evergreen perennial with rounded, dark green, 12cm long leaves with silver lines from the mid-ribs to the margins. The undersides are pale green or purple. The leaves spread out during the day, becoming erect in the evening. Pairs of small, 2-lipped, white flowers are produced in summer.

*Sow seed* at 16°C as soon as it is ripe.

🔲 *Softwood basal cuttings* in late spring in a propagator.

## MARRUBIUM INCANUM
Perennial with toothed, grey-green leaves, white felted on the underside. Whorls of pale lilac flowers are produced in early summer.

*Sow seed* in a garden frame in spring. Germination is erratic.

🔲 *Softwood cuttings* in spring.

Melianthus major

## MATTEUCCIA STRUTHIOPTERIS
(Ostrich fern)
Deciduous fern with lance-shaped, 1.2m long, pinnate, pale green, sterile fronds. Fertile fronds are 30cm long, lance-shaped and dark brown and appear in late summer.

*Sow spores* at 14°C as soon as they are ripe.

🔲 *Divide* large clumps in early spring. Pot the rhizomes into humus-rich, acid, soil-based compost.

## MATTHIOLA INCANA (Stock)
Perennial with lance-shaped, grey-green leaves. Upright racemes of highly fragrant, white, pink, mauve or purple flowers are produced from early summer to late autumn.

*Sow seed* in a garden frame in summer. Overwinter with frost protection. Plant out in late spring. Most gardeners prefer the double-flowered plants and, over the years, plant breeders have managed to develop strains of seed that allow you to choose. With some, when the temperature is lowered, the seedlings with the pale leaves are the double flowering. With others, it is the seedlings with a notch at the side of the leaf.

## MAZUS REPTANS
Perennial with short, coarsely toothed, mid-green leaves. Racemes of purple-blue flowers with red and yellow spots on the lower petals are produced in late spring and summer.

*Sow seed* in a garden frame in spring or autumn.

🔲 *Divide* in late spring.

## MECONOPSIS BETONICIFOLIA
(Himalayan blue poppy)
Deciduous perennial with rosettes of pale, bluish-green, 20–30cm long leaves covered in brown hairs. Saucer-shaped, bright blue, pendant, nodding flowers with orange-yellow stamens are carried on bristly stalks in early summer.

*Sow seed* as soon as it is ripe, in a garden frame. Use a peat-based compost and only apply a thin layer of sifted compost to keep the seed moist and still allow daylight to penetrate. Seedlings are prone to damping off during winter. If the seed can be stored in cool, dry conditions, then sow no later than late winter.

### MEDINILLA MAGNIFICA
Tender shrub with leathery, deep green, 25–30cm long leaves and prominent, pale green veins. Pendant panicles of cerise-red flowers with yellow stamens are produced below pairs of large, cupped, icing pink bracts.

*Sow seed* at 20°C in spring.
*Softwood cuttings* in spring.
🌢 *Semi-ripe cuttings* in summer in a propagator.
*Air layer* in late spring.

### MELALEUCA ELLIPTICA
(Granite bottlebrush)
Tender, evergreen shrub with peeling, corky bark and small, deep green leaves that are pale green on the underside. Dense spikes of crimson (sometimes bright pink) flowers are produced from spring to midsummer.

*Sow seed* at 22°C in spring.
🌢 *Semi-ripe cuttings* in a propagator in summer. Pot the rooted cuttings in autumn into soil-based compost and overwinter under glass.

### MELIA AZEDARACH (Bead tree)
Tender, deciduous tree with pinnate, bright green, 30–60cm long leaflets. Pendant panicles of fragrant, star-shaped, lilac flowers are produced in late spring and early summer. Deep yellow, bead-like fruit follows in autumn.

🌢 *Sow seed* at 16°C in spring.
*Softwood cuttings* in a propagator in summer.

### MELIANTHUS MAJOR (Honey bush)
Tender, evergreen shrub with hollow stems. Spreading, pinnate leaves, 30–45cm long, are sharply toothed and greyish blue-green. Racemes of brownish, brick-red flowers appear in late spring and early summer.

*Sow seed* at 16°C in spring.
*Softwood, basal cuttings* in early summer.
🌢 *Plant rooted suckers* in spring in a garden frame.

### MELIOSMA MYRIANTHA
Deciduous shrub or small tree with sharply toothed, mid-green leaves with soft, red-brown hairs on the mid-ribs. Panicles of fragrant, creamy-white flowers are produced in midsummer, followed by small, dark red fruit.

*Sow seed* in a garden frame in autumn.
🌢 *Softwood cuttings* in early summer.

### MELISSA OFFICINALIS (Lemon balm)
Perennial with hairy stems and wrinkled, light green, aromatic leaves. Spikes of pale yellow flowers fading to white are produced in summer.

*Sow seed* in a garden frame in spring.
🌢 *Divide* in early spring or late autumn.

### MELITTIS MELISSOPHYLLUM
(Bastard balm)
Perennial with hairy, square stems and hairy, wrinkled, aromatic leaves that smell of honey. Whorls of 2-lipped, tubular flowers appear in late spring and early summer; these may be white, pink or purple or white with purple lips.

*Sow seed* in a garden frame in autumn.
🌢 *Divide* in spring as the new growths emerge.

### MENTHA SUAVEOLENS (Apple mint)
Perennial with soft, hairy, wrinkled, greyish-green, aromatic leaves smelling of apple. Spikes of tiny, tubular, white or pink flowers are produced in summer. A rampant-growing herb that needs to be contained, otherwise it will become a weed.

*Seed* Sow the tiny seed on the surface of the compost in a container in a garden frame during autumn or spring. Mixing the seed with talcum powder will make it easier to sow the small seed. Don't sneeze!
*Softwood cuttings* in spring or summer.
*Divide* in autumn or spring.
*Insert pieces of rhizomes cut from the plant* horizontally in compost at any time of the year.

### MENYANTHES TRIFOLIATA (Bogbean)
Aquatic perennial with bright green, 3-palmate leaves. Racemes of white flowers opening from pink buds are produced in summer.

*Sow seed* in winter in containers of peaty compost standing in water.
🌢 *Divide* rhizomes in summer, cutting them into 20cm lengths. Lay them horizontally on mud in a container in shallow water.

Melissa officinalis

## MENZIESIA FERRUGINEA (Rusty leaf)
Deciduous shrub with mid-green leaves covered in soft, rust-brown hairs turning bright red in autumn. Umbels of urn-shaped, red-flushed, yellow flowers are produced in late spring and early summer.

**Sow seed** in a garden frame in autumn. Use ericaceous compost and leave the seed uncovered.
**Softwood cuttings** in early summer in a propagator, in ericaceous compost.

## MERTENSIA MARITIMA (Oyster plant)
Perennial with spoon-shaped, fleshy, glaucous leaves. Bell-shaped blue flowers open from pink buds in early summer.

**Sow seed** in a garden frame in autumn in moisture-retentive compost.
**Divide** carefully in early spring as new growths emerge.

## MESPILUS GERMANICA (Medlar)
Deciduous tree with long, dark green leaves that turn yellowish-brown in late autumn. Large white or pink-tinged white flowers appear in late spring or early summer. Fleshy, apple-like, edible fruit is produced in late autumn.

**Sow seed** in open ground in autumn.
**Layer** in summer.
**Whip and tongue graft** in early summer. Use *Cydonia oblonga* (quince) as a rootstock.

## METASEQUOIA GLYPTOSTROBOIDES
(Dawn redwood)
Deciduous conifer with orange-brown bark and soft, bright green leaves with 2 light green bands on the underside. The leaves turn yellow in autumn. It has light brown, female cones.

**Sow seed** in a garden frame in autumn.
**Semi-ripe cuttings** in summer in a propagator. Take with a 'heel'.
**Hardwood cuttings** in winter.

## MICHELIA FIGO
Tender, evergreen tree with rich, dark green leaves that are paler green on the underside. Cup-shaped, banana-scented, greenish-yellow flowers with deep red margins to the petals open from woolly brown bracts during spring and summer.

**Sow seed** in a garden frame in late summer.
**Softwood cuttings** in early summer.
**Semi-ripe cuttings** in late summer.
**Air layer** in late spring.

## MICROBIOTA DECUSSATA
Evergreen conifer with bright, mid-green leaves that turn brown in winter. Female cones have one fertile scale. Male cones are pale yellow. A conifer that is frequently dug up and dumped during the first winter as it looks dead.

**Sow seed** in open ground in autumn.
**Semi-ripe cuttings** in summer with a 'heel'. Do remember that the foliage turns brown in winter, so don't assume the worst.

## MILIUM EFFUSUM 'AUREUM'
(Bowles' golden grass)
Semi-evergreen, perennial grass with flat, strap-like, 30cm long, golden-yellow leaves. Nodding panicles of golden spikelets are produced from late spring to midsummer.

**Sow seed** in spring in open ground. It comes true from seed.
**Divide** in late spring.

## MILLA BIFLORA
Bulbous perennial with narrow, glaucous, mid-green leaves. Umbels of tubular, fragrant, white or white-flushed pink flowers with green central veins are produced in summer and autumn.

**Sow seed** at 16°C in spring.

**Remove offsets** in autumn after the leaves turn yellow. Pot into a free-draining, loam-based compost and place in a frost-free conservatory or greenhouse.

## MIMOSA PUDICA (Sensitive plant)
Tender, evergreen perennial with prickly stems. Bright green leaves are divided into 4 leaflets, made up of pairs of narrow segments that fold up like butterfly wings when touched. Light pink to lilac flowerheads are produced in summer.

**Sow seed** at 20°C in spring.
**Softwood cuttings** in early summer in a propagator.

## MIMULUS LUTEUS
(Yellow monkey flower)
Perennial with oblong leaves. Yellow flowers with dark red spots appear in late spring and early summer.

**Sow seed** in a garden frame in autumn or spring. Self-seeds freely.
**Divide** in spring.

## MIRABILIS JALAPA (Marvel of Peru)
Perennial with dull green leaves. Trumpet-shaped, fragrant, pink, red, yellow or white flowers are produced from early to late summer. The flowers open in the afternoon and die the following morning.

**Sow seed** at 16°C in spring.
**Divide** tubers in spring. Repot immediately.

## MISCANTHUS SINENSIS
Deciduous, perennial grass with basal, linear, 1.2m long, mid-green leaves. Panicles of silky, pale grey spikelets, tinted maroon, are produced in autumn.

**Sow seed** in a garden frame in early spring.
**Divide** in early spring. Keep the young plants in shade for a few weeks.

### MITCHELLA REPENS (Partridge berry)

Evergreen perennial with glossy, dark green, white-veined leaves. Fragrant, white, occasionally pink tinged, flowers are produced in early summer, followed by bright red berries.

*Sow seed* in a garden frame in autumn.
*Pot up rooted runners* in spring and plant out in the autumn.

### MITELLA BREWERI (Mitrewort)

Perennial with hairy, ovate, mid-green leaves. Racemes of tiny, greenish-yellow, bell-shaped flowers with fringed petals appear in late spring and early summer.

*Sow seed* in a garden frame in autumn.
*Divide* in spring.

### MITRARIA COCCINEA

Evergreen shrub with leathery, glossy, dark green, toothed leaves. Single, tubular, bright scarlet flowers are produced from spring to autumn.

*Sow seed* in a garden frame in spring.
*Semi-ripe cuttings* in summer in a propagator, using ericaceous compost.

### MOLINIA CAERULEA
(Purple moor grass)

Perennial grass with flat, mid-green, 45cm long leaves. Panicles of purple spikelets on straw-coloured stems are produced from spring to autumn.

*Sow seed* in a garden frame in spring.
*Divide* established clumps in spring. Plants are slow to become established.

### MOLUCCELLA LAEVIS (Bells of Ireland)

Annual with deeply scalloped, pale green leaves. Whorled spikes of fragrant, purple-pink or white flowers are produced in late summer. Each flower is cupped in a pale green calyx, turning white in late autumn.

Monarda 'Beauty of Cobham'

*Sow seed* in open ground in late spring or at 16°C in containers in early spring. Germination can be erratic at higher temperatures.

### MONARDA 'BEAUTY OF COBHAM'
(Bergamot)

Perennial with square stems and purplish-green leaves. Purplish-pink bracts surround the pale pink flowers from midsummer to mid-autumn.

*Sow seed* in a garden frame in autumn or spring.
*Softwood basal cuttings* in late spring.
*Divide* in early spring before the new growths emerge.

### MONSTERA DELICIOSA
(Swiss cheese plant)

Tender, evergreen climber with long-stalked, heart-shaped, leathery, glossy, deeply lobed mid-green leaves, often with oblong holes between the lateral veins. Juvenile leaves are smaller and solid. Creamy-white spathes, 20–30cm long, appear in summer, followed by cone-shaped, edible fruit.

*Sow seed* at 20°C as soon as it is ripe.
*Leaf cuttings* in a propagator in summer. Cut the leaf in half to reduce transpiration. Roll the leaf and hold with a rubber band to take up less space in the propagator.
*Layer* in autumn.

## MORAEA HUTTONII

Cormous perennial with a single, linear, channelled, 90cm long, mid-green, basal leaf. Fragrant, deep yellow flowers with brown marks are produced in spring and early summer.

*Sow seed* in a garden frame in autumn.

🛛 *Remove offsets* in late autumn.Plant them 5 cm deep in a free-draining, loam-based compost in a frost-free greenhouse.

## MORINA LONGIFOLIA (Whorlflower)

Perennial with rosettes of linear, aromatic, glossy, dark green, spiny-edged leaves. Tall stems with whorled clusters of white flowers with spiny bracts are produced in summer. After fertilization the flowers turn carmine-red.

*Sow seed* individually in pots of well-drained compost in a garden frame. Keep the seedlings cool and the frame well ventilated.

🛛 *Root cuttings* in winter in a garden frame.

## MORISIA MONANTHOS

Perennial with rosettes of lance-shaped, glossy, dark green leaves. The plant covers itself with cross-shaped, golden-yellow flowers in late spring and early summer.

*Sow seed* in a garden frame in spring.

*Root cuttings* in a garden frame in winter. Remove the portions of root without lifting the parent plant, as it forms a tap root and resents disturbance.

## MORUS NIGRA (Mulberry)

Deciduous tree with heart-shaped, rough-surfaced, mid-green leaves. Catkins of cup-shaped, green, female and male flowers appear in late spring, followed by edible fruit. Berries are green at first, turning red and then dark purple when ripe in late summer.

Morina longifolia

*Sow seed* in containers outside in autumn.

*Semi-ripe cuttings* in summer.

*Hardwood cuttings* in a garden frame in late autumn.

◨ *Hardwood stumps* – often referred to as truncheons – using thicker branches than a cutting. Hammer short 'pegs' into the ground in late autumn. The 'pegs' should be 15cm long and taken from long, 3-year-old branches that are 5cm thick.

### MUEHLENBECKIA AXILLARIS
(Wire plant)

Deciduous shrub with wiry-stems and crinkly margined, glossy, dark green leaves. Fragrant, greenish-white flowers are produced in late spring and summer.

*Sow seed* at 20°C in spring.

◨ *Semi-ripe cuttings* in a propagator in summer.

*Irishman's cuttings* Remove rooted sections in spring.

### MUSA ACUMINATA (Banana)

Suckering, evergreen perennial with large, 2–3m long, glaucous, paddle-shaped, mid-green leaves that have brown papery edges. Pendant, white or yellow flowers with purple bracts are followed by edible, yellow-skinned fruit.

*Plant rooted suckers* in early spring. Remove the older, large leaves. Use a loam-based compost and position in a frost-free conservatory or greenhouse..

### MUSCARI ARMENIACUM
(Grape hyacinth)

Bulbous perennial with lance-shaped, 20cm long, mid-green leaves. Dense racemes of tubular, bright blue flowers with a white mouth are produced in spring.

Myosotis sylvatica

*Sow seed* in a garden frame in autumn.

◨ *Remove offsets* in summer and replant immediately in a sheltered part of the garden, or pot and overwinter in a garden frame.

### MUTISIA DECURRENS

Evergreen climber with winged stems and 10cm long, dark green leaves, each with a tendril at the tip. Large, 12cm in diameter, bright orange flowerheads are produced in summer.

*Sow seed* in a garden frame in autumn.

*Softwood tip cuttings* in early summer. I have never managed to root more than one of a batch at any time!

*Layer* in late autumn. They can take ages to root.

◨ *Plant rooted suckers* in early spring in a garden frame. In summer, stand them out on a sheltered part of the garden for a year before planting out.

### MYOSOTIDIUM HORTENSIA
(Chatham Island forget-me-not)

Evergreen perennial with large, 30cm long, glossy, bright green basal leaves with wavy margins and prominent veins. Dense clusters of bell-shaped, dark or pale blue flowers, occasionally with white-edged lobes, are produced in early summer.

◨ *Seed* Sow the large, black seeds as soon as they are ripe, in a garden frame with frost protection. Use extra grit to provide a free-draining compost.

*Divide* in spring.

### MYOSOTIS SYLVATICA (Forget-me-not)

Short-lived perennial with lance-shaped, grey-green leaves. Masses of saucer-shaped, bright blue flowers with single, yellow eyes are produced in spring and early summer.

*Sow seed* in a garden frame in spring.

### MYRICA GALE (Bog myrtle)

Deciduous shrub with lance-shaped, aromatic leaves. The yellowish-brown catkins are followed by yellowish-brown fruit.

*Sow seed* outdoors in containers as soon as it is ripe.

◨ *Softwood cuttings* in early summer.

*Layer* in early spring. I take the lazy option and mound a mixture of peat and leaf mould over the lower third of the stems. Keep them damp and the stems will root into the compost. They can be cut off, complete with their roots, in late autumn.

## MYRIOPHYLLUM HIPPUROIDES
(Western milfoil)
Aquatic perennial with yellow-green submerged leaves and whorls of lance-shaped, olive-green or red leaves above water with tiny, white flowers in the leaf axils during summer.

**Softwood cuttings.** Insert young tip growths or lengths of stem under water in sand or mud.

## MYRRHIS ODORATA (Sweet cicely)
Perennial herb with hollow stems and aromatic, aniseed-flavoured, 45cm long, bright green leaves. Umbels of star-shaped, white flowers appear in early summer, followed by ridged, shiny brown fruit.

**Sow seed** in a garden frame in early autumn. Removing the flower stems as they develop improves the flavour but eliminates any chance of saving the seed.
- **Divide** in spring.

## MYRTUS COMMUNIS (Common myrtle)
Evergreen shrub with glossy, 5cm long, dark green, aromatic leaves. Bowl-shaped, fragrant, white flowers with prominent white stamens are produced in late summer and early autumn. Purple-black berries follow.

**Sow seed** in a garden frame in spring.
- **Semi-ripe cuttings** with a 'heel' in a propagator in early autumn.

## NANDINA DOMESTICA
(Heavenly bamboo)
Evergreen shrub with pinnate, 90cm long, bright green leaves. The young leaves are red-purple, turning mid-green in summer and reverting to deep red in winter. Conical panicles, 45cm long, of star-shaped, white flowers with bold, thick, yellow anthers are produced in summer, followed by bright red fruit.

*Myrtus communis*

- **Sow seed** in a garden frame as soon as it is ripe.
**Semi-ripe cuttings** with a 'heel' in summer.

## NARCISSUS (Daffodil)
Bulbous perennial with basal, strap-shaped, mid- to dark green leaves. Single or double, yellow, white, orange or bicoloured flowers appear during late winter, spring or late summer with a shallow or deep corona (trumpet).

**Sow seed** of the species as soon as it is ripe in a garden frame. It may take 7 years before it flowers.
- **Remove offsets** in early summer as the leaves turn yellow, or in early autumn before growth commences.

## NEILLIA SINENSIS
Deciduous shrub with peeling, brown bark and glossy, dark green, sharply toothed and lobed leaves. Racemes of small, tubular, pink-white flowers are produced in late spring and early summer.

**Softwood cuttings** in early summer.
- **Take rooted suckers** in autumn and either pot up for a season outdoors to allow more roots to develop or, if well rooted, plant out in the open ground.

## NELUMBO LUTEA (American lotus)
Aquatic perennial with deep, crescent-shaped, bluish-green, 50cm wide leaves carried on stalks that are 2m long. Rose-like, yellow flowers are produced in late summer.

**Sow seed** in spring at 25°C in loam-based compost submerged in water. As the seedlings grow, lower the pot into deeper water.
- **Divide** in spring. The lotus detests disturbance. Place the fleshy root on the soil surface and keep in shallow water until growth starts.

## NEMATANTHUS GREGARIUS
Tender, evergreen sub-shrub with fleshy, glossy, deep green leaves. Tubular, orange flowers with purple stripes, and green calyces with orange tips are produced in summer.

- **Softwood tip cuttings** in late spring. Spray the foliage with rainwater.

## NEMESIA CAERULEA
Perennial with lance-shaped leaves. Terminal racemes of tubular, 2-lipped, white, pink or pale blue flowers with yellow throats are produced in early summer and autumn.

**Sow seed** at 15°C in spring.
- **Softwood cuttings** of non-flowering shoots in late summer. Cover with horticultural fleece.

## NEMOPHILA MENZIESII
(Baby blue eyes)
Annual with grey-green leaves. Solitary, saucer-shaped, blue flowers with pale blue or bluish-yellow centres and a deep purple spot on each petal are produced in summer.

**Sow seed** in open ground in late spring.

*Narcissus poeticus*

Nerine bowdenii

**NEPENTHES 'DIRECTOR G. T. MOORE'**
(Pitcher plant)
Tender, evergreen climber with strap-like leaves. Pear-shaped, light green pitchers, 13cm long, have purple-red mottling and mottled wings.

**Sow seed** as soon as it is ripe, on the surface of moist peat in a propagator. Maintain high humidity.
🔲 **Softwood cuttings** in spring at 25°C in orchid compost with added sphagnum moss.
**Air layer** in late spring.

**NEPETA × FAASSENII** (Catmint)
Perennial with wrinkled, scalloped, aromatic, hairy, grey-green leaves. Spikes of lavender-blue flowers with dark purple spots are produced in summer and early autumn.

**Sow seed** in a garden frame in autumn.
🔲 **Softwood cuttings** in early summer under horticultural fleece. Pot up the cuttings as soon as they are rooted. Encourage some growth and root run in the container before late autumn.
**Divide** in spring as growth commences.

**NERINE BOWDENII**
Bulbous perennial with strap-like, 30cm long, bright green leaves after the flowers. Umbels of funnel-shaped, scented, pink flowers with wavy margins are produced before the leaves in autumn.

**Seed** Sow the fleshy seed as soon as it is ripe at 12°C. Don't cover the seed with compost. Germination is quick.
🔲 **Divide** clumps just after flowering. Keep the nose of the bulb at soil level.

**NERIUM OLEANDER** (Rose bay)
Tender, evergreen shrub with lance-shaped, deep green or greyish-green leaves. Clusters of white, pink or red flowers are produced in summer.

**Sow seed** at 16°C in spring.
**Semi-ripe cuttings** in a propagator in summer.
🔲 **Air layer** in late spring.

Handle this plant with care, as all parts of it are poisonous.

**NERTERA GRANADENSIS** (Bead plant)
Perennial with small, bright green leaves. Bell-shaped, yellowish-green flowers are produced in summer, followed by masses of orange or red berries.

🔲 **Sow seed** at 16°C in spring.
**Divide** in spring.

**NICANDRA PHYSALODES** (Shoo-fly)
Annual with wavy-margined, mid-green leaves. Violet-blue flowers with white throats are produced in summer and autumn, followed by brown berries enclosed in green calyces.

**Sow seed** in open ground in late spring. Self-seeds freely.

**NICOTIANA SYLVESTRIS**
(Ornamental tobacco plant)
Biennial with a basal rosette of 30cm long, dark green leaves. Panicles of nodding, long, trumpet-shaped, very fragrant, white flowers that close in full sun are produced from midsummer to autumn.

**Sow seed** at 16°C in spring on the surface of the compost.

**NIDULARIUM REGELIOIDES**
Perennial bromeliad with rosettes of strap-like, toothed, bright green leaves. Tubular, red flowers with purple-tipped white sepals surrounded by bright red bracts appear in summer.

**Sow seed** at 25°C in spring.
🔲 **Remove offsets** in spring or summer. Pot into an orchid compost and position in moderate light away from bright sunlight in a greenhouse or conservatory. Maintain a humid atmosphere.

**NIEREMBERGIA REPENS** (White cup)
Perennial with spoon-shaped, mid-green leaves. Bell-shaped, white flowers with yellow centres are produced in summer.

**Sow seed** at 16°C in spring.
**Softwood, tip cuttings** in early summer. I find it best to keep the cuttings shaded for a few weeks.
🔲 **Divide** in spring.

**NIGELLA DAMASCENA** (Love-in-a-mist)
Annual with divided, 12cm long, bright green leaves. Saucer-shaped, pale blue flowers, maturing to sky blue, are produced during summer and early autumn. Each flower is surrounded by a collar of finely divided foliage.

**Sow seed** in late spring in open ground. It also self-seeds freely.

## NOMOCHARIS PARDANTHINA

Bulbous perennial with small, lance-shaped, mid-green leaves. Racemes of nodding, white or pale pink flowers, which have dark centres, are heavily marked with deep red dots and fringed petal margins during early summer.

**Sow seed** at 10°C in autumn or in spring. The seedlings hate being disturbed, so plant only 3 seeds per pot. After germination, thin to a single seedling and plant it out from the pot. It will flower within 4–5 years.

## NOTHOFAGUS ANTARCTICA
(Southern beech)
Deciduous tree with ovate, glossy, dark green, crinkly leaves that turn yellow in autumn. Flowers and fruits are insignificant.

**Sow seed** singly in pots in a garden frame in autumn.

## NOTHOLIRION BULBULIFERUM

Bulbous perennial with 45cm long, basal, mid-green leaves. Racemes of trumpet-shaped, pale lilac-pink flowers with green tips appear in summer.

**Sow bulblets** in late summer in a garden frame.
🗐 **Remove offsets** in autumn and replant in a multi-purpose compost in a garden frame.

## NOTOSPARTIUM GLABRESCENS

Leafless shrub with dark, greenish-blue shoots. Racemes of pink, pea-like flowers with purple veins are produced in summer.

**Sow seed** in a garden frame in autumn or spring.
🗐 **Semi-ripe cuttings** in summer in a propagator. Double the amount of grit in the rooting compost. Overwinter the rooted cuttings in a frost-proof greenhouse.

## NUPHAR PUMILA
(Yellow pond lily, Spatterdock)
Aquatic perennial with ovate, bright green, floating leaves up to 12cm in diameter. Submerged leaves are rounded, wavy at the margins and pale green. Small, bright yellow flowers are produced in summer.

**Divide** rhizomes, making sure each piece is complete with a bud, and transplant into a container of clay-based soil. Place in the water or directly into the mud at the bottom of the pond.

## NYMPHAEA (Water lily)
Aquatic perennial with floating, bright green, rounded leaves with 2 lobes. White, yellow, pink, red or blue flowers with narrow petals appear during summer, followed by fruit that mature underwater.

**Sow seed** as soon as it is ripe, on the surface of the compost and submerge in 3cm of water at 13°C. To collect the seed, enclose the whole seed head in a muslin bag after flowering to prevent it sinking as it ripens.
🗐 **Divide** in early summer.

## NYMPHOIDES PELTATA (Floating heart)
Aquatic perennial with mottled, mid-green leaves that are 5–10cm in diameter. Funnel-shaped, bright yellow flowers are carried on long stems in summer.

**Plant rooted runners** in summer in an aquatic planting basket in water no deeper than 60cm.

## NYSSA SYLVATICA (Tupelo tree)
Deciduous tree with glossy, 15cm long, dark green leaves that turn yellow, orange or red in autumn. Tiny, green flowers are followed by small, blue fruit.

Nymphaea 'Mrs Richmond'

*Sow seed* in open ground in autumn.
*Softwood cuttings* in early summer.
    Use ericaceous compost.
🔲 *Semi-ripe cuttings* in late summer.

### OCHNA SERRULATA
(Micky mouse plant)
Tender, semi-evergreen tree with bronze shoots covered in raised, corky spots. The leaves are shiny and bright green. The saucer-shaped, bright yellow flowers appear in late spring and early summer. After the petals drop, the sepals become shiny red with glossy, black fruit.

*Sow seed* at 16°C in spring.
🔲 *Semi-ripe cuttings* in a propagator in
    summer.
*Air layer* in spring.

### ODONTOGLOSSUM CRISPUM
Tender orchid with linear, 30cm long, mid-green leaves. Racemes of white flowers with yellow lips and spotted centres appear in winter.

*Divide* established clumps in late
    summer.

### OENOTHERA MACROCARPA
(Ozark sundrops)
Perennial with red-tinted shoots and lance-shaped, mid-green leaves with white mid-ribs. Solitary, saucer-shaped, bright golden-yellow flowers appear from late spring to late autumn. Calyces are speckled red.

*Sow seed* in a garden frame in spring.
🔲 *Softwood cuttings* of non-flowering
    shoots in early summer.

### OLEA EUROPAEA (Olive)
Evergreen tree with leathery, grey-green leaves that are silvery-green on the underside. Panicles of small, fragrant, white flowers appear in summer followed by edible, green fruit that ripen to black.

*Sow seed* at 15°C in spring.
🔲 *Semi-ripe cuttings* in late summer. Use
    short cuttings with a 'heel' under
    horticultural fleece. I root them on a
    hot bed of rotting farmyard manure in
    a garden frame. After 6 weeks the bed
    will be cold and the rooted plants can
    be overwintered in the frame.

### OLEARIA MACRODONTA (Daisy bush)
Evergreen shrub with holly-like, sharply toothed, glossy, dark green leaves that are white felted on the underside. Masses of fragrant, daisy-like, white flowerheads with purple-brown centres are produced in summer.

*Softwood cuttings* in early summer.
🔲 *Semi-ripe cuttings* in midsummer.

In both cases, shorten the leaves by half to reduce transpiration.

### ONOCLEA SENSIBILIS (Sensitive fern)
Deciduous fern with pinnate, 90cm long, pale green, sterile fronds. Fertile fronds are lance-shaped and 60cm long and appear in late summer. Bead-like, black lobes enclose the sori.

*Sow spores* at 16°C as soon as they
    are ripe.
🔲 *Divide* in early spring.

### ONONIS FRUTICOSA
(Shrubby restharrow)
Deciduous shrub with 3-palmate, leathery leaves. Clusters of pea-like, pink flowers with pale pink wings and cerise central markings are produced during summer.

*Sow seed* in a garden frame in autumn
    or spring.
🔲 *Softwood cuttings* in early summer.

Onopordum acanthium

### ONOPORDUM ACANTHIUM
(Scotch thistle)
Biennial with spiny toothed, green-grey, 30cm long leaves. Spiny pale green stems support round, thistle-like, pale purple flowerheads that are enclosed in spine-tipped bracts.

*Sow seed* in a garden frame in early
    autumn.

### ONOSMA ALBOROSEA
Evergreen perennial with spoon-shaped, white hairy, grey-green leaves. Nodding, tubular, white flowers with the tips maturing to deep pink-purple are produced in summer.

*Sow seed* in a garden frame in autumn.

### OPHIOPOGON PLANISCAPUS
(Lilyturf, Mondo grass)
Perennial grass with strap-like, curving, dark green leaves. Racemes of bell-shaped, white-purple flowers appear in summer followed by fleshy, blue-black fruit.

*Sow seed* in a garden frame as soon
as it is ripe.
- *Divide* in early spring. Take care to retain
the fleshy roots on the plants.

---

**OPUNTIA ERINACEA** (Prickly pear)
Tender, perennial cactus with blue-
green stems in flattened segments with
white spines. Bowl-shaped, yellow, pink
or red flowers are produced in summer,
followed by pale green, spiny fruit.

*Sow seed* at 20°C as soon as it is ripe.
Pre-soak the seed for 24 hours.
- *Softwood cuttings* Root portions of
stem in free-draining, gritty compost.
Allow the cut surface to dry before
inserting in the compost.

---

**ORIGANUM 'KENT BEAUTY'** (Marjoram)
Semi-evergreen sub-shrub with small,
bright green, aromatic leaves. Whorls
of tubular, pale pink or mauve flowers
with deep rose-pink bracts appear
during summer.

*Sow seed* in a garden frame in autumn.
- *Softwood, basal cuttings* in late spring.
*Divide* in spring.

---

**ORNITHOGALUM NARBONENSE**
(Star-of-Bethlehem)
Bulbous perennial with basal, linear,
60cm long, grey-green leaves. Pyramidal
racemes of star-shaped, white flowers
appear in late spring and early summer.

*Sow seed* in a garden frame in spring.
- *Remove offsets* in late summer when
dormant and replant in containers of
soil-based compost in a garden frame.

---

**ORONTIUM AQUATICUM** (Golden club)
Aquatic perennial with submerged and
floating 20cm long, mid-green leaves
that are tinted purple on the underside.
Small, golden-yellow flowers appear in
late spring and early summer at the tips
of white spadices.

*Sow seed* as soon as it is ripe, in loam-
based compost. Cover with 2cm of
rainwater and put in a garden frame.
- *Divide* in spring.

---

**OSMANTHUS DELAVAYI**
Evergreen shrub with glossy, dark green,
leathery leaves. Clusters of very fragrant,
white, tubular flowers are produced in
spring, followed by blue-black fruit.

*Sow seed* in a garden frame as soon
as it is ripe.
- *Semi-ripe cuttings* in summer in a
propagator.
*Layer* in late autumn or spring.

---

**OSMUNDA REGALIS** (Royal fern)
Deciduous fern with 2-pinnate, 90cm
long, bright green, sterile fronds. Fertile
fronds are 2m long, with tassel-like tips
of brown sporangia, and are produced
in summer.

*Sow spores* at 16°C as soon as possible,
since the viability period only lasts for
a few days.
- *Divide* established clumps in spring.
Keep the sections as large as possible.
The loose fibre on the rootstock is
used in orchid compost.

---

**OSTEOMELES SCHWERINIAE**
Deciduous or semi-evergreen shrub
with bright green, pinnate leaves. Cup-
shaped, white flowers appear in early
summer, followed by dark brown fruit
that ripen to blue-black.

*Sow seed* in a garden frame in autumn.
- *Semi-ripe cuttings* in summer.

---

**OSTEOSPERMUM 'WHIRLYGIG'**
Evergreen sub-shrub with lance-shaped,
toothed, grey-green leaves. The daisy-
like flowers, which are spoon-shaped
and crimped with white ray-florets, are
light blue on the underside and are
produced from spring to autumn.

*Sow seed* at 16°C in early spring.
*Softwood cuttings* in late spring.
- *Semi-ripe cuttings* in late summer.
Remove any flower buds.

---

**OSTROWSKIA MAGNIFICA**
(Giant bellflower)
Perennial with whorls of glaucous,
10–15cm long leaves. Racemes of
outward-facing, bell-shaped, blue
or blue-purple flowers, with deeper
coloured veins, are produced in
early summer.

*Sow seed* individually in containers, in a
garden frame, as soon as it is ripe.
Avoid root disturbance. It is slow to
flower from seed, taking up to 4 years.
- *Root cuttings* in early winter in a garden
frame. Have patience, as they take up
to 6 months to become established.

---

**OSTRYA CARPINIFOLIA**
(Hop hornbeam)
Deciduous tree with many veined, dark
green leaves that turn yellow in autumn.
The male catkins are deep yellow and
pendulous and are produced in autumn,
but open in spring. Female catkins are
inconspicuous and consist of white,
hop-like clusters of fruit that turn brown
in autumn.

*Sow seed* as soon as it is ripe, in a
garden frame.

---

**OURISIA MICROPHYLLA**
Semi-evergreen perennial with tiny,
heather-like, pale green leaves. Small,
pale pink, tubular flowers with white
centres are produced in late spring and
early summer.

*Sow seed* in a garden frame in early
spring.
- *Softwood tip cuttings* in early summer
under horticultural fleece.

## OXALIS ENNEAPHYLLA

Perennial with hairy, blue-grey leaves made up of tiny, pleated leaflets. Single, funnel-shaped, white to deep pink, fragrant flowers appear during late spring and early summer.

**Sow seed** at 16°C in early spring.
**Divide** clumps in spring.
⬤ **Divide** rhizomes in early summer and root in a propagator.

## OXYDENDRUM ARBOREUM

(Sorrel tree)
Deciduous shrub or small tree with lance-shaped, 20cm long, glossy, dark green leaves that turn yellow, brilliant red and purple in autumn. Large panicles of urn-shaped, small, white flowers are produced in late summer and autumn.

**Sow seed** in a garden frame in autumn.
⬤ **Semi-ripe cuttings** with a 'heel' in summer in ericaceous compost. Trim leaves to reduce transpiration.

## PACHYSANDRA TERMINALIS

Evergreen perennial with toothed, glossy, dark green leaves. Spikes of tiny, white, male, petal-less flowers appear in early summer.

⬤ **Softwood cuttings** in early summer.
**Divide** in spring.

## PACHYSTACHYS LUTEA (Lollipop plant)

Tender, evergreen shrub with strongly veined, 15cm long, deep green leaves. Spikes of 2-lipped, tubular, white flowers, surrounded by bright yellow bracts, appear in spring and summer.

⬤ **Softwood cuttings** in a propagator in summer. Cut leaves in half to reduce transpiration. Make sure the leaves are free of whitefly and red spider.

## PAEONIA CAMBESSEDESII

(Majorcan peony)
Perennial with young leaves flushed purple. Mature leaves are dark green with purple veins and are reddish-purple on the underside. Single, bowl-shaped, wavy-margined, pink flowers with yellow stamens and red filaments are produced in late spring and early summer.

**Sow seed** in containers in a garden frame in autumn. Seedlings may take 18 months to appear. The roots are produced in the first year, with the shoot and leaves appearing in the second year. It may take 5 years for them to flower, but they are well worth the wait.
⬤ **Divide** in autumn or early spring.
**Semi-ripe cuttings** of tree peonies, such as *P. lutea* var. *ludlowii*, in late summer.

## PALIURUS SPINA-CHRISTI

(Jerusalem thorn)
Deciduous shrub with thorny shoots and glossy, dark green leaves. Tiny, star-shaped, yellow flowers appear in summer, followed by hard fruit with a green wing ripening to black.

**Sow seed** in a garden frame in autumn.
⬤ **Softwood cuttings** in summer. Wear protective gloves.

## PAMIANTHE PERUVIANA

Bulbous perennial with a false stem formed by the bases of the strap-shaped, 50cm long, mid-green leaves. Umbels of fragrant, bell-shaped, white flowers with green stripes and creamy-white outer petals appear in spring.

**Sow seed** at 20°C when ripe.
⬤ **Remove offsets** in autumn and pot up in containers.

## PANCRATIUM MARITIMUM

(Sea daffodil)
Bulbous perennial with narrow, strap-like, grey-green basal leaves that are 45cm long. Umbels of up to 6 fragrant, white flowers appear in late summer.

**Sow seed** at 14°C when ripe.
⬤ **Remove offsets** in winter. Pot into a free-draining, gritty compost in a frost-free greenhouse or conservatory.

## PAPAVER ORIENTALE (Oriental poppy)

Perennial with white-bristly stems and 30cm long, mid-green leaves. Solitary, cup-shaped, orange-scarlet flowers without bracts appear from late spring to midsummer with large, blue-black or white basal spots.

**Seed** To aid seed collection, lift the poppies (roots and all) after flowering and hang, upside down, in an airy shed. Contain the seed heads in a paper bag. When ripe, the seed will fall into the bag ready for sowing or storing. Sow in autumn in a garden frame. Leave the seed uncovered, as light is required for germination.
◨ **Divide** in early spring.
⬤ **Root cuttings** in late autumn in a garden frame.

## PAPHIOPEDILUM (Slipper orchid)

Evergreen orchid with leathery, grey or mid- to dark green leaves that are occasionally mottled. Racemes of petals and sepals with a pouch appear in winter and spring in a range of colours.

**Softwood cuttings** in early summer under horticultural fleece. Shorten the leaves by half.
**Side shoots** taken from close to the base of the orchid in orchid compost in summer.
Don't try to divide the clump.

Paeonia cambessedesii

### PARAHEBE CATARRACTAE

Evergreen sub-shrub with lance-shaped, toothed, dark green leaves, purple-tinged when young. Racemes of saucer-shaped, white flowers with purple veins and a bright red eye appear in summer.

***Sow seed*** in a garden frame in spring.
▯ ***Semi-ripe cuttings*** with a 'heel' in early summer.

### PARIS POLYPHYLLA

Perennial with whorls of lance-shaped, mid-green leaves. Spider-like flowers with thread-like, pale green-yellow inner tepals and narrow, green outer tepals appear in summer. These are followed by green pods that split open when ripe to show shiny, red seeds.

***Sow seed*** in containers outside in autumn.
***Divide*** in late autumn.

### PARNASSIA PALUSTRIS

(Grass of Parnassus)
Perennial with rosettes of heart-shaped, small, pale green leaves. Solitary, white flowers with green veins and yellow nectar glands appear in late spring and early summer.

***Sow seed*** in a garden frame in autumn. Use moisture-retentive compost.
▯ ***Divide*** in autumn. Where the soil is wet, divide in early spring.

### PARROTIA PERSICA (Iron tree)

Deciduous tree with glossy, 12cm long, bright green leaves turning brilliant yellow, orange, red and purple in autumn. Tiny clusters of red flowers appear in late winter before the leaves.

***Sow seed*** in a garden frame in autumn.
***Softwood cuttings*** in early summer.
▯ ***Semi-ripe cuttings*** in late summer in ericaceous compost. Cut the leaves in half to reduce transpiration. Wounding

Paris polyphylla

the sides of the cutting close to the 'heel' is more successful than crossing your fingers!

## PARROTIOPSIS JACQUEMONTIANA
Deciduous shrub with 10cm long, mid-green leaves. Flowerheads of petal-less flowers with white bracts and yellow stamens appear in spring and early summer.

**Sow seed** in a garden frame in autumn.
🛛 **Softwood cuttings** in early summer. Trim the leaves by half to reduce transpiration.
**Semi-ripe cuttings** in late summer.

## PARTHENOCISSUS QUINQUEFOLIA
(Virginia creeper)
Deciduous climber with palmate, mid-green, dull leaves that turn brilliant red in early autumn.

**Sow seed** in a garden frame in autumn.
🛛 **Softwood cuttings** in early summer.
**Semi-ripe cuttings** in late summer.
**Hardwood cuttings** in winter.

## PASSIFLORA CAERULEA
(Blue passion flower)
Climber with angular stems and deeply lobed, rich green leaves. Bowl-shaped, white or pink-tinged flowers with purple and white ringed coronas are produced from early summer to autumn, followed by barely edible orange fruit.

**Sow seed** at 16°C in spring.
**Semi-ripe cuttings** in summer.
🛛 **Layer** in late autumn or late spring.

## PAULOWNIA TOMENTOSA
(Empress tree, Foxglove tree)
Deciduous tree with bright mid-green, 30cm wide leaves that are hairy on both sides. Upright panicles of tubular, pale lilac and fragrant flowers with purple and pale yellow markings appear in late spring from felted overwintering buds.

🗉 **Sow seed** in a garden frame in autumn or spring. Every seed will germinate, so space the seed.
🛛 **Root cuttings** in early winter in a garden frame. Ensure the cuts are clean, without ragged edges.

## PELARGONIUM
Tender perennial, evergreen in mild climates. with various leaf shapes. Many are aromatic and most are carried on long stalks. Clusters of 5-petalled, star-, funnel- or saucer-shaped flowers in colours from white and pink through red and deep purple are produced from spring to autumn.

**Sow seed** of species and F1 hybrid varieties at 16°C in early spring.
🛛 **Softwood cuttings** from late spring until early autumn. Keep the foliage dry and the humidity low to avoid botrytis disease. Avoid using thick-stemmed cuttings as they are slower to root.

## PELTANDRA VIRGINICA (Arrow arum)
Aquatic perennial with arrow-shaped leaves on long stalks. Green spathes, margined white or cream, in early summer are followed by green berries.

🛛 **Divide** in spring.

## PENNISETUM VILLOSUM (Feathertop)
Deciduous, perennial grass with 15cm long, mid-green leaves. Plume-like panicles of white or pale green, feathery bristles are produced in early autumn maturing to purple.

**Sow seed** at 16°C in late spring. This plant is often treated as an annual, with seed sown every year.
🛛 **Divide** in early summer.

## PENSTEMON NEWBERRYI
Evergreen sub-shrub with leathery leaves. Dense racemes of funnel-shaped, deep pink flowers appear in early summer.

Pelargonium 'Lord Bute'

**Sow seed** at 10°C in late winter.
**Softwood cuttings** in early summer.
🛛 **Semi-ripe cuttings** in midsummer. Cover with horticultural fleece.

## PENTAS LANCEOLATA (Star cluster)
Tender, evergreen perennial with 15cm long, bright green, hairy leaves. Tubular, white, pink, lilac or blue flowers appear from spring through to autumn.

**Sow seed** at 16°C in spring.
🛛 **Softwood cuttings** from spring to late summer.

## PEPEROMIA CAPERATA
Tender, evergreen perennial with rosettes of dark green, deeply veined, heart-shaped leaves. Upright spikes of tiny, white flowers appear in late summer.

**Sow seed** at 20°C as soon as it is ripe.
**Softwood cuttings** during summer.
🛛 **Leaf or leaf bud cuttings** during spring and summer.

Perovskia 'Blue Spire'

## PERILLA FRUTESCENS
Annual with deeply toothed, mid-green leaves occasionally with purple speckles. Spikes of tiny, white flowers appear in summer.

***Sow seed*** at 16°C in spring.

## PERIPLOCA GRAECA (Silk vine)
Deciduous climber with glossy, dark green leaves. Star-shaped, greenish-yellow flowers, purple-brown on the inside, are produced in late summer. They have an unpleasant odour and are followed by 12cm long seed pods that, when ripe, produce silky-tufted seeds.

***Sow seed*** at 16°C in spring. Rub the seed first to remove the tufted outer coat.
🔳 ***Semi-ripe cuttings*** in midsummer. Trim the leaves by half to reduce transpiration.

## PEROVSKIA 'BLUE SPIRE'
Deciduous sub-shrub with grey-white stems and deeply divided, green-grey leaves. Masses of tubular, lavender-blue flowers appear in panicles during late summer and early autumn.

🔳 ***Softwood cuttings*** in late spring under horticultural fleece.
***Semi-ripe cuttings*** in midsummer.

## PERSICARIA AFFINIS
Evergreen perennial whose leaves turn maroon-bronze in autumn. Spikes of rose-red flowers in summer and autumn fade to pale pink.

***Sow seed*** in a garden frame in spring.
🔳 ***Divide*** in spring or late autumn.

## PETASITES FRAGRANS
(Winter heliotrope)
Perennial with kidney-shaped basal leaves, hairy on the underside. Panicles of deep pink to purple, fragrant flower-heads appear at the same time as the leaves in late winter and early spring.

🔳 ***Divide*** in early spring or late autumn.

## PETROPHYTUM CAESPITOSUM
(Rock spiraea)
Evergreen sub-shrub with small, spoon-shaped, bluish-green, hairy leaves. Racemes of small, creamy-white flowers with prominent stamens appear in summer.

***Sow seed*** in a garden frame in autumn.
🔳 ***Semi-ripe cuttings*** in midsummer. Insert small cuttings with a 'heel' in well-drained, alkaline compost.
***Remove rooted offsets*** in late spring and plant in their permanent positions outside.

## PETTERIA RAMENTACEA
(Dalmatian laburnum)
Deciduous shrub with 3-palmate, dark green leaves. Racemes of fragrant, bright yellow flowers are produced in late spring and early summer.

***Sow seed*** in containers in autumn in a well-drained compost. Over-winter outside in a sheltered part of the garden.
🔳 ***Softwood cuttings*** in early summer.

## PETUNIA
Perennials treated as annuals with mid- to dark green leaves. Single or double, trumpet- or saucer-shaped, white, pink, magenta, purple or bicolour flowers appear in early summer and autumn.

***Sow seed*** at 16°C in autumn or late spring on the surface of peat-based compost. Cover with cling film to keep the seed moist but remove it as soon as the first leaves appear. Dust fine compost over the seedlings to hold the roots in place.
🔳 ***Softwood cuttings*** in summer, overwintered with frost protection.

## PHACELIA SERICEA
Perennial with rosettes of silver-haired, lobed leaves. Small, bell-shaped, deep blue flowers with pale blue anthers are produced in summer.

*Sow seed* in a garden frame in autumn.

## PHALAENOPSIS (Moth orchid)
Evergreen orchid with a stem-like rhizome and 2–5 fleshy, mid- to dark green, oval leaves. Racemes of flowers are produced from the base of the plant at any time of the year.

*Side shoots* taken from close to the base in orchid compost in a propagator.

## PHALARIS ARUNDINACEA
(Ribbon grass)
Evergreen perennial with flat, mid-green leaves, sometimes with yellow stripes. Panicles of light green spikelets that mature to buff are produced in early summer.

*Divide* in late spring.

## PHELLODENDRON AMURENSE
(Amur cork tree)
Deciduous tree with corky, pale brown bark on mature trees. The aromatic, glossy, dark green leaves turn yellow in autumn. Tiny, cup-shaped, male and female flowers are produced on separate plants. With cross pollination, blue-black fruit appear in autumn.

*Sow seed* in autumn in a soil-based compost and position outdoors in a sheltered part of the garden. Germination is poor, so this is not the most efficient way to propagate this tree.
- **J** *Semi-ripe cuttings* in midsummer taken with a 'heel'. Trim the leaves to one third their length to reduce transpiration.

## PHILADELPHUS 'LEMOINEI'
(Mock orange)
Deciduous shrub with mid-green leaves. Racemes of single, highly fragrant, cup-shaped, pure white flowers are produced in early summer.
- **E** *Softwood cuttings* in summer.
- **J** *Hardwood cuttings* in late autumn or winter.

## PHILESIA MAGELLANICA
Evergreen shrub with small, dark green leaves, bluish-white on the underside. Single, trumpet-shaped, deep red-pink, waxy flowers appear in midsummer.

*Semi-ripe cuttings* in midsummer.
- **J** *Collect rooted suckers* in spring and pot up for a year in a free-draining, acid compost before planting out in their permanent position.

## PHILLYREA ANGUSTIFOLIA
Evergreen shrub with thin, dark green leaves. Clusters of small, greenish-white, fragrant flowers appear in late spring and early summer, followed by small, blue-black fruit.

*Semi-ripe cuttings* in a propagator in summer.

## PHILODENDRON SCANDENS
(Heart leaf)
Tender, evergreen climber with glossy, deep green, 30cm long leaves that are pointed at the tips. The green spathes are white on the inside and 15cm long, appearing at any time of the year.

*Sow seed* at 20°C in spring. Sow on the surface of the compost.
*Leaf bud cuttings* in early summer.
- **J** *Layer* or air layer in late spring.

## PHLOMIS FRUTICOSA (Jerusalem sage)
Evergreen shrub with lance-shaped, wrinkled, grey-green, sage-like leaves that are woolly on the underside. Deep, golden-yellow flowers are produced in early and midsummer.

*Sow seed* at 16°C in spring.
- **J** *Softwood cuttings* in summer in free-draining compost.

## PHLOX PANICULATA
Perennial with lance-shaped, mid-green leaves. The fragrant, white, pale lilac or pink-purple flowers appear in summer and early autumn.

*Sow seed* in a garden frame in spring.

Phlomis fruticosa

*Phormium tenax 'Sundowner'*

🔲 *Softwood basal cuttings* in spring.
*Divide* in autumn or in early spring.
*Root cuttings* in autumn or early winter in a garden frame.

## PHOENIX CANARIENSIS
(Canary Island date palm)
Evergreen palm with arching, 3–6m long, deep green leaves. Pendant panicles of cream or orange-yellow flowers are produced in summer, followed by edible yellow fruit flushed with red.

*Sow seed* at 20°C in spring.

## PHORMIUM TENAX (New Zealand flax)
Evergreen perennial with rigid, upright, sword-like, dark green leaves that are blue-green on the underside. Panicles of tubular, red flowers are produced in summer on strong, 4m long, upright stems

*Sow seed* at 16°C in spring. Germination can be difficult.
🔲 *Divide* in spring.

## PHOTINIA DAVIDIANA
Evergreen tree with lance-shaped, dark green leaves that turn red in autumn.

Panicles of small, white flowers are produced in summer, followed by bright red fruit.

*Sow seed* in a garden frame in autumn.
🔲 *Semi-ripe cuttings* in summer in a propagator.

## PHUOPSIS STYLOSA
Perennial with whorls of musk-scented, mid-green leaves. Masses of tiny, scented, funnel-shaped, deep pink flowers are produced in summer.

*Sow seed* in a garden frame in autumn.
*Softwood tip cuttings* in late spring and early summer.
🔲 *Divide* in late spring or early summer.

## PHYGELIUS CAPENSIS (Cape figwort)
Evergreen shrub with dark green leaves. Upright, 60cm long panicles of orange flowers, with bright yellow throats and red lobes, are produced throughout the summer.

*Sow seed* in a garden frame in spring.
*Softwood cuttings* in early summer.
🔲 *Plant rooted suckers* in spring in containers of well-drained, gritty compost outside.

## PHYLLODOCE EMPETRIFORMIS
Evergreen shrub with small, linear, glossy, bright green leaves. Umbel-like clusters of bell-shaped, rose-pink flowers are produced in late spring and early summer.

*Sow seed* at 10°C in early spring in ericaceous compost.
*Semi-ripe cuttings* in summer. Cover with horticultural fleece.
*Layer* in spring. This plant will layer itself in peat mulch, producing 'Irishman's cuttings'. Simply spread a 5cm layer of peat or leaf mould over the trailing stems and wash it down to soil level to provide a rich rooting medium. By autumn the stems will be well rooted in the mulch.

## PHYLLOSTACHYS NIGRA
(Black bamboo)
Evergreen bamboo with green canes that turn jet black in the second or third year and lance-shaped, dark green leaves.

*Divide* in spring.

## PHYSALIS ALKEKENGI
(Chinese lantern)
Perennial with mid-green leaves. Small, creamy-white, bell-shaped flowers are produced in midsummer, followed by papery, red calyces enclosing the bright orange-red berries. With the exception of the berries, all parts of the plant are toxic.

*Sow seed* in a garden frame in spring.
🔲 *Divide* in spring.

## PHYSOCARPUS OPULIFOLIUS
(Ninebark)
Deciduous shrub with lobed, mid-green leaves. Clusters of small, pink-tinged white flowers appear during early summer followed by tiny, bladder-like, greenish-red fruit.

***Sow seed*** in a container outside in spring or autumn.

🌱 ***Softwood cuttings*** in summer.

***Plant rooted suckers*** in spring. Grow in a container of ericaceous, well-drained compost until autumn before planting out in the garden.

## PHYSOSTEGIA VIRGINIANA

(False dragonhead, Obedient plant)
Deciduous perennial with sharply toothed, 10cm long, mid-green leaves. Racemes of white, lilac-pink or purple flowers appear in summer and early autumn.

***Sow seed*** in a garden frame in autumn.

Pieris formosa

🌱 ***Divide*** in early spring before growth starts.

## PHYTEUMA HUMILE

Perennial with lance-shaped, dull green basal leaves. Clusters of violet-blue flowers with linear bracts are produced in summer.

***Sow seed*** in a garden frame in autumn.

## PHYTOLACCA AMERICANA

(Pokeweed, Red ink plant)
Deciduous perennial with lance-shaped, mid-green, 20–30cm long leaves becoming purple-tinged in autumn. Racemes of white or pink flowers are produced in late summer and early autumn followed, by dark maroon berries. Be warned: all parts of this plant are highly toxic.

***Sow seed*** at 16°C in early spring.

## PICEA GLAUCA VAR. ALBERTIANA 'CONICA' (Spruce)

Evergreen conifer with a tight, cone-shaped habit of growth and tiny, needle-like, blue-green leaves.

🌱 ***Semi-ripe cuttings*** in late summer with a 'heel'.

## PICRASMA QUASSIOIDES (Quassia)

Deciduous tree with pinnate, 30cm long, glossy, mid-green leaves that turn bright yellow, orange and maroon in autumn. Panicles of tiny, bowl-shaped, green flowers are produced in early summer.

***Sow seed*** in a garden frame in autumn.

## PIERIS FORMOSA

Evergreen shrub with glossy, dark green, 10cm long leaves that are bronze when young. The panicles of urn-shaped, white flowers are produced in mid-spring.

***Sow seed*** in a garden frame in autumn.

***Softwood cuttings*** in early summer.

🌱 ***Semi-ripe cuttings*** in late summer in a propagator.

## PILEA CADIEREI (Aluminium plant)

Tender, evergreen perennial with dark green leaves marked with 4 rows of raised, silver blotches.

***Sow seed*** at 20°C in spring.

🌱 ***Softwood tip cuttings*** in spring in a propagator.

***Divide*** in spring.

## PILEOSTEGIA VIBURNOIDES

Evergreen climber with leathery, 15cm long, dark green leaves. Dense panicles of small, star-shaped, creamy-white flowers with prominent stamens are produced in late summer and early autumn.

- *Semi-ripe cuttings* in summer.
- *Layer* in spring.

## PIMELEA PROSTRATA
Evergreen shrub with green-grey, leathery leaves often margined red. Small, tubular, fragrant, white flowers appear in summer, followed by white or red fruit.

- *Sow seed* in a garden frame in spring.
- *Semi-ripe cuttings* in summer in a propagator.

## PIMPINELLA MAJOR
Perennial with pinnate, mid-green basal leaves. Umbels of greenish-white or pink flowers appear in spring.

- *Sow seed* in a garden frame as soon as it is ripe. Sow 2 seeds in a deep pot to avoid damaging the brittle tap root.

## PINGUICULA GRANDIFLORA
(Butterwort)
Perennial with rosettes of small, sticky, pale green leaves. Trumpet-shaped, deep blue flowers with white throats are produced during summer.

- *Sow seed* at 16°C as soon as it is ripe, on the surface of damp sphagnum moss.

## PINUS WALLICHIANA (Bhutan pine)
Evergreen conifer with grey-green or glaucous-blue leaves, up to 20cm long, that are held in groups of five. The green, female cones ripen to brown, with forward-pointing scales.

- *Sow seed* in late autumn in a garden frame. Protect seedlings from frost.

## PIPER NIGRUM (Black pepper)
Evergreen, perennial climber with deep-veined, leathery, 12cm long, dark green leaves.

- *Sow seed* at 24°C in early spring.
- *Semi-ripe cuttings* in summer. Cut leaves in half to avoid transpiration.

## PIPTANTHUS NEPALENSIS
(Evergreen laburnum)
Evergreen shrub with 3-palmate, dark blue-green leaves that are blue-white on the underside. Racemes of bright yellow, pea-like flowers are produced in late spring and early summer, followed by bright green seed pods.

- *Sow seed* in a garden frame in spring. Score the seed coat with sandpaper beforehand and every one will germinate.
- *Semi-ripe cuttings* in midsummer, taken with a 'heel'.

## PISONIA UMBELLIFERA (Parapara)
Tender, evergreen shrub with glossy, bright green, 15–40cm long leaves. Panicles of tiny, yellow or pink flowers appear at any time.

- *Sow seed* at 16°C in spring.
- *Softwood cuttings* in early summer.
- *Semi-ripe cuttings* in late summer. Shorten long leaves to reduce transpiration.
- *Air layer* in late spring.

## PISTACIA LENTISCUS (Mastic tree)
Evergreen shrub or bushy tree with glossy, pinnate, aromatic, dark green leaves. Dense panicles of male (red stamens) and female (brownish-green stamens) flowers are produced in late spring and early summer, followed by red fruit that ripen to black. The sticky sap is used to manufacture mastic and varnish.

Pinus wallichiana

*Sow seed* at 22°C in spring.
*Softwood cuttings* in late spring.
  Remove half of the leaflets to reduce
  transpiration.
◻ *Semi-ripe cuttings* in summer.

### PITTOSPORUM TENUIFOLIUM
(Kohuhu)
Evergreen tree with black young stems
and wavy-margined, glossy, mid-green
leaves. Bell-shaped, honey-scented,
small, red-black flowers are produced in
late spring and early summer, followed
by dark grey seed capsules.

◻ *Sow seed* in a garden frame as soon
  as it is ripe. It will self-seed under
  mature trees.
*Semi-ripe cuttings* in summer.
*Layer* in spring. Or so some people say.
  It doesn't work for me.

### PLANTAGO NIVALIS
Evergreen perennial with rosettes
of lance-shaped, silver-green, silky-
haired leaves. Spikes of small, tubular,
pale brown flowers are produced
in summer.

*Sow seed* in a garden frame in autumn.
◻ *Divide* in spring.

### PLATANUS × HISPANICA
(London plane)
Deciduous tree with cream, grey and
brown, flaking bark and bright green,
lobed, 30cm long leaves. Green clusters
of fruit turn brown and hang on the tree
from autumn to winter.

*Sow seed* in autumn in a garden frame.
◻ *Hardwood cuttings* in winter.

### PLATYCARYA STROBILACEA
Deciduous tree with pinnate, 30cm
long, mid-green leaves. Greenish-yellow
catkins made up of several male flowers
surrounding a single female flower are

produced in late summer, followed by
racemes of small, winged, brown fruit
which last well into the winter.

*Sow seed* in autumn in containers in a
  garden frame.

### PLATYCERIUM BIFURCATUM
(Staghorn fern)
Tender, evergreen fern with sterile
fronds that are mid-green, turning
brown. The fertile fronds are grey-green
and divided into strap-like sections.

*Sow spores* at 21°C as soon as they are
  ripe.
◻ *Remove plantlets* from the root tips of
  mature plants and pot up.

### PLATYCODON GRANDIFLORUS
(Balloon flower)
Perennial with whorls of lance-shaped,
blue-green leaves. The bell-shaped,
deep blue flowers have darker veins
and open from large, balloon-like buds
during late summer.

*Sow seed* outdoors in spring in seed
  compost with extra grit for drainage,
  or in well-cultivated soil in the garden.
  This plant dislikes having its roots
  disturbed, so plant it in its permanent
  position in autumn.
◻ *Remove and pot up rooted basal
  shoots* in summer.
*Divide* in summer.

### PLATYSTEMON CALIFORNICUS
(Cream cups)
Annual with hairy, grey-green leaves.
Creamy-yellow, 6-petalled, single
flowers are produced in spring.

*Sow seed* in open ground in spring.

### PLECTRANTHUS FORSTERI
Tender, evergreen perennial with hairy,
scallop-margined, pale green leaves.
Racemes of whorled, white or pale

Platycodon grandiflorus

purple, tubular flowers are produced
throughout the year.

*Sow seed* at 20°C as soon as it is ripe.
◻ *Softwood tip cuttings* at any time.
*Divide* rooted sections in late spring.

### PLEIONE FORRESTII
Orchid with pseudobulbs, each with a
single, folded 10cm long leaf. Solitary,
yellow flowers with red-flecked lips
appear in late winter and spring.

*Divide* in spring. Discard the old
  pseudobulbs.

### PLUMBAGO AURICULATA
(Cape leadwort)
Tender, evergreen, climbing shrub with
spoon-shaped, matt green leaves.
Racemes of sky blue, tubular flowers are
produced in late summer and autumn.

*Sow seed* at 16°C in spring.
◻ *Semi-ripe cuttings* in summer in a
  propagator.

Plumeria rubra f. acutifolia

**PLUMERIA RUBRA** (Frangipani)
Tender, deciduous shrub with mid-green, 25–40cm long leaves. Racemes of rose-pink or red, yellow-centred flowers appear from summer to mid-autumn. The variety *P. rubra* f. *acutifolia* has white flowers with yellow centres.

*Sow seed* at 18°C in spring.
🔲 *Semi-ripe cuttings* of stem tips in early spring before leaves form. Allow the wound to dry for a few hours before inserting it in cactus compost.

**POA ALPINA** (Alpine meadow grass)
Perennial grass with short, mid-green leaves. Dense, purplish-green panicles appear from early summer to early autumn.

*Sow seed* in a garden frame in autumn or spring.
🔲 *Divide* in early summer.

**PODOCARPUS SALIGNUS**
(Willowleaf podocarp)
Evergreen conifer with peeling, red-brown bark and sickle-shaped, bluish-green leaves that are yellowish-green on the underside. Catkin-like, yellow cones contain the male flowers, with the female flowers held in a cone-like cluster. Small, egg-shaped, green or violet fruit appear in autumn.

*Sow seed* in a garden frame in spring. It may take 24 months to germinate.
🔲 *Semi-ripe cuttings* with a 'heel' in late summer. Take them from upright, leading growths.

**PODOPHYLLUM PELTATUM**
(American mandrake)
Perennial with 30cm long, glossy, dark green leaves. Saucer-shaped, waxy, white, fragrant flowers, 5cm in diameter, are produced from spring to early summer, followed by edible, pale green fruit.

*Sow seed* in a garden frame as soon as it is ripe.
🔲 *Divide* in spring or early autumn.

**POLEMONIUM CARNEUM**
(Jacob's ladder)
Perennial with mid-green, pinnate, 20cm long leaves. Open, bell-shaped, yellow, pale pink or lavender flowers with bright yellow centres are produced in early summer.

*Sow seed* in a garden frame in spring.
🔲 *Divide* in late spring.

### POLIANTHES TUBEROSA (Tuberose)
Tuberous perennial with a basal rosette of 45cm long, dark green leaves. Spikes of incredibly fragrant waxy-white flowers are produced in summer.

*Sow seed* at 20°C as soon as it is ripe.
🗓 *Remove* and pot up offsets in autumn.

### POLYGALA CALCAREA (Milkwort)
Evergreen perennial with rosettes of leathery, mid-green leaves. Racemes of deep blue flowers with white-edged lips appear in late spring and early summer.

*Sow seed* in a garden frame in autumn.
*Softwood cuttings* in early summer.
🗓 *Semi-ripe cuttings* in late summer. Cover with horticultural fleece.

### POLYGONATUM MULTIFLORUM
(Solomon's seal)
Perennial with lance-shaped, bright green leaves. Pendant, tubular, white flowers with green tips are produced in late spring, followed by black fruit.

*Sow seed* in a garden frame in autumn. Alternatively, chill at 1°C for 10 days and sow in spring.
🗓 *Divide* in spring as growth starts. Take care not to damage the brittle shoots.

### POLYPODIUM VULGARE
(Common polypody)
Evergreen fern with pinnate, leathery, 45cm long, dark green fronds.

*Sow spores* at 16°C as soon as they are ripe.
🗓 *Divide* in late spring.

### POLYSTICHUM SETIFERUM
(Soft shield fern)
Evergreen fern with soft, dark green, shuttlecock fronds 45–120cm long.

*Sow spores* at 16°C in autumn as soon as they are ripe.

🗓 *Divide* rhizomes in spring. Keep in shade for a few days to allow the rhizomes to recover.

### PONCIRUS TRIFOLIATA
(Japanese bitter orange)
Deciduous shrub with sharp spines and 3-palmate, dark green leaves that turn yellow in autumn. Saucer-shaped, fragrant, white flowers, measuring 5cm in diameter, appear in late spring and early summer, followed by inedible green fruit turning orange.

*Sow seed* in a garden frame in autumn.
🗓 *Semi-ripe cuttings* in summer in a propagator. Watch out for the sharp spines.

### PONTEDERIA CORDATA (Pickerel weed)
Marginal, aquatic perennial with glossy, 20cm wide, bright green leaves. Spikes of tubular, blue flowers appear in late summer.

*Sow seed* as soon as it is ripe, in containers outside.
🗓 *Divide* in late spring, as growth commences.

### POPULUS BALSAMIFERA
(Balsam poplar)
Deciduous tree with balsam-scented buds and glossy, dark green, 12cm long leaves that are pale green on the underside. Pendant, green catkins are produced in early spring.

🗓 *Hardwood cuttings* during winter. It is possible to root year-old branches up to 2m long.

### PORTULACA GRANDIFLORA (Sun plant)
Tender annual with red stems and fleshy, bright green leaves. White, yellow, light pink or carmine, single or double flowers appear in summer.

*Sow seed* at 16°C in late spring.

### POTAMOGETON CRISPUS
(Curled pondweed)
Aquatic perennial with branching stems, up to 3m long, and leathery, mid-green, floating leaves. Fleshy spikes of inconspicuous, white and red flowers appear on the water surface in summer.

*Softwood cuttings* in late spring.

### POTENTILLA FRUTICOSA
Deciduous shrub with pinnate, dark green leaves. Saucer-shaped, yellow flowers appear from late spring to late summer.

*Sow seed* in a garden frame, in autumn or spring.
🗓 *Softwood cuttings* in early summer.
*Divide* perennials such as
*P. atrosanguinea* in spring.

### PRATIA PEDUNCULATA
Evergreen perennial with small, rounded, dark green leaves. Small, star-shaped, pale blue flowers are produced throughout summer.

Polystichum setiferum

*Divide* at any time of the year. Keep the young plants in a shaded position until well rooted.

## PRIMULA DENTICULATA
(Drumstick primula)
Deciduous perennial with a rosette of spoon-shaped, mid-green leaves that are white and mealy on the underside. Dense umbels of purple flowers with yellow centres are held on stout stems during spring and early summer.

*Seed* Most gardeners sow seed in a garden frame as soon as it is ripe. I find it difficult to manage the seedlings through the winter and, for that reason, I prefer to sow in spring. Primula seed needs light for germination and must be sown on the surface of the compost. If the temperature is allowed to rise above 65°F, the seed will become dormant. Never allow the compost to dry out.
*Softwood basal cuttings* in early spring.
▯ *Rooted offsets* in autumn.
*Divide* in late autumn.
*Root cuttings* in winter in a garden frame.

## PROSTANTHERA CUNEATA (Mint bush)
Evergreen shrub with tiny, glossy, mid- to dark green, aromatic leaves. Racemes of tubular, white flowers, with yellow and purple markings on the insides, appear during summer.

*Sow seed* at 16°C in spring.
▯ *Semi-ripe cuttings* in summer.

## PROTEA CYNAROIDES (King protea)
Tender, evergreen shrub with leathery, greyish-green, 7–12cm long leaves. Bowl-shaped flowerheads that are 10–25cm across, with cream, light pink or crimson bracts, are produced in late spring and early summer.

*Sow seed* at 18°C as soon as it is ripe.
▯ *Semi-ripe cuttings* in summer.

## PRUNELLA GRANDIFLORA (Self heal)
Semi-evergreen with deep green leaves. Spikes of whorled, purple flowers appear during summer.

*Sow seed* at 10°C in spring.
*Divide* in late autumn or spring.

## PRUNUS (includes cherry and laurel)
Deciduous trees and evergreen shrubs with a range of different leaves. Many of the deciduous species colour well in autumn. Flowers range from white through yellow to many shades of pink. Fruit ripen to yellow, red or black and include dessert cherries.

*Sow seed* of species (not varieties – it will not come true) in containers in autumn outside. Cover the surface with fine wire mesh to deter vermin.
*Softwood cuttings* of deciduous species in early summer.
▯ *Semi-ripe cuttings* of evergreens in midsummer in a propagator.
*Bud graft* cultivars in summer.
▯ *Whip and tongue graft* in early spring.

## PSEUDOLARIX AMABILIS (Golden larch)
Deciduous conifer with purple young shoots and soft, bright green, linear leaves turning orange-yellow in early autumn. Erect, greenish-yellow female cones mature to brown.

*Sow seed* in an ericaceous compost outside in containers in spring.
▯ *Softwood cuttings* in early summer.

## PSEUDOPANAX FEROX
(Toothed lancewood)
Evergreen tree with narrow, sharply pointed and toothed, 45cm long, bronze-green juvenile leaves marked grey. Mature plants bear linear, 15cm long, dark green leaves. Panicles of green flowers appear in summer and early autumn, followed by small, black fruit.

*Sow seed* in a garden frame in late autumn.
▯ *Semi-ripe cuttings* in summer.
*Air layer* in summer.

## PSEUDOTSUGA MENZIESII (Douglas fir)
Evergreen conifer with corky, red-brown bark. The linear, dark green leaves have 2 white bands on the underside. The female cones have erect bracts.

*Sow seed* in ericaceous compost, outside in containers in spring.

## PTELEA TRIFOLIATA (Hop tree)
Deciduous shrub with aromatic bark and 3-palmate, dark green leaves. Star-shaped, greenish-white flowers are produced in midsummer, followed by pale green, winged and flattened fruit.

*Sow seed* in containers of free-draining compost in spring, outside in a sheltered position.
▯ *Softwood cuttings* in early summer.

## PTEROCARYA × REHDERIANA (Wingnut)
Deciduous tree with pinnate, 20cm long, glossy, dark green leaves. Pendant spikes of winged, green fruit are produced in summer.

*Sow seed* in seed compost in containers, outside in autumn.
▯ *Take rooted suckers* in spring and plant directly into their permanent position or pot them into a soil-based compost until autumn, before planting out.

## PULMONARIA ANGUSTIFOLIA
(Blue cowslip)
Perennial with lance-shaped, mid- to dark green (unspotted) leaves. Bright blue, funnel-shaped flowers appear in spring.

*Sow seed* as soon as it is ripe, in humus-rich compost outside. Seedlings seldom come true to the species, resulting in colours ranging from white through pink to blue and mauve.

**Root cuttings** in winter in a garden frame.

◫ **Divide** after flowering.

## PULSATILLA VULGARIS (Pasque flower)

Perennial with pinnate, light green leaves. Bell-shaped, silk-haired, white or purple flowers are produced in spring.

**Sow seed** as soon as it is ripe in a garden frame with the nose down and the tail upwards. That way, the seed will twist itself into the compost. If sowing in spring, remove the little tail.

◫ **Root cuttings** in winter in a garden frame.

## PUNICA GRANATUM (Pomegranate)

Deciduous shrub or small tree with glossy, bright green leaves that are coppery-green when they first open. Clusters of funnel-shaped, bright orange-red flowers appear throughout summer, followed by pale brown-yellow, edible fruit.

**Sow seed** at 16°C in late spring.

◫ **Semi-ripe cuttings** in a propagator in summer.

## PUSCHKINIA SCILLOIDES (Squill)

Bulbous perennial with linear, 15cm long basal leaves. Racemes of bell-shaped, pale, whitish-blue flowers, with a deeper blue stripe on each petal, are produced in spring.

**Sow seed** in a garden frame in autumn.

◫ **Remove offsets** in midsummer as the leaves die.

## PUYA CHILENSIS

Tender bromeliad with rosettes of stiff, leathery, grey-green, 90cm long leaves with sharp spines along the margins. In summer yellow or green, trumpet-shaped flowers, with green bracts up to 5cm long, are carried on tall, 1.2m high panicles.

**Sow seed** at 24°C as soon as it is ripe.

## PYRACANTHA ATALANTIOIDES (Firethorn)

Evergreen shrub with spiny stems and lance-shaped, glossy, dark green leaves. Clusters of small, white flowers appear in late spring, followed by bright, orange-red berries that last through the winter.

**Sow seed** in a garden frame in late autumn.

◫ **Semi-ripe cuttings** in a propagator in summer.

## PYRUS CALLERYANA (Pear)

Deciduous tree with glossy, dark green leaves turning red in late autumn or early winter. Racemes of up to 10 white flowers appear in mid-spring, followed by small brown fruit in early autumn.

**Sow seed** outside in autumn.

◫ **Whip and tongue graft** in winter. **Bud graft** in summer.

## QUERCUS RUBRA (Red oak)

Deciduous tree with deeply lobed, matt, dark green leaves turning brilliant yellow, orange and red-brown in autumn. Acorns are small.

◫ **Sow seed** in containers outside as soon as it is ripe. Protect from vermin using wire mesh.

## RAMONDA MYCONI

Evergreen perennial with rosettes of hairy, dark green leaves. Panicles of 5-petalled, violet-blue flowers with golden-yellow anthers appear in late spring and early summer.

Pulsatilla vulgaris var. rubra

*Sow seed* in a container in a garden frame as soon as it is ripe. Growth is slow and it may be weeks before the seedlings are large enough to prick out.

*Leaf cuttings* in early autumn.

▯ *Softwood rosettes* in early summer. Water the compost from below to avoid excess moisture rotting the leaves.

## RANUNCULUS FICARIA

(Lesser celandine)

Tuberous, deciduous perennial with glossy, dark green, toothed basal leaves with silver or brown markings. Cup-shaped, shiny, golden-yellow flowers that fade to white appear in early spring.

*Sow seed* as soon as it is ripe, in a container in a garden frame. It is the devil to germinate. The seedlings of some species of ranunculus may take 2 years to appear.

▯ *Divide* tubers in late autumn or in early spring.

## RAOULIA HOOKERI var. ALBOSERICEA

Evergreen perennial with tiny, overlapping, white, silk-haired leaves. Pale green or yellow flowers are produced in midsummer.

*Divide* in spring. Pot up the rooted stems.

## REBUTIA FIEBRIGII

Clustering cactus with spherical, ribbed, dark green stems and white areolas with white radial spines. Bright orange, red or pale brown flowers are produced in summer.

*Sow seed* at 20°C in early spring.

*Remove offsets* in late spring or early summer and root in free-draining, cactus compost.

## REHMANNIA GLUTINOSA

Perennial with rosettes of scalloped, basal, mid-green leaves that are tinted red on the underside. Racemes of reddish-brown, tubular flowers, with pale, yellow-brown lips and purple veins, are produced in late spring and summer.

*Sow seed* at 15°C in early spring.

*Softwood cuttings* of basal shoots in early spring.

▯ *Rooted runners* in spring.

*Root cuttings* in early winter in a garden frame.

## REINWARDTIA INDICA (Yellow flax)

Tender, evergreen shrub with greyish-green, finely toothed leaves. Funnel-shaped, butter-yellow flowers are produced from late autumn to late spring.

*Sow seed* at 18°C in late spring in a propagator.

▯ *Softwood cuttings* in early summer.

## RESEDA ODORATA (Mignonette)

Annual with mid-green, 3-lobed leaves. Small, star-shaped, highly perfumed, pale green or white flowers with orange stamens are produced from midsummer to autumn.

*Sow seed* in open ground in early spring or in a garden frame in autumn.

## RHAMNUS ALATERNUS

(Italian buckthorn)

Evergreen shrub with leathery, glossy, dark green leaves. Clusters of green-yellow flowers appear in late spring and early summer, followed by red fruit maturing to black.

Ranunculus ficaria 'Brazen Hussy'

**Sow seed** as soon as it is ripe, in a container in a garden frame.

- **Semi-ripe cuttings** in summer with a 'heel'.
**Layer** in autumn or late spring.

### RHAPHIOLEPIS UMBELLATA

Evergreen shrub with leathery, dark green, 7cm long leaves. Racemes of fragrant, white flowers, occasionally tinted pink, are produced in early summer.

- **Semi-ripe cuttings** in late summer with a 'heel'.
**Layer** in autumn.

### RHAPIS EXCELSA (Fan palm)

Tender, clump-forming palm with bamboo-like stems and deeply-lobed, dark green, 20–30cm long leaves. Panicles of tiny, cream flowers are produced in summer.

**Sow seed** at 26°C in spring.
- **Divide** in spring. Avoid direct sunlight for a few days.

### RHEUM PALMATUM (Chinese rhubarb)

Hardy perennial with a large fleshy root and palmate, coarsely toothed, 90cm long, dark green leaves. These are deep red on the underside and carried on thick leaf stalks. Tall, 2m high panicles of tiny, star-shaped, pale green to deep red flowers are produced in early summer.

**Sow seed** in a garden frame in autumn.
- **Divide** in late winter. Take care not to damage the roots. Make a clean cut where the roots are broken.

### RHODOCHITON ATROSANGUINEUS
(Purple bell vine)

Tender, deciduous climber with rich green, heart-shaped leaves. Solitary, tubular, pendant, reddish-purple flowers, with cup-shaped, rose-pink calyces, are produced in midsummer and autumn on long stalks.

Rheum palmatum 'Atrosanguineum'

**Sow seed** at 18°C in spring.

### RHODODENDRON (including deciduous and evergreen azaleas)

Leaves can be deciduous or evergreen, mid- or dark green, leathery or glossy. Flowers are produced in racemes and may be funnel- or saucer-shaped, sometimes fragrant. There are many different colours, some with darker marks on the petals.

**Sow seed** of the hybrid varieties and dwarf species in containers of ericaceous compost, in a garden frame in spring. Plants hybridize freely and seed that you have saved yourself is unlikely to come true – an inferior plant is the most probable result.
- **Semi-ripe cuttings** in late summer.
- **Simple layer** between mid-spring and late summer. Layers may take up to 2 years to form a good root system.
**Saddle graft** in late winter.

### RHODOHYPOXIS BAURII

Perennial with basal rosettes of lance-shaped, folded, grey-green, hairy leaves. Deep red or pale pink flowers are produced in summer.

**Sow seed** at 10°C, as soon as it is ripe or in spring.
**Divide** clumps in autumn.
- **Remove corm-like rhizomes** in late autumn and pot up in ericaceous compost in a garden frame until late spring.

### RHODOTYPOS SCANDENS
(White kerria)

Deciduous shrub with deeply veined, mid-green leaves. White, 4-petalled flowers are produced in late spring and early summer, followed by glossy, black berries.

**Sow seed** in a garden frame in autumn.
- **Softwood cuttings** in early summer.
**Semi-ripe cuttings** in late summer with bottom heat.

**RHOICISSUS CAPENSIS** (Cape grape)
Tender, evergreen climber with long,
forked tendrils and leathery, dark green
leaves. Tiny, pale green flowers appear
in spring, followed by dark red, grape-
like berries.

*Sow seed* at 12°C in late spring.
◪ *Semi-ripe cuttings* in summer in a
    propagator.
*Layer* in late spring.

**RHUS TYPHINA** (Stag's horn sumach)
Deciduous shrub or small tree with
velvety red shoots and pinnate, 60cm
long, dark green leaves that turn
brilliant red in early autumn. Conical
panicles of greenish-yellow flowers are
produced in summer, followed by
clusters of dark red, hairy fruits.

*Sow seed* outdoors in autumn.
*Semi-ripe cuttings* in summer. Shorten
    the leaves to reduce transpiration.
*Root cuttings* in winter in a garden
    frame.
◪ *Take rooted suckers* in winter. Pot up
    outside or plant out in the garden
    where they are to grow. They quickly
    form large clumps, so don't accept too
    many free gifts of this plant.

**RIBES ODORATUM** (Buffalo currant)
Deciduous shrub with bright green
leaves that turn deep red and purple in
late autumn. Pendant racemes of
fragrant, tubular, yellow flowers appear
in late spring, followed by black fruit.

*Hardwood cuttings* in winter.

**RICINUS COMMUNIS** (Castor oil plant)
Evergreen, branching shrub, usually
grown as an annual, with deeply
toothed, glossy, mid-green or bronze-red
leaves. Spikes of greenish-yellow flowers
appear in summer. The female flowers
appear above the male flowers, each

with a prominent red stamen, followed
by reddish-brown capsules covered in
brown spines. All parts are toxic,
especially the seeds.

*Seed* Sow the large, speckled seeds in
    spring, singly in small pots at 21°C.
    Pre-soak the seeds for 24 hours. Plant
    out after risk of frost is over.

**ROBINIA PSEUDOACACIA**
(False acacia, Locust)
Deciduous tree with spiny shoots and
pinnate, dark green, 30cm long leaves.
Pendant racemes of fragrant, white
flowers appear in early summer,
followed by 10cm long, brown seed pods.

*Sow seed* in a garden frame in autumn.
    Rub the seed with sandpaper
    beforehand to soften the hard coat.
*Root cuttings* in winter in a garden frame.
◪ *Take rooted suckers* in late autumn, pot
    into a well-drained, soil-based compost
    and overwinter in a garden frame.

**RODGERSIA PINNATA**
Perennial with reddish stalks and
palmate, deeply veined, 90cm long, dark
green leaves. Panicles, 30–60cm high, of
star-shaped cream, pink or red flowers
appear in late summer and early autumn.

*Sow seed* in a garden frame in spring.
◪ *Divide* in early spring. Take care not to
    damage the young emerging shoots.

**ROMNEYA COULTERI**
(Californian tree poppy)
Deciduous sub-shrub with glaucous,
grey-green leaves. Solitary, saucer-
shaped, white flowers, 12cm in diameter
with prominent, golden-yellow stamens,
appear throughout the summer.

*Sow seed* at 15°C in spring.
◪ *Softwood basal cuttings* in spring.
*Root cuttings* in winter in a garden
    frame.

*Plant rooted suckers* in late winter, in a
    soil-based compost in a garden frame.

**ROMULEA BULBOCODIUM**
Cormous perennial with linear, mid-
green basal leaves. Funnel-shaped, lilac-
purple flowers, with white or yellow
centres, appear in spring.

*Sow seed* at 10°C in autumn.
◪ *Remove offsets* in late autumn.

**ROSA** (Rose)
Deciduous shrubs with spiny stems
and glossy, mid- to dark green leaves.
Flowers are single or double, often
fragrant, in a wide range of colours, and
are followed by bright orange or red
fruit (hips).

*Sow seed* of the species as soon as the
    hips are fully red. Open the hips and
    remove the seed.
*Semi-ripe cuttings* in late summer with
    a 'heel' under horticultural fleece.
Ⅎ *Hardwood cuttings* in winter outside.
*Bud graft* in summer.

**ROSCOEA CAUTLEYOIDES**
Tuberous perennial with linear, deep
green, 40cm long leaves. White, yellow
or purple, orchid-like flowers appear in
the leaf axils in midsummer.

*Sow seed* in a garden frame as soon as it
    is ripe. Protect the young seedlings
    from strong sunlight. Alternatively,
    sow in spring but chill the seed in a
    refrigerator for 14 days beforehand.
◪ *Divide* in spring.

**ROSMARINUS OFFICINALIS**
(Rosemary)
Evergreen shrub with aromatic, leathery,
dark green leaves that are white felted
on the underside. Whorls of tubular,
white, pale blue or blue-purple, 2-lipped
flowers are produced in spring and early
summer and again in early autumn.

Rhus typhina

*Sow seed* in a container in a garden frame, in spring. I always find that a large percentage of seed is not viable, so I tend to sow thickly.

*Semi-ripe cuttings* in summer with a short 'heel'.

### RUBUS TRICOLOR

Evergreen shrub with conspicuous, soft red bristles on the stems and glossy, dark green leaves, covered with white hairs on the underside. Terminal racemes of saucer-shaped, white flowers are produced in summer, followed by edible, raspberry-like, red fruit.

*Sow seed* in autumn in a garden frame. A tip for separating the seed from the flesh is to mix the berries with water and put through the kitchen blender. If the seed is sown in spring, it will be slow to germinate.

*Semi-ripe cuttings* in summer.

*Remove rooted sections* of stem in winter or spring.

### RUDBECKIA FULGIDA

(Black-eyed Susan)
Perennial with lance-shaped, 12cm long, mid-green basal leaves. Daisy-like flowerheads, with orange-yellow ray-florets and dark brown disc-florets, are produced during late summer and autumn.

*Sow seed* in a garden frame in autumn.

*Divide* in late autumn or early spring.

### RUMEX SANGUINEUS (Bloody dock)

Rosette-forming perennial whose mid- to dark green leaves have red or purple veins. Panicles of tiny, star-shaped, green flowers turning deep red-brown are produced in early summer, followed by brown fruit.

*Sow seed* in open ground in spring.

### RUSCUS ACULEATUS (Butcher's broom)

Evergreen sub-shrub with spine-tipped, glossy, dark green cladophylls (the broom family's equivalent of leaves). Female plants produce red berries on the upper surface of the cladophylls during autumn and winter.

*Sow seed* in a garden frame as soon as it is ripe.

*Divide* in spring.

### RUTA GRAVEOLENS (Common rue)

Evergreen shrub with aromatic, blue-green, lobed leaves. Cup-shaped, insipid-looking, yellow flowers appear in summer.

*Sow seed* in a garden frame in spring.

*Semi-ripe cuttings* in summer.

### SACCHARUM RAVENNAE

(Plume grass)
Perennial grass with long, grey-green leaves with a central white stripe. Silvery-white or purple plumes appear in late summer and autumn.

*Sow seed* in a garden frame in late summer.

*Divide* in early summer.

### SAGINA BOYDII (Pearlwort)

Perennial with rosettes of glossy, dark green leaves. Tiny, pale green flowers without petals appear in summer.

*Seed* Sow the tiny seeds on the surface of the compost in a cold frame in autumn. Water from the base of the pot to avoid washing the fine seed all over the surface

*Root softwood rosettes* in early summer.

### SAGITTARIA LATIFOLIA (Duck potato)

Marginal, aquatic perennial with arrow-shaped, mid-green leaves. Racemes of white flowers appear in whorls in summer. The flower stalks are triangular in cross-section.

*Sow seed* as soon as it is ripe, in containers of wet compost. Stand the pots in a tray of water.

*Divide* tubers in spring.

### SAINTPAULIA IONANTHA

(African violet)
Tender perennial with rosettes of mid-green, hairy leaves on succulent stems. Pale to dark blue flowers are produced at intervals throughout the year.

*Sow seed* at 20°C in early spring.

*Leaf cuttings* in summer. Water from the base of the container to avoid damaging the leaf.

### SALIX ALBA (White willow)

Deciduous tree with saw-toothed, lance-shaped, grey-green leaves that are blue-green on the underside. The male catkins are yellow. Female catkins are greenish-yellow and appear in spring at the same time as the leaves.

Ruscus aculeatus 'Tricolor'

**Sow seed** as soon as the capsules are ripe. Do not allow the seed to dry out. Ideal for gardeners who can't wait; the seedlings will emerge within 2 days.

**Softwood cuttings** in midsummer.

E **Hardwood cuttings** in winter. Cuttings up to 1.8m high will root if they are inserted in a hole made with a crow bar.

### SALPIGLOSSIS SINUATA

Annual with lance-shaped, wavy-margined, mid-green leaves. Single, funnel-shaped, 5-lobed flowers, in a wide range of colours that are heavily veined in a different colour, are produced in summer and autumn.

**Sow seed** at 18°C in late spring. Alternatively, if sown in autumn and containerized in a heated greenhouse, they will flower in late winter.

### SALVIA OFFICINALIS (Common sage)

Evergreen perennial or sub-shrub with aromatic, grey-green, woolly leaves. Racemes of pale blue flowers are produced in early summer.

**Sow seed** in a garden frame in spring.

J **Softwood cuttings** in late spring.

**Semi-ripe cuttings** in early autumn in a propagator.

### SAMBUCUS NIGRA

(Black elder, Bourtree)

Deciduous shrub with stout stems and pinnate, mid-green leaves that are 25cm long. Panicles of tiny, fragrant, white flowers are produced in early summer, followed by shiny, black fruit.

**Sow seed** in a garden frame in autumn, after soaking in water at room temperature for 24 hours. Seed stored at 1°C for 12 weeks prior to sowing will germinate quickly in spring.

**Softwood cuttings** in early summer.

J **Hardwood cuttings** in winter.

Salvia officinalis 'Tricolor'

### SANGUINARIA CANADENSIS

(Bloodroot)

Perennial with broad, 20–30cm wide, bluish-green leaves. Cup-shaped, white flowers (occasionally pink) are produced in spring.

**Sow seed** in a garden frame in autumn.

J **Divide** immediately after flowering. The rhizomes exude a red sap when they are wounded.

### SANGUISORBA OFFICINALIS

(Greater burnet)

Perennial with pinnate, 60cm long, greyish-green basal leaves. Spikes of small, red-brown flowers are produced in summer.

**Sow seed** in a garden frame in autumn.

J **Divide** in early spring or late autumn.

### SANSEVIERIA TRIFASCIATA

(Mother-in-law's tongue)

Tender perennial with lance-shaped, 1.2m long, fleshy leaves with horizontal bands of light and mid-green. Racemes of tiny, tubular, greenish-white flowers are produced at any time of the year.

E **Leaf cuttings** in summer in a propagator. (Variegated varieties will produce all-green leaves.)

J **Plant rooted suckers** in spring, in loam-based compost in a propagator with bottom heat.

### SANTOLINA CHAMAECYPARISSUS

(Cotton lavender)

Evergreen shrub with greyish-white, finely toothed leaves. Small, bright yellow flowerheads appear in summer and early autumn.

*Sow seed* in a container in a garden
frame in autumn.
- *Semi-ripe cuttings* in late summer in
a propagator.

## SANVITALIA PROCUMBENS
(Creeping zinnia)
Prostrate annual with mid-green leaves.
Bright yellow flowerheads with black
centres are produced during summer
and autumn.

*Sow seed* in open ground in late spring.

## SAPINDUS SAPONARIA VAR.
DRUMMONDII (Western soapberry)
Deciduous tree with pinnate, glossy,
mid-green, 45cm long leaves turning
deep yellow in autumn. Panicles of
creamy-white flowers appear in late
spring and early summer, followed by
small, deep orange-yellow fruit.

*Sow seed* at 16°C in spring.

## SAPONARIA OCYMOIDES
(Tumbling Ted)
Perennial with lance-shaped, hairy,
bright green leaves. A mass of pink
flowers cover the plant in summer.

*Sow seed* in a container in a garden
frame, in spring or autumn.
- *Softwood cuttings* in early summer.

## SARCOCOCCA CONFUSA
(Sweet box, Christmas box)
Evergreen shrub with glossy, 5cm long,
dark green leaves. Clusters of small,
highly fragrant, pure white flowers
are produced in winter, followed by
shiny black fruit.

*Sow seed* in containers outside in
spring.
- *Semi-ripe cuttings* in late summer
or autumn.

## SARRACENIA FLAVA
(Yellow trumpet pitcher)
Perennial with yellowish-green pitchers
with raised lids, occasionally with deep
red veins. Nodding, yellow, 8cm wide
flowers are produced in late spring.

*Seed* Stratify seed for 3–4 weeks and sow
at 16°C in spring. Stand the container
in a tray of rainwater.
- *Divide* in early spring.

## SASA VEITCHII (Bamboo)
Bamboo with purple canes and ribbed,
glossy, dark green, 20cm long leaves
that wither along the margins in
autumn, turning bleached white.

*Divide* clumps in spring, retaining the
young outer pieces of rhizome for
propagating.

## SASSAFRAS ALBIDUM
Deciduous tree with aromatic, deep
green, 15cm long, lobed leaves that turn
purple or yellow, then orange, in
autumn. Racemes of tiny, yellow-green
flowers appear in spring at the same
time as the leaves, followed by deep blue
fruit on long stalks.

- *Sow seed* as soon as it is ripe, in a
container in a garden frame.
*Root cuttings* in early winter in a
garden frame.

## SAXIFRAGA OPPOSITIFOLIA
(Purple saxifrage)
Evergreen perennial with rosettes of
small, dark green leaves. Cup-shaped,
small, white, pink or deep purple
flowers are produced in early summer.

*Sow seed* in a container in a garden
frame in autumn.
- *Softwood rosette cuttings* in early
summer. Remove the flower buds
before you start.

## SCABIOSA CAUCASICA
(Pincushion flower)
Perennial with grey-green, 15cm long
basal leaves. Lavender-blue flowers, 7cm
wide, are produced in late summer.

*Sow seed* in containers in a garden frame,
as soon as it is ripe or in spring.
- *Softwood basal cuttings* in spring.
*Divide* in spring.

## SCHEFFLERA ELEGANTISSIMA
(False aralia)
Tender, evergreen shrub with linear,
toothed, glossy, dark green leaflets that
are 15–20cm long and brown-green on
the underside with white mid-ribs.
Umbels of yellowish-green flowers
appear in autumn and winter, followed
by black fruit.

*Sow seed* at 22°C in spring.
- *Semi-ripe cuttings* in a propagator in
summer. Reduce the length of the
leaflets to prevent transpiration.
*Air layer* in spring.

## SCHISANDRA RUBRIFLORA
Deciduous climber with lance-shaped,
10cm long, dark green leaves that turn
yellow in autumn. Solitary, dark red
flowers appear in late spring and
summer, followed by pendant spikes of
fleshy, bright red fruit.

*Sow seed* in a container in a garden
frame as soon as it is ripe.
- *Softwood cuttings* in early summer.
*Semi-ripe cuttings* in late summer.

## SCHIZANTHUS PINNATUS
(Poor man's orchid, Butterfly flower)
Tender annual with pale green leaves.
Tubular, 2-lipped flowers, in a wide
range of colours often with a bright
yellow throat and contrasting spots,
are produced from late spring until
mid-autumn.

Scabiosa caucasica

Sow seed at 16°C in mid-spring. If sown at 16°C in late summer they will flower that winter.

## SCHIZOPHRAGMA INTEGRIFOLIUM

Deciduous climber with dark green, 15cm long leaves. Clusters of small, fragrant, creamy-white flowers with cream bracts are produced in midsummer.

- **Softwood cuttings** in early summer. Pot the cuttings up as soon as they are rooted to establish a good root system before late autumn.
  **Semi-ripe cuttings** in late summer.

## SCHIZOSTYLIS COCCINEA (Kaffir lily)

Evergreen perennial with narrow, upright, 45cm long, sword-like, mid-green leaves. Gladiolus-like spikes of cup-shaped, scarlet flowers are produced in autumn.

- **Sow seed** at 15°C in spring.
- **Divide** in spring. Use moisture-retentive compost.

## SCHLUMBERGERA TRUNCATA
(Christmas cactus)

Perennial cactus with bright green stem segments. Bright, carmine-red, 7.5cm long flowers are produced in late winter and early spring.

- **Sow seed** at 19°C in cactus compost in spring.
- **Softwood stem sections** 5-7.5cm long in late spring or early summer. Do not cover with polythene.

## SCIADOPITYS VERTICILLATA
(Japanese umbrella pine)

Evergreen conifer with red-brown, peeling bark and whorls of linear, 5–10cm long, glossy, dark green leaves that are paler green on the underside. The tiny, male cones are borne in clusters; female cones are 5cm long and take 2 years to ripen.

- **Sow seed** in a garden frame in spring.
- **Semi-ripe cuttings** in late summer with a 'heel'. They will root under polythene in a garden frame or on the windowsill.

## SCILLA BIFOLIA

Bulbous perennial with bright green, linear basal leaves. One-sided racemes of star-shaped, blue or deep blue flowers appear in spring at the same time as the leaves.

- **Sow seed** in a garden frame as soon as it is ripe. Self-seeds readily.
- **Divide** offsets in early autumn.

## SCROPHULARIA AURICULATA
(Water figwort)

Aquatic perennial, often grown as a herbaceous perennial, with square-stemmed stems and toothed and wrinkled, dark green leaves. Clusters of 2-lipped, greenish-yellow flowers with a brown upper lip appear in summer and early autumn.

- **Sow seed** outdoors in spring or autumn.
  **Softwood basal cuttings** in a garden frame in late spring.
- **Softwood cuttings** in early summer. Pot the rooted cuttings into moisture-retentive compost.
  **Divide** in spring.

## SCUTELLARIA ALPINA (Skull cap)

Perennial with hairy, grey-green leaves. Racemes of purple flowers with cream lower lips are produced in summer.

- **Sow seed** in a garden frame as soon as it is ripe.
- **Softwood cuttings** in early summer. Pot into alkaline compost
  **Divide** in early spring.

## SEDUM SPATHULIFOLIUM

Evergreen perennial with fleshy stems supporting rosettes of small, mid-green or silvery, spoon-shaped leaves. Star-shaped, bright yellow flowers are produced in summer.

- **Sow seed** in a garden frame in autumn.
  **Divide** in spring.

- *Softwood rosette cuttings* in summer. The stems are brittle and broken rosettes will often root where they fall.

### SELAGINELLA LEPIDOPHYLLA
(Resurrection plant)
Tender, evergreen perennial with clumps of dark green leaves that curl into a ball when dry. When watered it opens to a flat, rosette-shaped plant.

- *Sow spores* at 20°C as soon as they are ripe.
- *Pot up* rooted stems in spring, using alkaline compost.

### SELENICEREUS GRANDIFLORUS
(Queen of the night)
Tender cactus with mid-green, ribbed stems and areoles of yellow spines that mature to grey. The fragrant, white, 30cm long flowers, with pale brown outer segments, open at night.

- *Sow seed* at 19°C in spring.

- *Softwood stem segments* 2.5-5cm long, in cactus compost in a propagator in summer. Allow the cut ends of the cutting to dry for a day before inserting in the compost. Keep the cuttings and the young, rooted plants shaded.

### SEMIAQUILEGIA ECALCARATA
Perennial with mid-green leaves that are purple on the underside. Panicles of pendant, bell-shaped, dark purple-red flowers appear in early summer.

- *Sow seed* in a garden frame as soon as it is ripe.

### SEMPERVIVUM TECTORUM
(Common houseleek)
Evergreen, succulent perennial with rosettes of bristle-tipped, bluish-green, purple-tinted leaves. Deep red-purple flowers appear in summer.

- *Sow seed* in a garden frame in early summer.
- *Remove offsets* in early summer and root in a gritty compost in a shaded garden frame.

### SENECIO CINERARIA
Evergreen sub-shrub, usually grown as an annual, with felted, silvery-grey, 15cm long leaves. Deep orange-yellow flower-heads are produced in midsummer in the second year after sowing.

- *Sow seed* at 20°C in spring.
- *Semi-ripe cuttings* in late summer, under horticultural fleece.

### SEQUOIA SEMPERVIRENS
(Coastal redwood)
Evergreen conifer with soft, red-brown bark and sharp-pointed, linear, deep green leaves that are silver on the underside. The green, female cones ripen in the first year.

Sempervivum tectorum

*Sow seed* in a garden frame in spring.
- *Softwood cuttings* in summer.
*Semi-ripe cuttings* in autumn with a 'heel'.

## SEQUOIADENDRON GIGANTEUM
(Giant redwood, Wellingtonia)
Evergreen conifer with tiny, grey-green leaves. Mid-green, female cones ripen and turn brown in the second year.

*Sow seed* in a garden frame in spring.
- *Softwood cuttings* in summer.
*Semi-ripe cuttings* with a 'heel' in early autumn.

## SHIBATAEA KUMASASA
Evergreen bamboo with pale brown canes and lance-shaped, dark green leaves.

*Divide* and plant the young portions in early spring. The new shoots appear in late winter or early spring.

## SHORTIA GALACIFOLIA (Oconee bells)
Evergreen perennial with small, glossy, dark green, wavy-margined leaves that turn bronze-purple in autumn. Funnel-shaped, white flowers, often flushed pink, with toothed petals appear in late spring.

*Sow seed* in containers in a garden frame as soon as it is ripe.
*Softwood basal cuttings* in early summer. Keep the compost moist and the cuttings and seedlings shaded.
- *Replant rooted runners* in spring, in containers of ericaceous compost with added leaf mould. Plant the runners in their permanent positions without disturbing the roots.

## SIDALCEA MALVIFLORA
(Checkerbloom)
Perennial with lobed, bright green leaves. Racemes of funnel-shaped, pink flowers are produced in early summer.

- *Sow seed* in a garden frame in spring or autumn.
*Divide* in spring.

## SILENE DIOICA 'ROSEA PLENA'
(Catchfly)
Semi-evergreen perennial with dark green leaves. Basal leaves are larger then those on the stalks. Clusters of double, dark pink flowers, with a white base to the petals, appear from late spring to late summer.

*Sow seed* in a garden frame in autumn.
*Separate rooted side shoots* in mid- to late summer.
*Softwood basal cuttings* in spring.

## SILYBUM MARIANUM
(Blessed Mary's thistle, Milk thistle)
Biennial with a basal rosette of 50cm long, spiny, deeply lobed, glossy, dark green leaves that are marbled white with white veins. Thistle-like, purple-red, fragrant flowerheads are produced in summer and autumn.

*Sow seed* outside where it is to flower. Thin seedlings to 50cm apart.

## SINNINGIA CARDINALIS
(Cardinal flower)
Tender, tuberous perennial with white-haired, mid-green leaves. Clusters of tubular, deep red flowers appear during late summer and autumn.

*Seed* Sow the tiny seeds at 20°C on the surface of the compost in spring. Mixing the seed with talcum powder to bulk it up makes uniform sowing a simple task.
*Leaf cuttings* in spring and summer in a propagator.
- *Divide* tubers in spring.

## SISYRINCHIUM STRIATUM
Evergreen perennial with iris-like, grey-green, strap-like leaves that are 45cm long. Clusters of cup-shaped, pale yellow flowers, with reddish-brown, striped tepals, are produced in early summer.

*Sow seed* in containers in a garden frame, in autumn or spring.
- *Divide* in spring.

## SKIMMIA JAPONICA
Evergreen shrub with dark green, 10cm long, slightly aromatic leaves. Panicles of fragrant white flowers appear in mid- to late spring, followed by red fruit on female plants.

*Sow seed* in a garden frame in autumn.
- *Semi-ripe cuttings* in a propagator in early autumn. Take the cuttings with a 'heel' and trim the leaves to reduce transpiration. If large amounts of callus form without any roots, scrape away the callus and re-insert the cutting. It will now root.

## SMILACINA RACEMOSA
(False Solomon's seal)
Perennial with mid-green, heavily veined leaves that are downy on the underside and turn yellow in autumn. Panicles of creamy-white flowers are produced in late spring, followed on female plants by green berries that mature to red.

*Sow seed* at 12°C after putting up with a whole lot of trouble. The seeds suffer from double dormancy, so need to be chilled for 90 days, then placed in the warmth for 90 days, followed by a further 90 days in the cold. After all that, they need to be brought into the warmth for germination. Lady gardeners could give birth in the time!
- *Divide* rhizomes in spring. Use ericaceous compost and keep the young plants shaded until established.

## SMILAX CHINA
Deciduous climber with dark green, 7cm long leaves. Umbels of yellowish-green flowers appear in spring, followed on female plants by small, bright red berries.

*Sow seed* in a garden frame in autumn.

### SMITHIANTHA 'ORANGE KING'

Tender perennial with heart-shaped, 15cm long, mid-green, purple-haired leaves with purple markings along the veins. Red-spotted, orange flowers, with yellow on the inside of the lips, appear in summer and autumn.

***Sow seed*** at 18°C in late spring. Seedlings are prone to damping off disease.
- ***Divide*** rhizomes in spring.

### SOLANDRA MAXIMA (Cup of gold)

Tender, evergreen climber with leathery, rich green, 15cm long leaves. Large, trumpet-shaped, golden-yellow flowers with purple veins are produced in summer.

***Sow seed*** at 16°C in spring.
***Semi-ripe cuttings*** in summer in a propagator.
- ***Air layer*** in late spring.

### SOLANUM CRISPUM

(Chilean potato tree)
Evergreen or semi-evergreen climber with dark green, 12cm long leaves. Clusters of lilac-blue, fragrant flowers appear in summer, followed by creamy-white fruit.

***Sow seed*** at 18°C in spring.
- ***Semi-ripe cuttings*** in a propagator in summer and early autumn.

### SOLDANELLA ALPINA

(Alpine snowbell)
Evergreen perennial with thick, rounded, dark green leaves. Funnel-shaped, nodding, violet-purple flowers, with red blotches on the inside and deeply fringed petals, are produced in early spring, often through lying snow.

***Sow seed*** as soon as it is ripe in a garden frame in well-drained compost with a surface of washed grit.
- ***Divide*** in early spring. Repot immediately.

### SOLEIROLIA SOLEIROLII

(Mind-your-own-business)
Evergreen perennial with tiny, rounded, mid-green leaves. Solitary, tiny, pink-tinged white flowers appear in summer.

***Divide*** in early summer.

### SOLIDAGO 'LODDON GOLD'

(Golden rod)
Perennial with mid-green leaves. Panicles of flowers coloured a deep butter-yellow are produced in late summer and early autumn.

***Divide*** in spring or late autumn.

### × SOLIDASTER LUTEUS

Deciduous perennial with lance-shaped, mid-green, 15cm long leaves. Panicles of daisy-like flowers, with pale yellow ray-florets and deep yellow disc-florets, are produced in summer and early autumn.

- ***Softwood, basal cuttings*** in spring.
***Divide*** in early spring.

### SOPHORA TETRAPTERA (Kowhai)

Evergreen tree with dark green, pinnate leaves that are 15cm long. Racemes of golden-yellow, 5cm long flowers, with forward-pointing petals, are produced in late spring.

***Sow seed*** as soon as it is ripe, in containers in a garden frame. Soak the seed for 2 hours before sowing.
- ***Semi-ripe cuttings*** in a propagator in late summer.

### SORBARIA SORBIFOLIA

Deciduous shrub with 25cm long, dark green leaves. Conical panicles of tiny, white flowers appear in late summer.

***Sow seed*** in a garden frame in autumn.
- ***Semi-ripe cuttings*** in summer. Shorten the leaves to reduce transpiration.
***Replant rooted suckers*** in late autumn in a garden frame.

Solandra maxima

### SORBUS AUCUPARIA

(Mountain ash, Rowan)
Deciduous tree with pinnate, mid- to dark green leaves that colour to yellow, orange or red in autumn. Clusters of white flowers in spring are followed by large clusters of orange-red berries.

- ***Sow seed*** in a garden frame in autumn. Spring-sown seed may take as long as 18–24 months to germinate.
***Softwood cuttings*** in late spring. They are difficult to root. I have managed a good 'strike' of cuttings only once.
***Bud graft*** in summer.
***Whip and tongue graft*** in winter.

### SPARAXIS TRICOLOR

Tender, cormous perennial with basal fans of dark green, lance-shaped, 30cm long leaves. The funnel-shaped, orange, red or purple flowers carry a dark red or black central mark and are produced in spring and early summer.

**Sow seed** in a garden frame as soon as it is ripe.

▯ **Remove offsets** when the plants are dormant in autumn and pot up in soil-based compost in a frost-free greenhouse.

## SPARTIUM JUNCEUM (Spanish broom)

Deciduous shrub with dark green shoots and small, lance-shaped, dark green leaves. Terminal racemes of fragrant, golden-yellow, pea-like flowers are produced from early summer to mid-autumn, followed by flattened, dark brown seed pods.

**Sow seed** in a garden frame, in autumn or spring.

## SPATHIPHYLLUM WALLISII

Tender, evergreen perennial with wavy-margined, dark green, 30cm long leaves. Fragrant, white spathes that are

15–20cm long appear in spring and summer, and mature to green with green and white spadices.

**Sow seed** as soon as it is ripe at 26°C on moist sphagnum moss.

▯ **Divide** in late winter or after flowering.

## SPIRAEA DOUGLASII

Deciduous shrub with dark green, 10cm long leaves that are grey and felted on the underside. Panicles of pink-purple flowers appear in early summer.

▯ **Softwood cuttings** in summer.

**Take rooted suckers** in late autumn and plant them outside in their permanent positions. Prune the sucker in early summer (before removing it from the parent) to encourage it to form a branched habit.

## STACHYS BYZANTINA (Lamb's ears)

Evergreen perennial with rosettes of thick, wrinkled, grey-green leaves that are densely covered with white wool. Erect spikes of woolly, pink-purple flowers are produced in summer and early autumn.

**Sow seed** in a garden frame in spring or autumn.

▯ **Irishman's cuttings.** Remove rooted portions of stem in early spring.

## STACHYURUS PRAECOX

Deciduous shrub with 15cm long, mid-green leaves. Racemes of bell-shaped, greenish-yellow flowers are produced in late winter and early spring.

**Sow seed** in a garden frame in autumn.

▯ **Semi-ripe cuttings** with a 'heel' in summer. Shorten the leaves to reduce transpiration.

Stachys byzantina

### STAPELIA GRANDIFLORA

(Carrion flower)

Tender succulent with fleshy, mid-green stems. Purplish-red flowers, with wrinkled lobes lined with purple and yellow, appear in summer.

***Sow seed*** at 20°C in spring.
- ***Softwood stem sections*** in summer, in free-draining, gritty compost.

### STAPHYLEA PINNATA (Bladder nut)

Deciduous shrub with pinnate, dark green leaves. Pendant panicles of bell-shaped, fragrant, white-tinged pink flowers appear in late spring and early summer, followed by greenish-white fruit.

***Sow seed*** in a garden frame in autumn.
***Softwood cuttings*** in early summer.
- ***Semi-ripe cuttings*** in midsummer in a propagator.

### STAUNTONIA HEXAPHYLLA

Evergreen climber with palmate, leathery, dark green leaves. Racemes of fragrant, cup-shaped, purple-tinged, white flowers appear in spring, followed by edible, purple fruit.

***Sow seed*** at 16°C in spring.
- ***Semi-ripe cuttings*** with a 'heel' in summer.

### STEPHANANDRA INCISA

Deciduous shrub with mid-green leaves turning deep yellow in autumn. Panicles of greenish-white flowers are produced in early summer.

***Softwood cuttings*** in early summer under horticultural fleece.
***Semi-ripe cuttings*** with a 'heel' in midsummer.
- ***Hardwood cuttings*** in early winter.
***Plant rooted suckers*** in a soil-based compost in autumn and overwinter in a garden frame.

Stapelia grandiflora

### STEPHANOTIS FLORIBUNDA

(Madagascar jasmine)

Tender, evergreen climber with glossy, deep green, thick leaves that are 10cm long. Clusters of fragrant, waxy, white flowers are produced in spring and summer.

***Sow seed*** at 18°C in spring.
- ***Semi-ripe cuttings*** in a propagator in summer.

### STERNBERGIA LUTEA

(Autumn daffodil)

Bulbous perennial with lance-shaped, 30cm long, deep green leaves. Goblet-shaped, dark yellow flowers appear in autumn at the same time as the leaves.

***Sow seed*** at 16°C in spring.
- ***Remove offsets*** in late autumn when the plant is dormant, and replant immediately.

### STEWARTIA PSEUDOCAMELLIA

Deciduous tree with peeling, pink and grey bark and dark green, 10cm long leaves that turn yellow, orange and purple in autumn. Cup-shaped, white flowers with creamy yellow stamens are produced in summer.

***Sow seed*** in a garden frame in autumn.
- ***Softwood cuttings*** in early summer with a pair of leaves.
***Semi-ripe cuttings*** in late summer.
***Layer*** in late autumn.

### STIPA GIGANTEA (Great feather grass)

Evergreen perennial grass with mid-green leaves that are 60cm long. Panicles of purplish-green spikelets appear in summer, turning golden-yellow when fully ripe.

***Sow seed*** in a garden frame in spring.
- ***Divide*** in early summer.

**STOKESIA LAEVIS** (Stokes' aster)
Evergreen perennial with lance-shaped, mid-green basal leaves and pale green mid-ribs. Cornflower-like flowerheads, with purple-blue, fringed ray-florets and paler disc-florets, are produced in summer and early autumn.

*Sow seed* in a cold frame in autumn.
🗍 *Root cuttings* in late winter in a garden frame.
*Divide* in spring.

**STRATIOTES ALOIDES** (Water soldier)
Aquatic perennial with rosettes of lance-shaped, sharp-pointed, olive-green, 50cm long leaves. Cup-shaped, white or pink-tinged white flowers appear in midsummer.

*Separate* young plantlets in spring.

**STRELITZIA REGINEA** (Bird of paradise)
Tender, evergreen perennial with lance-shaped, 45cm long, deep green leaves. Purple and orange-tinted, green spathes, with orange or yellow calyces and bright blue corollas, are produced in winter and spring.

*Sow seed* at 20°C in spring.
🗍 *Plant rooted suckers* in spring, in loam-based compost in a propagator.

**STREPTOCARPUS CAULESCENS**
(Cape primrose)
Tender perennial with soft and hairy, mid-green leaves. Clusters of 8–12 white or violet flowers with purple throats appear off and on during the year.

*Sow seed* at 18°C in winter or spring. Sow the seed on the surface of the compost.
🗍 *Leaf cuttings* in early summer.
*Softwood stem tip cuttings* in spring in a propagator.
*Divide* in early summer.

**STREPTOSOLEN JAMESONII**
(Marmalade bush)
Tender, evergreen shrub with deep green leaves. Orange-yellow flowers with twisted tubes are produced from late spring to late summer.

*Softwood cuttings* in early summer.
🗍 *Semi-ripe cuttings* in late summer in a propagator.
*Layer* in late summer.

**STROBILANTHES ATROPURPUREA**
Deciduous perennial with deep green leaves. Spikes of tubular, purple flowers appear in summer.

*Sow seed* at 16°C in spring.
🗍 *Softwood basal cuttings* in early summer in a propagator.

**STYRAX JAPONICUS**
(Japanese snowbell)
Deciduous tree with glossy, dark green, 10cm long leaves, maturing to red or yellow in autumn. Bell-shaped, fragrant, white or pink-tinged flowers are produced along the lower side of the branches in early summer.

*Sow seed* as soon as it is ripe, at 15°C for 12 weeks, then reduce the temperature to 2°C for a further 12 weeks. Germination may be erratic.
🗍 *Softwood cuttings* in summer.

**SUCCISA PRATENSIS** (Blue buttons)
Perennial with rosettes of mid-green, 30cm long basal leaves. Solitary, pincushion-like, violet flowerheads appear from summer to late autumn.

*Sow seed* in a garden frame, in spring or autumn.
🗍 *Softwood basal cuttings* in spring.

**SYCOPSIS SINENSIS**
Evergreen shrub with 10cm long, leathery, dark green leaves that are paler green on the underside. Clusters of light brown, felted buds open to petal-less flowers with red anthers and yellow filaments in spring.

*Sow seed* in a garden frame in ericaceous compost.
🗍 *Semi-ripe cuttings* in summer with a 'heel' and no more than 3 leaves.

**SYMPHORICARPOS × CHENAULTII**
(Snowberry)
Deciduous shrub with dark green leaves that are hairy on the underside. Clusters of small, greenish-white flowers appear in late summer, followed by white fruit marked with red.

🗍 *Softwood cuttings* in summer.
*Hardwood cuttings* in late autumn.

**SYMPHYANDRA WANNERI**
Perennial with rosettes of hairy, lance-shaped, 10cm long, dark green leaves. Panicles of pendant, bell-shaped, violet-blue flowers are produced throughout summer.

*Sow seed* at 12°C in late winter or early spring.

**SYMPHYTUM OFFICINALE**
(Common comfrey)
Perennial with hairy, 10cm long, dark green leaves. Creamy-white, pink or purple flowers appear in late spring and summer.

*Sow seed* in a garden frame, in autumn or spring.
🗍 *Root cuttings* in late autumn in a garden frame.
*Divide* in spring.

## SYMPLOCOS PANICULATA
(Sapphire berry)
Evergreen tree or bushy shrub with dark green, 7.5cm long leaves. Terminal panicles of star-shaped, fragrant, white flowers with prominent stamens are produced during late spring and early summer.

*Sow seed* in autumn, in ericaceous compost, in containers in a garden frame.
▯ *Softwood cuttings* in early summer.

## SYNGONIUM PODOPHYLLUM
(Goose foot)
Tender, evergreen climber with heart-shaped, juvenile leaves, maturing to arrow-shaped, dark green leaves with grey-green markings. Clusters of cream or greenish-yellow spathes are produced in summer.

▯ *Softwood cuttings* from the tips of stems in summer in a propagator.
*Leaf-bud cuttings* in summer in a propagator.

## SYRINGA MEYERI (Lilac)
Deciduous shrub with mid-green, oval leaves. Small panicles of fragrant, lavender-pink flowers appear in late spring and early summer.

*Sow seed* in a garden frame as soon as it is ripe or in spring.
▯ *Softwood cuttings* in early summer.
*Layer* in early summer.

## TAGETES ANTIGUA SERIES
(African marigold)
Annual with pinnate, mid-green leaves. Pompom-like, terminal flowerheads, 12.5cm across, in lemon-yellow, golden-yellow or orange, are produced from early summer to autumn.

*Sow seed* at 20°C in early spring.

## TAMARIX TETRANDRA (Tamarisk)
Deciduous shrub or small tree with tiny, scale-like, mid-green, feathery leaves. Racemes of pale pink flowers are produced in late spring.

*Sow seed* as soon as it is ripe, in a garden frame.
*Semi-ripe cuttings* in summer with a 'heel'.
▯ *Hardwood cuttings* in winter.

## TANACETUM PARTHENIUM (Feverfew)
Woody based, short-lived perennial with hairy, mid-green, aromatic basal leaves. Masses of daisy-like flowerheads, with white ray-florets and bright yellow disc-florets, appear in summer.

*Sow seed* at 12°C in early spring.
*Softwood basal cuttings* in spring.
▯ *Softwood cuttings* in early summer.

## TAXODIUM DISTICHUM
(Swamp cypress)
Deciduous conifer with small, pale green leaves turning bright brown in autumn. Male cones are red; female cones are green, ripening to brown.

*Sow seed* in a garden frame in spring.

## TAXUS BACCATA (Yew)
Evergreen conifer with linear, glossy, dark green leaves that are paler on the underside. Male cones are yellow. Green seeds are surrounded by red arils. The arils are fleshy.

*Sow seed* in a garden frame in late autumn. Germination can take up to 36 months.
▯ *Semi-ripe cuttings* in late summer. Take cutting material from upright shoots to encourage a strong, leading shoot.

Taxus baccata

## TECOMA STANS
(Trumpet bush, Yellow elder)
Tender, evergreen large shrub or small tree with lance-shaped, bright green, 40cm long, pinnate leaves. Panicles of bright yellow, funnel-shaped flowers appear from late winter to early summer.

*Sow seed* at 20°C in spring.
- *Semi-ripe cuttings* in a propagator in summer.

## TECOPHILAEA CYANOCROCUS
(Chilean blue crocus)
Cormous perennial with lance-shaped, dark green basal leaves. Funnel-shaped, gentian-blue flowers with white veins are produced in spring.

*Sow seed* in a garden frame in early autumn.
- *Remove offsets* in late summer. Plant 5cm deep and surface mulch in frosty areas.

## TELLIMA GRANDIFLORA (Fringe cups)
Perennial with rosettes of mid-green, scalloped leaves. Racemes are 30cm long with greenish-white flowers in late spring and early summer.

*Sow seed* in a garden frame in spring.
- *Divide* in spring as growth starts.

## TELOPEA OREADES
(Gippsland waratah)
Tender, evergreen shrub with lance-shaped, matt, dark green, 15cm long leaves. Flowerheads consisting of tubular, red flowers surrounded by pale green or pink bracts appear in late spring and summer.

*Sow seed* in a garden frame as soon as it is ripe. Check that the seed is intact by breaking it open. Most seed is unlikely to be viable.

- *Semi-ripe cuttings* with a 'heel', in a propagator in summer.
- *Leaf-bud cuttings* in a propagator in summer.

## TETRANEMA ROSEUM
(Mexican foxglove)
Tender, evergreen perennial with dark green leaves. Trumpet-shaped, 2-lipped, mauve flowers appear in summer.

*Sow seed* at 20°C in spring.
- *Divide* in spring.

## TEUCRIUM FRUTICANS
(Shrubby germander)
Evergreen shrub with white woolly shoots and aromatic, lance-shaped, grey-green leaves. Terminal racemes of pale blue flowers with prominent stamens are produced in summer.

*Sow seed* in a garden frame, as soon as it is ripe.
- *Softwood cuttings* in early summer under polythene.
- *Semi-ripe cuttings* in midsummer in a propagator.

## THALICTRUM FLAVUM (Meadow rue)
Perennial with pinnate, 40cm long, mid-green leaves. Panicles of fragrant, yellow flowers with erect, bright yellow stamens are produced in summer.

*Sow seed* in a garden frame, as soon as it is ripe.
- *Divide* in early spring. Keep in shade until well rooted.

## THELYPTERIS PALUSTRIS (Marsh fern)
Deciduous fern with pinnate, 40cm long, sterile, pale green fronds. The fertile fronds differ, being 90cm long with narrow pinnae at the base.

*Sow spores* at 16°C, as soon as they are ripe.
- *Divide* in early summer.

## THERMOPSIS VILLOSA (Carolina lupin)
Perennial with 3-palmate, bright mid-green leaves covered with glaucous, silky hairs on the underside. Racemes of pale yellow flowers are produced in late spring and early summer.

- *Sow seed* at 10°C in spring. Transplant the seedlings when small, as the roots resent disturbance.
- *Divide* in spring. I have never had success with this method. Established plants resent being disturbed.

## THUJA PLICATA (Western red cedar)
Evergreen conifer with red-brown, mature bark and mid- to dark green, scale-like, aromatic leaves that are grey-green on the underside. The small, female cones have 5 pairs of scales with a small hook on each scale.

*Sow seed* in late winter in a garden frame.
- *Semi-ripe cuttings* with a 'heel' in late autumn.

## THUJOPSIS DOLABRATA (Hiba)
Evergreen conifer with scale-like, glossy, dark green leaves that are silvery-white on the underside. Blue-grey, female cones ripen to brown; male cones are dark purple.

*Sow seed* in a garden frame in early spring.
- *Semi-ripe cuttings* with a 'heel' in late summer.

## THUNBERGIA ALATA
(Black eyed Susan)
Tender, evergreen climber, often treated as an annual, with mid-green leaves. Solitary yellow or orange flowers, often with rich brown-purple centres, are produced from midsummer to autumn.

- *Sow seed* at 16°C in spring.

*Softwood cuttings* in early summer.
*Semi-ripe cuttings* in late summer in a propagator.
*Layer* in late spring.

### THYMUS × CITRIODORUS
(Lemon-scented thyme)
Evergreen shrub with small, mid-green, aromatic leaves (there is also a variegated form). Pale, lavender-pink flowers are produced in summer.

*Sow seed* in a garden frame in spring.
*Softwood cuttings* in early summer.
*Semi-ripe cuttings* in late summer.
◧ *Irishman's cuttings* in late spring. Pot into free-draining, gritty compost.
*Divide* in spring.

### TIARELLA CORDIFOLIA (Foam flower)
Perennial with pale green leaves, turning bronze-red in autumn. Racemes of creamy-white flowers appear in summer.

*Sow seed* in a garden frame in spring.
◧ *Divide* in spring.

Thymus × citriodorus 'Variegatus'

### TIBOUCHINA ORGANENSIS (Glory bush)
Tender, evergreen shrub with angular, hairy stems and greyish-green, 15cm long leaves that are covered with soft hairs. Panicles of saucer-shaped, blue-purple flowers are produced in summer and autumn.

*Sow seed* at 16°C in spring.
*Softwood cuttings* in late spring under horticultural fleece.
◧ *Semi-ripe cuttings* in summer in a propagator.

### TIGRIDIA PAVONIA (Tiger flower)
Tender, bulbous perennial with a basal fan of lance-shaped, 25–50cm long, dark green leaves. Iris-like, white, yellow, orange, pink or red flowers, with contrasting central spots, are produced in summer.

*Sow seed* at 16°C in spring.
◧ *Remove offsets* in late autumn and pot into a gritty, free-draining compost in a garden frame.

### TILIA × EUROPAEA (Common lime)
Deciduous, suckering tree with rounded, dark green, 10cm long leaves, paler green on the underside. Pale yellow flowers appear in midsummer.

*Seed* Stratify seed for 16–20 weeks and sow in a garden frame in spring.

### TILLANDSIA ARGENTEA (Air plant)
Tender, evergreen perennial with rosettes of linear, white-scaly, pale, silvery-green leaves. Spikes of tubular, red or bright blue flowers, with pale pink bracts, are produced in spring.

*Sow seed* at 27°C onto small bundles of larch twigs wrapped in sphagnum moss. Mist daily with rainwater.

### TOLMIEA MENZIESII (Pick-a-back-plant)
Perennial with basal, 12.5cm long, kidney-shaped, lime-green leaves. Young plants are produced on the leaves where the leaf and stalk join. One-sided racemes of fragrant flowers with purple-brown petals, pale green sepals marked purple-brown, and orange anthers are produced in late spring and early summer.

*Sow seed* in a garden frame in spring.
*Leaf cuttings* on the surface of compost. Pot up plantlets when well rooted.
*Divide* in spring.
◧ *Remove and plant up plantlets* in late summer.

### TORREYA CALIFORNICA
(California nutmeg)
Evergreen tree with lance-shaped, yellowish-green leaves. The female, cone-like seed pods are purplish-green and take 2 years to mature.

*Sow seed* in a garden frame as soon as it is ripe. Germination may take 24–30 months.
◧ *Semi-ripe cuttings* in late summer using upright growing shoots.

## TRACHELIUM ASPERULOIDES

Perennial with small, glossy, mid-green leaves. Masses of tubular, white or lavender-blue flowers appear in late summer.

**Sow seed** in a garden frame as soon as it is ripe
**Softwood cuttings** in summer.

## TRACHELOSPERMUM JASMINOIDES

(Star jasmine)
Evergreen climber with 10cm long, glossy, dark green leaves, turning bronze-red in winter. Pure white, fragrant flowers are produced in mid- to late summer.

**Semi-ripe cuttings** in a propagator in summer.
**Layer** in autumn.

## TRACHYCARPUS FORTUNEI

(Chusan palm)
Evergreen palm with fan-shaped, dark green, 45–70cm long leaves. Pendant panicles of small, yellow flowers appear in early summer, followed by blue-black fruit on female plants.

**Sow seed** in spring at 24°C.

## TRADESCANTIA FLUMINENSIS

(Wandering Jew)
Tender, trailing, evergreen perennial with light green leaves that are purple on the underside. White flowers are produced throughout the year.

**Softwood tip cuttings** at any time of the year.

## TRICYRTIS FORMOSANA (Toad lily)

Perennial with glossy, purple-spotted, dark green, 12.5cm long leaves. Star-shaped, white, white-tinged pink or deep purple-pink flowers, with white stigmas spotted deep pink, appear in autumn.

**Sow seed** as soon as it is ripe, in a garden frame with frost protection for the first winter.
**Divide** in early spring before growth starts.

## TRIFOLIUM REPENS 'PURPURASCENS QUADRIFOLIUM' (Clover)

Perennial with 4-palmate, deep purple leaves with bright green margins. Racemes of white, pea-like flowers appear in summer.

**Sow seed** in a garden frame in spring.
**Divide** separate rooted stems in spring. Pot up in free-draining compost.

## TRILLIUM GRANDIFLORUM

(Wake robin)
Perennial with rounded, dark green, 30cm long leaves. Pure white flowers with green sepals appear above the leaves in spring and early summer.

**Sow seed** as soon as it is ripe, in a garden frame in constantly moist, peaty compost. It may take 2 years for the leaves to appear and a further 4–5 years for the plants to produce flowers.
**Divide** after flowering. Each rhizome must have at least one growing bud.
**Offsets** If the growing bud is removed from the plant after it has flowered, offsets will form. Remove and pot them up immediately.

## TRITONIA CROCATA

Cormous perennial with lance-shaped, mid-green basal leaves. Spikes of funnel-shaped, pink, deep orange or red flowers are produced in summer.

**Sow seed** at 16°C as soon as it is ripe, or in spring.
**Remove offsets** in late autumn and plant in loam-based, free-draining compost.

## TROCHODENDRON ARALIOIDES

(Wheel tree)
Evergreen tree or large shrub with spirals of glossy, dark green, 10cm long leaves. Racemes of bright green flowers, comprising green stamens emerging from a green disc, appear in late spring and early summer.

**Sow seed** in a garden frame in autumn.
**Semi-ripe cuttings** in midsummer in ericaceous compost.

## TROLLIUS CHINENSIS (Globeflower)

Perennial with 5-lobed, mid-green basal leaves that are 10–12.5cm long. Bowl-shaped, deep orange-yellow flowers are produced in summer.

**Sow seed** in a garden frame in autumn. Alternatively, chill for 14 days and sow in spring. Germination is erratic and can take up to 2 years.
**Divide** immediately after flowering, unless the ground is cold and wet, in which case wait until early spring.

Trollius chinensis

## TROPAEOLUM SPECIOSUM
(Flame nasturtium)
Perennial climber with palmate, dark green leaves. Bright red flowers with long spurs appear in summer and autumn, followed by blue fruit with red calyces.

*Sow seed* as soon as it is ripe. Allow 8 weeks stratification and then place in a garden frame.

*Divide* in late winter. Do not allow the white rhizomes to dry out.

## TSUGA HETEROPHYLLA
(Western hemlock)
Evergreen conifer with tiny, glossy, dark green leaves. Female cones are mid-brown.

*Sow seed* in a garden frame in spring.

*Semi-ripe cuttings* with a 'heel' in late summer.

## TULBAGHIA ALLIACEA
Semi-evergreen perennial with linear, basal, mid-green, aromatic leaves. Umbels of fragrant, greenish-white flowers, with a purple tinge and dark red stamens, are produced in late spring and early summer.

*Sow seed* at 16°C in early spring. Quick to germinate and come into flower.
*Divide* in late summer.

## TULIPA (Tulip)
Bulbous perennial with mid- to dark green leaves that are basal or held on a stem. Upright, terminal flowers have 6 tepals (petals). They are usually bowl- or goblet-shaped and come in a range of colours, including mixed.

*Seed* Sow species in a garden frame in autumn. From germination to flowering will take 5–7 years.

*Remove offsets* in autumn and pot up immediately.

## TWEEDIA CAERULEA
Tender, evergreen sub-shrub with white-hairy stems and lance-shaped, light green leaves. Small clusters of sky-blue flowers open from pink buds and fade to purple in summer and autumn.

*Sow seed* at 12°C in spring.

*Softwood cuttings* in a propagator in summer.

## TYPHA LATIFOLIA (Bulrush)
Aquatic perennial with strap-like, mid-green, 1.8m long leaves. Dark brown flower spikes, held on 180cm long stalks, appear in summer. Female flowers mature to white.

*Divide* in spring.

## ULEX EUROPAEUS (Gorse, Whin, Furze)
Evergreen shrub with spine-tipped shoots and stiff, dark green leaves narrowing to spines. Pea-like, bright yellow, coconut-scented flowers are produced throughout the year, with masses in spring.

*Sow seed* in a garden frame in spring. Self-seeds readily.

*Softwood cuttings* in summer under clear polythene.

## ULMUS GLABRA (Wych elm)
Deciduous tree with dark green, 15cm long leaves that are downy on the underside and turn yellow in autumn. Tiny, red flowers are produced in spring, followed by winged, dark green fruit.

*Sow seed* outdoors in autumn or spring.

*Softwood cuttings* in summer.

## UMBELLULARIA CALIFORNICA
(California laurel)
Evergreen tree with leathery, bright green leaves that are very aromatic. The aroma from the crushed leaves can cause a headache. Umbels of greenish-yellow flowers appear in late winter and early spring, followed by purple berries.

*Sow seed* in a garden frame in autumn.

*Semi-ripe cuttings* in late summer. Do not inhale deeply when working with the foliage.

## URSINIA ANETHOIDES
Tender, evergreen perennial, usually grown as an annual, with small, deeply divided, dark green leaves. Solitary, golden-yellow flowerheads, with purple disc-florets, are produced in summer and early autumn.

*Sow seed* at 16°C in spring.

*Softwood cuttings* in summer under horticultural fleece.

## UVULARIA GRANDIFLORA
(Large merrybells)
Perennial with downward-pointing, lance-shaped, mid-green, 10cm long leaves. Tubular, bell-shaped, pendant, pale yellow flowers with twisted tepals appear in late spring and early summer.

*Sow seed* in a garden frame, as soon as it is ripe.

*Divide* in early spring.

## VACCINIUM MACROCARPON
(Cranberry)
Evergreen shrub with dark green leaves turning bronze in winter. Clusters of pendant, bell-shaped, pink flowers are produced in summer, followed by edible, red berries.

*Sow seed* in a garden frame in spring, on the surface of ericaceous compost. Sieve fruit to separate the seeds. If the seed is stored dry, germination will be rapid.

*Semi-ripe cuttings* with a 'heel'in late summer.
*Layer* in early autumn.

Uvularia grandiflora

**VALERIANA OFFICINALIS** (Valerian)
Perennial with aromatic, pinnate, bright green, 20cm long leaves. Pink or white flowers are produced in summer.

**Sow seed** outdoors in containers in spring.
J **Divide** in autumn or early spring.

**VELTHEIMIA CAPENSIS**
Tender, bulbous perennial with basal rosettes of thick, glaucous, blue-green, lance-shaped, 30cm long, wavy-margined leaves. Terminal racemes of pendant, tubular, white flowers with red spots or pink flowers with green spots are produced in spring on stout, purple-spotted, green stems.

**Sow seed** at 24°C in autumn.
J **Remove offsets** in late summer and repot immediately in a loam-based compost with the neck of the bulb at compost level.

**VERATRUM ALBUM** (False hellebore)
Perennial with basal, pleated 30cm long leaves. Panicles of star-shaped, white or greenish-white flowers are produced in early summer.

**Sow seed** in a garden frame as soon as it is ripe.
J **Divide** in autumn or early spring. Wear gloves as the black rhizomes are poisonous.

**VERBASCUM OLYMPICUM** (Mullein)
Perennial with rosettes of lance-shaped, mid-green, 20–60cm long basal leaves that are covered with grey-white wool. Branching stems with panicles of saucer-shaped, bright yellow flowers are produced in early and midsummer.

E **Sow seed** in a garden frame in spring or early summer.
**Root cuttings** in early winter in a garden frame.

## VERBENA BONARIENSIS
Perennial with lance-shaped, wrinkled leaves that are hairy on the underside. Tall panicles of small, lilac-purple flowers appear in midsummer and early autumn.

- **Sow seed** at 18°C in autumn or early spring. Self-seeds readily in mild autumns.
  **Softwood stem-tip cuttings** in late summer.

## VERNONIA NOVEBORACENSIS
Perennial with lance-shaped, 20cm long, dark green leaves. Clusters of tubular, white or red-purple, fluffy-headed flowers are produced from late summer to mid-autumn.

- **Sow seed** in a garden frame in spring.
- **Divide** in spring.

## VERONICA SPICATA
Perennial with lance-shaped, hairy leaves. Terminal racemes of star-shaped, bright blue flowers with long, purple stamens appear throughout the summer.

- **Sow seed** in a garden frame in autumn.
  **Divide** in autumn or early spring.

## VESTIA FOETIDA
Evergreen shrub with glossy, dark green leaves that, when crushed, emit an unpleasant odour. Clusters of pendant, tubular, pale yellow flowers with protruding stamens are produced from late spring to midsummer.

- **Sow seed** in a garden frame in autumn.
- **Semi-ripe cuttings** in summer.

## VIBURNUM FARRERI
Deciduous shrub with 10cm long, dark green leaves that are bronze when young and turn red-purple in autumn. Clusters of fragrant, tubular, plain white or white-tinged pink flowers are produced from autumn through winter and into spring, followed by bright red fruit.

- **Sow seed** in a garden frame in autumn, or outdoors in pots in spring. Protect from vermin for 24 months.
- **Softwood cuttings** in summer under clear polythene. Reduce the length of the leaves to prevent transpiration.

## VINCA MAJOR (Greater periwinkle)
Evergreen shrub with lance-shaped, dark green leaves. Star-like, violet-blue flowers are produced from spring through to autumn.

- **Semi-ripe cuttings** in summer.
- **Divide** in autumn or spring.

## VIOLA CORNUTA (Horned violet)
Evergreen perennial with bright green, toothed leaves. Masses of fragrant, lilac-blue flowers, with the lower petals marked white, are produced during spring and summer.

- **Sow seed** in an open garden frame as soon as it is ripe and allow to become frosted. Germination may be slow.
  **Divide** in spring or autumn.

## VITIS DAVIDII (Vine)
Deciduous climber with heart-shaped, lobed, glossy, dark green, 25cm long leaves that are blue-grey on the underside and turn bright red in late autumn. Small, edible, black grapes are produced in autumn.

- **Hardwood cuttings** in late winter.
  **Bud cuttings** in early spring.
  **Layer** in late autumn.

## VRIESEA CARINATA (Painted feather)
Tender, evergreen, perennial bromeliad with funnel-shaped rosettes of arching, glossy, mid-green leaves. Spike-like racemes of scapes (flower stalks) with red, purple or green bracts and narrow, green-tipped, yellow petals appear in summer or early autumn.

- **Sow seed** at 24°C as soon as it is ripe.
- **Remove offsets** in spring and pot into bromeliad compost.

## WALDSTEINIA TERNATA
Semi-evergreen perennial with 3-palmate, dark green leaves. Saucer-shaped, bright yellow flowers are produced in late spring and early summer.

- **Sow seed** in a garden frame in spring.
- **Divide** in early spring.
  **Rooted stolons** in autumn, in a soil-based compost in a garden frame.

## WATSONIA MARGINATA
Tender, cormous perennial with mid-green, 80cm long, sword-like basal leaves. Branched spikes of tubular, mauve-pink flowers, with purple and white markings, are produced from spring to early summer.

- **Sow seed** at 18°C in autumn.
- **Divide** in spring.

## WEIGELA MIDDENDORFFIANA
Deciduous shrub with bright green, 10cm long leaves. Clusters of bell-shaped, pale yellow flowers with red or deep yellow markings are produced from late spring to midsummer.

- **Sow seed** in a garden frame in autumn. The seed will not come true.
- **Softwood cuttings** in early summer.
- **Semi-ripe cuttings** in a propagator in midsummer.
  **Hardwood cuttings** in late autumn.

## WISTERIA FLORIBUNDA
(Japanese wisteria)
Deciduous climber with pinnate, dark green leaves. Pendant racemes of pea-

like, white, pink, blue or purple, fragrant flowers are produced in early summer.

**Seed** Sow the large seeds individually in small pots, in a garden frame, as soon as they are ripe. Soaking the seed for 24 hours prior to sowing is supposed to speed up germination, but it is difficult to tell, as germination is erratic (1–6 months). If you are not the patient type, forget sowing, as it will take 7 years before the wisteria flowers.

**Softwood basal cuttings** in midsummer in a propagator.

**Layer** in autumn.

**Saddle graft** in winter.

### WOODWARDIA RADICANS
(European chain fern)
Evergreen fern with lance-shaped, pinnate, dark green, 180cm long fronds.

**Sow spores** at 16°C in late summer.

**Remove bulbils** from leaf tips in autumn and pot up in moisture-retentive compost in a garden frame.

**Divide** in early spring.

### WULFENIA CARINTHIACA
Evergreen perennial with rosettes of glossy, dark green, 20cm long leaves. One-sided racemes of small, tubular, deep purple-blue flowers appear in summer.

**Sow seed** in a garden frame in autumn.

**Divide** in spring into well-drained compost.

### XANTHOCERAS SORBIFOLIUM
Deciduous shrub with glossy, dark green, pinnate, 30cm long leaves. Upright panicles of white, star-shaped flowers appear in late spring as the young leaves emerge. The yellowish-green marks at the base of the petals mature to pale brown.

**Sow seed** outdoors in autumn.

**Root cuttings** in early winter.

**Plant rooted suckers** in well-drained compost in winter and overwinter in a garden frame. Trim any damaged roots to reduce the risk of coral spot disease.

### XANTHORHIZA SIMPLICISSIMA
(Yellowroot)
Deciduous shrub with 30cm long, bright green, lobed leaflets, opening bronze and turning red-bronze in late autumn. Pendant racemes of star-shaped, brown-purple flowers are produced in spring.

**Sow seed** outdoors in autumn.

**Divide** in spring or late autumn.

### YUCCA GLORIOSA (Spanish dagger)
Evergreen shrub with stiff, sword-like, sharply pointed, 60cm long, blue-green leaves. Upright panicles of pendant, bell-shaped, white or purple-tinged white flowers are produced in summer and autumn.

**Sow seed** at 18°C in spring.

**Root cuttings** in winter in bottom heat, or in pots of gritty compost on a hot bed in a garden frame. Choose only the fleshy roots.

**Plant rooted suckers** in spring in free-draining compost. Use a heated propagator if it is tall enough – the plants will root much more quickly than in a garden frame.

Weigela middendorffiana

### ZANTEDESCHIA AETHIOPICA
(Arum lily)

Evergreen perennial with arrow-shaped, glossy, bright green, 45cm long leaves. Large, pure white, 20cm long spathes with creamy-yellow spadices are produced during late spring and early summer.

*Sow seed* at 25°C as soon as it is ripe.

▯ *Divide* in spring.

### ZEA MAYS (Sweetcorn, Maize)

Annual grass with bright green, lance-shaped, 90cm long leaves and a panicle of male flowers and female inflorescences. The female flowers are followed in late summer and early autumn by cobs with yellow, edible grain.

*Sow seed* at 18°C in early spring.

### ZEPHYRANTHES CANDIDA
(Rain flower)

Deciduous, bulbous perennial with linear, basal, 45cm long leaves. Crocus-like, white flowers, tinted red on the back of the petals, are produced in summer and early autumn.

*Sow seed* at 16°C as soon as it is ripe.

▯ *Remove offsets* in spring. Pot in a free-draining compost in a garden frame until all risk of frost is over, then plant out into their permanent positions.

### ZINNIA HAAGEANA (Mexican zinnia)

Tender annual with lance-shaped, mid-green, hairy leaves. Daisy-like, bright orange flowerheads are produced in summer.

*Sow seed* at 16°C in early spring.

Zantedeschia aethiopica

# Glossary

**Aril** The outer covering of some seeds, often brightly coloured, as with yew.

**Axil** The upper area between the leaf or stem and the branch it is attached to. This is where the bud will grow when a camellia is propagated by leaf bud.

**Basal shoot** A shoot that emerges at ground level, as with delphiniums.

**Basal plate** The fleshy plate at the base of a corm or bulb.

**Bulbils** Small, immature bulbs that form in the leaf axils of some bulbs, such as lilies. In time they will grow into bulbs.

**Bulblets** Small, immature bulbs that form around the parent bulb during the growing season. Grown on for a few years, they become bulbs large enough to flower.

**Callus** The white growth that appears around the wound of a cutting before the roots form. It is also the protective tissue that gradually closes over any tree wound.

**Calyx** The modified leaves (sepals) that enclose the flower bud.

**Cambium** A layer of living cells immediately below the bark that encourage growth.

**Clone** An exact replica of the parent plant obtained by propagating by any vegetative method (*see right*).

**Cormlets** Also called cormels. Small, immature corms attached to mature corms during the growing season.

**Corona** A crown-like growth, like the trumpet of a narcissus flower.

**Cotyledon** The first two leaves (dicotyledon) or single leaf (monocotyledon) to emerge as seed germinates. These simple leaves are the first to produce the food to allow the seedling to grow.

**Dormancy** Short-term slowing down of growth, usually in winter. With seeds, it is a state of suspended growth while waiting for the right conditions for germination.

**Floret** One flower in a closely packed inflorescence.

**Heel** A small strip of the main stem attached to the side shoot when it is pulled from the parent plant to form a cutting. It improves the chances of some plants rooting, especially conifers.

**Inflorescence** The flowering part of a plant, which may consist either of individual florets or of a collection forming a flowerhead.

**Involucre** A whorl of bracts enclosing and surrounding a number of flowers, as with a daisy.

**Keel** The two lower petals of a flower joined or partially connected to resemble the keel of a boat. Common in members of the legume family, such as the pea or sweet pea.

**Nectary** The organ in a flower that secretes nectar.

**Node** The area of the stem where a leaf appears.

**Offset** A small portion of the parent plant pulled off without lifting the plant. It is often available with roots, as in the case of globe artichokes.

**Photosynthesis** The process where the green colouring matter (chlorophyll) in plant leaves utilizes solar energy to convert water and carbon dioxide into carbohydrates and food. The cotyledons of a seedling perform this function as soon as they emerge from the compost.

**Pinnate** Said of leaflets arranged in pairs on either side of the leaf stalk, as in the common ash tree.

**Pseudobulb** Thickened, bulb-like storage organ found above ground on many orchids.

**Raceme** A flowerhead on which individual flowers are carried on stems of equal length on an unbranched main stem.

**Rhizome** A horizontal creeping stem on or just below soil surface. It produces roots that grow down and shoots that grow up, as in the case of bearded iris.

**Rootstock** The rooted plant on to which another plant without roots (the scion) is grafted.

**Rosette** Leaves closely arranged around a central stem.

**Runner** A thin stem that is produced above ground by the parent plant (strawberries are a good example). It roots at the nodes, forming plants.

**Scarify** To scrape or abrade the surface coat of a seed to allow water to penetrate and encourage germination.

**Scion** A bud or shoot grafted onto the rootstock of a different plant.

**Sepal** Part of the flower calyx found at the base of the flower. It resembles a thin leaf and protects the unopened flower.

**Sorus** (plural sori) A cluster of sporangia (seed pods) in a fern.

**Spadix** A flower spike partially enclosed by a fleshy bract (spathe).

**Spathe** A broad fleshy bract partially enclosing a central flower spike (spadix)

**Spore** The reproductive part of a fern, fungus or moss.

**Stolon** A thin stem produced above ground, differing from a runner in that it roots only at the tip of the stem.

**Stratification** Chilling or warming seed to overcome dormancy and allow the seed to germinate.

**Sucker** A shoot arising from the base of the plant or from the rootstock onto which a scion is grafted.

**Tepal** A part of a flower not clearly identifiable as a sepal or petal as in crocus.

**True** Identical to its parent.

**Union** The joint between the rootstock and the scion in grafted plants.

**Vegetative propagation** Propagation using a portion of the living plant, as opposed to propagating by seed. Whereas plants grown from seed do not always come 'true', with vegetative propagation the new plants will be identical to the parent plant the cuttings were taken from.

# Acknowledgements

My grateful thanks, as ever, to Kyle, Caroline and Vicki, for making this book happen, and to Isobel for making it look so handsome. Thanks also to Ray Broughton and Mark Ekin at Sparsholt College Hampshire for their help with photography; and to Anne and John Swithinbank for helpfully filling in photo gaps at the last minute.

All step-by-step photography is by Mark Winwood, except for page 33 top left by Jonathan Buckley (design by Carol Klein); pages 60–61, 89 (bottom left); & top right) and 101 by John Swithinbank.

Other photographs:
JB: Jonathan Buckley
MM: Marianne Majerus
CN: Clive Nichols
GPL: Garden Picture Library

page 2 MM; 4 MM; 6 GPL/Mark Bolton; 7 GPL/Darrell Gulin; 8 GPL/Suzie Gibbons; 9 GPL/Alec Scaresbrook; 10 (left) GPL/Stephen Hamilton; (right) GPL/Chris Burrows; 12 GPL/William Deering; 13 GPL/James Baigrie; 14 left GPL/left Jason Ingram, right GPL/Botanica; 15 GPL/Mel Watson; 16 GPL/John Glover; 17 GPL/Juliette Wade; page 18 MM; 19 (top) MM; (bottom) GPL/Lamontagne; 20 GPL/ Frederic Didillon; 24 GPL/Evan Sklar; 25 GPL/Flora Press; 28 (top) GPL/Brian Carter; (bottom) FLPA/Nigel Cattlin; 29 MM

page 34 (top) MM; (bottom) GPL/François De Heel; 35 MM; 36 JB (design Christopher Lloyd); 40 CN; 41 MM; 44 MM (RHS Wisley); 45 CN; 50 JB; 56 MM; 58 (top) JB (design Christopher Lloyd); (bottom) MM; 62 (top) John Glover; (bottom) FLPA/Rosie Mayer

page 64 CN (design Elisabeth Woodhouse); 65 MM (design Declan Buckley); 68 MM; 69 JB (design Sue and Wol Staines); 72 (top left) MM; 74 (top left) MM (Hillier Arboretum); 76 (top left) MM; 78 (top left) FLPA/Nigel Cattlin; 80 MM; 81 MM; 82 (top left) MM; 84 (top left) MM; 86 (top left) GPL/Jason Ingram;

page 88 JB (design Christopher Lloyd); 90 MM; 91 CN; 98 (top) JB (design Alan Titchmarsh); (bottom) MM (Hodsock Priory, Notts)

page 102 MM; 103 GPL/Mark Bolton; 104 FLPA/Nigel Cattlin; 105 FLPA/ Gary K Smith; 106 FLPA/Nigel Cattlin; 109 photolibrary; 113 MM

page 114 JB; 115 MM; 117 CN; 119 (left) JB; (right) JB; 121 JB; 122 CN; 124 JB (design Sue & Wol Staines); 125 JB (design Christopher Lloyd); 127 JB (design Alan Gray & Graham Robeson); 129 (left) MM; (right) JB (design Pam Schwerdt & Sibylle Kreutsberger); 130 GPL/Richard Bloom; 131 CN (design Christopher Bradley-Hole; 132–138 MM; 139 GPL/ David Cavagnaro; 140 MM; 143 JB (design Veronica Cross); 145 JB; 146 JB (design Beth Chatto);148 (top) CN; (bottom) JB (design Helen Yemm); 149 JB; 150–152 MM; 153 CN (Pettifers, Oxfordshire); 154 JB (design Christopher Lloyd); 155 CN; 157 MM; 158 CN (Hadspen Garden, Somerset); 159 CN; 160 (left) MM; (right) MM; 162 (left) JB (design Veronica Cross); (right) CN; 163 JB (design Sue & Wol Staines); 165 CN; 167 JB (design Sue & Wol Staines); 168 JB; 170 CN (Pettifers Garden, Oxon);

171 JB; 172 JB (design Helen Yemm); 173 CN (Meadow Plants, Berkshire); 174 CN; 175 JB; 176 MM; 177 JB; 178 JB (design Sue & Wol Staines); 179 JB (design Maureen Sawyer); 180 JB (design David & Mavis Seeney); 181 MM; 182 MM; 183 JB; 185–6 MM; 187 JB; 189 (left) CN (design Christopher Bradley-Hole); (right) CN; 190 MM; 191 (left) MM; (right) JB (design Christopher Lloyd); 192 MM; 193 (left) JB (design Christopher Lloyd); (right) MM; 194 CN; 195 (left) CN; (right) MM; 196 JB 197 CN; 198 JB (design Christopher Lloyd); 199 JB (design Virginia Kennedy); 200 JB (design Susan Sharkey); 201 (left) CN; (right) MM; 202 JB (design Paul Kelly); 203–206 CN; 207 JB (design Christopher Lloyd); 208 MM; 209 JB (design Sarah Raven); 210–211CN; 212 CN (design Olivia Clarke); 215 CN; 216 JB (design Christopher Lloyd); 217 JB (design Anthony Goff); 218 MM; 219 CN (design Dan Pearson; 220 CN; 221 MM; 222 photolibrary; 223 GPL/Chris Burrows; 224 MM; 225 CN; 227 MM; 228 MM (design Beth Chatto); 229 MM; 231–232 MM; 233 MM; 235 CN (design Wendy Lauderdale); 236 MM; 238 GPL/Lisa Romerein; 239 CN (Mottisfont Abbey, Hampshire); 240–244 MM; 245 CN; 247 CN; 249 MM; 250 CN

# Index